Unlikely LEADERS

Ellen G. White

Pacific Press® Publishing Association
Nampa, Idaho
Oshawa, Ontario, Canada
www.pacificpress.com

Cover design by Doug Church
Cover illustration by Eric Joyner
Inside design by Aaron Troia

Additional copies of this book are available by
calling toll-free 1-800-765-6955 or
online at www.adventistbookcenter.com.

Unless otherwise noted, Scripture quotations are from
The New King James Version, copyright © 1979, 1980, 1982,
Thomas Nelson, Inc., Publishers.

Scripture texts credited to NRSV are from the New Revised Standard Version
of the Bible, copyright © 1989 by the Division of Christian
Education of the National Council of the Churches of Christ in the USA.
Used by permission. All rights reserved.

Scripture texts credited to KJV are from the King James Version.

ISBN 13: 978-0-8163-2401-9
ISBN 10: 0-8163-2401-8

10 11 12 13 14 • 5 4 3 2 1

Contents

Foreword

Unlikely Leaders tells the story of the Christian church's beginning. Jesus left the work in the care of eleven men who seemed, humanly speaking, to be poor choices for establishing a world-wide movement to bring a rebellious planet back to its Creator. Their number included a brash fisherman who crumpled under pressure, a young man and his brother who were so hot-headed that they earned the nickname "sons of thunder," a tax collector who had enriched himself by working for the enemy, a patriot ("Zealot") who may have belonged to a group known for assassinating enemy collaborators, and a loyal but doubt-filled man who could rarely see the bright side of anything. A little later someone else joined them who had originally done his best to destroy them. What could come of a group like this?

Their story is a thrilling account of what God can do with unpromising material. It should give courage and hope to anyone who wants to serve God but is carrying the baggage of the past. God specializes in doing wonderful things with people who give themselves to His cause, to follow His leading. The Bible's book of Acts ends abruptly, suggesting that there is more to come in the story. We may be a part of that ongoing story today, as we near its completion.

Unlikely Leaders is an adaptation of *From Trials to Triumph,* a 1984 condensed edition of Ellen G. White's classic volume, *The Acts of the Apostles.* The condensed volume included all the chapters of the original, using only Mrs. White's own words but shortening the account.

The current adaptation goes a step beyond this, using some words, expressions, and sentence constructions more familiar to twenty-first century readers. Most of the Bible quotations come from the New King James Version, which closely resembles the King James Version that Ellen White commonly used. It is hoped that readers who are new to her writings will enjoy this adaptation and that it will encourage them to read the original editions of her works.

This volume presents insights into the Bible's account that will help the reader not only to understand the stories and instructions found there but also to see how they apply to the Christian's life today.

There are five powerful volumes in the Conflict of the Ages series. *Unlikely Leaders* was condensed and adapted from the fourth of the five. That many more readers may be drawn to God through these books and their presentation of Bible themes is the hope and prayer of

The Trustees of
The Ellen G. White Estate

God's Purpose for His Church

The church is God's appointed agency to save lost men and women. Its mission is to carry the gospel to the world. Through the church eventually everyone, including even "the principalities and powers in the heavenly places," will see the final and full display of God's love. (Ephesians 3:10.)

In the Scriptures are many wonderful promises about the church. "My house shall be called a house of prayer for all nations" (Isaiah 56:7).

"I will preserve you and give you
As a covenant to the people,
To restore the earth,
To cause them to inherit the
    desolate heritages;
That you may say to the prisoners,
    'Go forth,'
To those who are in darkness,
'Show yourselves.'"

Isaiah 49:8, 9

"Can a woman forget her nursing
    child,
And not have compassion on
    the son of her womb?
Surely they may forget,
Yet I will not forget you."

Isaiah 49:15

The church is God's fortress, His city of refuge, which He holds in a world in revolt. Any betrayal of the church is treason against Him who has bought mankind with the blood of His only Son. From the beginning, the church has been made up of faithful people. In every age the Lord's watchmen have faithfully given His message to their own generation. God has sent out His angels to minister to His church, and the gates of hell have not been able to prevail against His people. Not one opposing force has risen to counteract His work that God did not see ahead of time. He has not left His church forsaken, but has outlined in prophecy what would happen. All His plans will be fulfilled. God inspires and guards truth, and it will triumph over all opposition.

Feeble and defective as it may appear, the church is the one object that God regards above all others. It is the theater of His grace, in which He delights to reveal His power to transform hearts.

Earthly kingdoms rule by physical power, but Christ banishes every instrument of force from His kingdom. His rule is to uplift humanity and make it more noble. God has filled His church with various gifts and has given it the Holy Spirit.

From the beginning God has worked through His people to bring blessings to the world. God made Joseph a fountain of life to the ancient Egyptian nation. Through him God preserved that whole people. Through Daniel God saved the life of all the wise men of Babylon. These deliverances illustrate the spiritual blessings offered to the world through the God whom Joseph and Daniel worshiped. Everyone who will reveal Christ's love to the world is a worker with God for blessing humanity.

God desired Israel to be like wells of salvation in the world. The nations of the world had lost the knowledge of God. They had once known Him, but because "they did not glorify Him as God, nor were thankful, but became futile in their thoughts, . . . their foolish hearts were darkened" (Romans 1:21). Yet God did not blot them out. He decided to give them the opportunity to become acquainted with Him through His chosen people. Through the sacrificial service, Christ was to be lifted up, and all who would look to Him would live. The whole system of types and symbols was a condensed prophecy of the gospel.

But the people of Israel forgot God and failed to fulfill their holy mission. They clung to all their advantages for their own glorification. They shut themselves away from the world in order to escape temptation. They robbed God of service, and they robbed other people of a holy example.

Priests and rulers became satisfied with a legal religion. They thought their own righteousness was more than enough. They did not accept the goodwill of God as something apart from themselves, but connected it with their own merit because of their good works. The faith that works by love could find no place in the religion of the Pharisees.

God declared about Israel:

"I had planted you a noble vine,
    a seed of highest quality.
How then have you turned before
    Me
Into the degenerate plant of an alien
    vine?"

Jeremiah 2:21

"For the vineyard of the Lord of hosts
    is the house of Israel,
And the men of Judah are His
    pleasant plant.
He looked for justice, but behold,
    oppression;
For righteousness, but behold, a cry
    for help."

Isaiah 5:7

"The weak you have not strengthened, nor have you healed those who were sick, nor bound up the broken, nor brought back what was driven away, nor sought what was lost; but with force and cruelty you have ruled them" (Ezekiel 34:4).

The Savior turned from the Jewish leaders to entrust others with the privileges they had abused and the work they had scorned. God's glory must be revealed; His kingdom must be established. The disciples were called to do the work that the Jewish leaders had failed to do.

The Training of the Twelve

To carry on His work, Christ chose humble, unschooled men. Then He set about to train and educate them. They in turn were to educate others and send them out with the gospel message. They were to be given the power of the Holy Spirit so that they could proclaim the gospel by the power of God, not by human wisdom.

For three and a half years the disciples were under the instruction of the greatest Teacher the world has ever known. Day by day He taught them, sometimes sitting on the mountainside, sometimes beside the sea or walking along the road. He did not command the disciples to do this or that but said, "Follow Me." He took them with Him on His journeys through country and cities. They shared His simple food, and like Him, they were sometimes hungry and often tired. They saw Him in every phase of life.

The ordination of the Twelve was the first step in organizing the church. The record says, "He appointed twelve, that they might be with Him and that He might send them out to preach" (Mark 3:14). By these feeble messengers, through His Word and Spirit, He planned to place salvation within the reach of all. The words the disciples spoke as they witnessed would echo from generation to generation till the close of time.

The disciples' work was the most important that human beings had ever been given, second only to that of Christ Himself. They were workers together with God for saving men and women. As the twelve sons of Jacob stood as representatives of Israel, so the twelve apostles stand as representatives of the gospel church.

No "Wall" Between Jews and Gentiles

Christ began to break down the "middle wall of separation" (Ephesians 2:14) between Jew and Gentile and to preach salvation to everyone. He mingled freely with the despised Samaritans, setting aside the customs of the Jews. He slept under their roofs, ate at their tables, and taught in their streets.

The Savior longed to unfold to His disciples the truth that "the Gentiles should be fellow heirs" with the Jews and "partakers of His promise in Christ through the gospel" (Ephesians 3:6). He rewarded the faith of the centurion at Capernaum; He preached to the people living in Sychar; and on His visit to Phoenicia, He healed the daughter of the Canaanite woman.

Among those whom many thought were unworthy of salvation, there were people hungering for truth.

In this way Christ tried to teach the disciples that in God's kingdom there are no territorial lines, no rigid social classes, no aristocracy. They must bring all nations the message of a Savior's love. But not until later did they fully realize that God "made from one blood every nation of men to dwell on all the face of the earth" (Acts 17:26).

These first disciples represented a wide variety in types of character. Differing in natural characteristics, they needed to come into unity. To achieve this end, Christ tried to bring them into unity with Himself. He expressed His burden for them in His prayer to His Father, "That they all may be one, . . . that the world may know that You have sent Me, and have loved them as You have loved Me" (John 17:21–23). He knew that truth would conquer in the battle with evil, and that the blood-stained banner would someday wave triumphantly over His followers.

As Christ realized that soon He must leave His disciples to carry on the work, He tried to prepare them for the future. He knew that they would suffer persecution, be put out of the synagogues, and be thrown into prison. Some would even be killed. In speaking of their future, He was clear and definite, so that in their coming trials they would remember His words and be strengthened to believe in Him as the Redeemer.

"Let not your heart be troubled," He said. "I go to prepare a place for you. And if I go and prepare a place for you, I will come again and receive you to Myself; that where I am, there you may be also" (John 14:1–3). When I go away I will still work earnestly for you. I go to My Father and yours to cooperate with Him for your good.

"He who believes in Me, the works that I do he will do also; and greater works than these he will do, because I go to My Father" (verse 12). Christ did not mean that the disciples would do a better or higher work than He had done, but that their work would have greater extent. He was speaking of all that would take place under the power of the Holy Spirit.

What the Holy Spirit Accomplished

These words were wonderfully fulfilled. After the Spirit's arrival, the disciples were so filled with love that hearts were melted by the words they spoke and the prayers they offered. Under the influence of the Spirit, thousands were converted.

As Christ's representatives the apostles were to make a clear impression on the world. Their words of courage and trust would assure everyone that they were not working in their own power but in the power of Christ. They would declare that He whom the Jews had crucified was the Prince of life and that in His name they did the works that He had done.

On the night before the Crucifixion the Savior did not speak of the suffering He had endured and must yet endure. He tried to strengthen their faith, leading them to look forward to the joys that are in store for the overcomer. He would do more for His followers than He had promised. From Him would flow love and compassion, making people like Him in character. Armed with the power of the Spirit, His truth would go forward conquering and to conquer.

Christ did not fail, neither was He discouraged, and the disciples were to show the same kind of faith. They were to work as He worked. By His grace they were to go forward, never despairing, and hoping for everything.

Christ had finished the work God had given Him. He had gathered out those who were to continue His work. And He said: "I do not pray for these alone, but also for those who will believe on Me through their word; that they all may be one, . . . that the world may know that You have sent Me, and have loved them as You have loved Me" (John 17:20–23).

The Good News to Go Everywhere

After the death of Christ the disciples were almost overcome by discouragement. The sun of their hope had set, and night settled down on their hearts. Lonely and sick at heart, they remembered Christ's words, "If they do these things in the green wood, what will be done in the dry?" (Luke 23:31).

Several times Jesus had tried to open the future to His disciples, but they had not wanted to think about what He said. This left them completely hopeless when He died. Their faith did not penetrate the shadow Satan threw across their horizon. If they had believed the Savior's words that He was to rise on the third day, how much sorrow they might have avoided!

Crushed by depression and despair, the disciples met together in the upper room and locked the doors, fearing that what happened to their beloved Teacher might also happen to them. After His resurrection, the Savior appeared to them there.

For forty days Christ remained on earth, preparing the disciples for the work ahead of them. He spoke of the prophecies of His rejection by the Jews and His death, showing that every detail had been fulfilled. "And He opened their understanding," we read, "that they might comprehend the Scriptures." And He added, "You are witnesses of these things" (Luke 24:45, 48).

As the disciples heard their Master explaining the Scriptures in the light of all that had happened, their faith in Him was fully established. They reached the place where they could say, "I know whom I have believed" (2 Timothy 1:12). The events of Christ's life, death, and resurrection, the prophecies pointing to these events, the plan of salvation, and the power of Jesus to forgive sins—they had been witnesses to all these things, and they were to make them known to the world.

Before ascending to heaven, Christ told His disciples that they were to be the executors of the will in which He left to the world the treasures of eternal life. Although priests and rulers have rejected Me, He said, they will still have another opportunity to accept the Son of God. To you, My disciples, I commit this message of mercy, to be given to Israel first, and then to all nations. All who believe are to be gathered into one church.

The gospel commission is the great missionary blueprint of Christ's kingdom. The disciples were to work earnestly to bring people to Jesus. They were to go to the people with their message. Their every word and act was to fasten attention on Christ's name, which alone possessed that vital power to save sinners. His name was to be their badge of distinction, the authority for their actions, and the source of their success.

Successful Weapons in the Great Warfare

Christ plainly set before the disciples the need to maintain simplicity. The less pomp and show, the greater would be their influence for good. The disciples were to speak simply, the same way that Christ had spoken.

Christ did not tell His disciples that their work would be easy. They would have to fight "against principalities, against powers, against the rulers of the darkness of this age, against spiritual hosts of wickedness in the heavenly places" (Ephesians 6:12). But they would not be left to fight alone. He would be with them. If they would go out in faith, One who is mightier than angels would be with them—the General of the armies of heaven. He took on Himself the responsibility for their success. As long as they worked in connection with Him, they could not fail. He told them, Go to the people at the farthest part of the globe, and be assured that My presence will be with you even there.

Christ's sacrifice was full and complete. He had fulfilled the conditions of the atonement. He had taken the kingdom back from Satan and become heir of all things. He was on His way to the throne of God, to be honored by the heavenly host. Clothed with boundless authority, He gave His disciples their commission: "Go therefore and make disciples of all the nations, baptizing them in the name of the Father and of the Son and of the Holy Spirit, teaching them to observe all things that I have commanded you; and lo, I am with you always, even to the end" (Matthew 28:19, 20).

Just before leaving His disciples, Christ once more plainly stated that He did not intend to establish a worldly kingdom, to reign as an earthly ruler on David's throne. Their work was to proclaim the gospel message.

Christ's visible presence was about to be withdrawn, but a new infusion of power was to be theirs. The Holy Spirit was to be given to them in its fullness. "I send the Promise of My Father upon you," the Savior said, "but tarry in the city of Jerusalem until you are endued with power from on high." "You shall receive power when the Holy Spirit has come upon you; and you shall be witnesses to Me in Jerusalem, and in all Judea and Samaria, and to the end of the earth." (Luke 24:49; Acts 1:8.)

The Savior knew that His disciples must receive the heavenly gift. A vigilant, determined leader was in command of the forces of darkness, and the followers of Christ could battle for the right only through the help that God would give them by His Spirit.

Christ's disciples were to begin their work at Jerusalem, the scene of His amazing sacrifice for the human race. In Jerusalem there were many who secretly believed that Jesus of Nazareth was the Messiah and many who had been deceived by priests and rulers. The disciples were to call these people to repentance. And it was while all Jerusalem was stirred by the thrilling events of the past few weeks that the preaching of the disciples would make the deepest impression.

During His ministry, Jesus had constantly reminded the disciples that they were to unite with Him in recovering the world from the slavery of sin. And the last lesson He gave His followers was that they held in trust for the world the good news of salvation.

When the time came for Christ to ascend to His Father, He led the disciples out as far as Bethany. Here He paused, and they gathered around Him. With His hands stretched out as if to assure them of His protecting care, He slowly ascended from among them. "While He blessed them, . . . He was parted from them and carried up into heaven" (Luke 24:51).

While the disciples were gazing upward to catch the last glimpse of their ascending Lord, heavenly angels received Him and escorted Him to the courts above. The disciples were still looking toward heaven when "two men stood by them in white apparel, who also said, 'Men of Galilee, why do you stand gazing up into heaven? This same Jesus, who was taken up from you into heaven, will so come in like manner as you saw Him go into heaven'" (Acts 1:10, 11).

Christ's Second Coming—the Hope of the Church

Jesus' disciples were always to keep fresh in their minds the promise of Christ's second coming. The same Jesus would come again to take to Himself those who give themselves to His service here below. His voice would welcome them to His kingdom.

As in the symbolic service the high priest laid aside his special robes and officiated in the white linen garment of an ordinary priest, so Christ laid aside His royal robes, clothed Himself with humanity, and offered sacrifice, Himself the priest, Himself the victim. As the high priest came out to the waiting congregation in his special robes after performing his service in the Most Holy Place, so Christ will come the second time, clothed in His own glory and in the glory of His Father, and all the millions of angels will escort Him on His way.

In this way Christ will fulfill His promise: "I will come again and receive you to Myself" (John 14:3). The righteous dead will come from their graves, and those who are alive will be caught up with them, "to meet the Lord in the air" (1 Thessalonians 4:17). They will hear the voice of Jesus, sweeter than music, saying, "Come, you blessed of My Father, inherit the kingdom prepared for you from the foundation of the world" (Matthew 25:34).

How the disciples could rejoice in the hope of their Lord's return!

Pentecost: The Apostles Begin Their Work*

As the disciples returned from the Mount of Olives to Jerusalem, the people expected to see confusion and defeat on their faces, but they saw gladness and triumph. The disciples had seen the risen Savior, and His parting promise echoed in their ears.

In obedience to Christ's command, they waited in Jerusalem for the Holy Spirit's outpouring, where they were "continually in the temple, praising and blessing God" (Luke 24:53). They knew they had an Advocate at the throne of God. In awe they bowed in prayer, repeating the assurance, "Whatever you ask the Father in My name He will give you" (John 16:23). They extended the hand of faith higher and still higher.

As the disciples waited, they humbled their hearts in repentance and confessed their unbelief. Truths that had passed from their memory God brought again to their minds, and they repeated them to one another. Scene after scene of the Savior's life passed before them. As they meditated on His pure life, they felt that no work would be too hard, no sacrifice too great, if only their lives could bear witness to the loveliness of Christ's char-acter. If they could live the past three years over again, they thought, how differently they would act! But the thought that they were forgiven comforted them, and they determined, as far as possible, to make up for their unbelief by bravely testifying about Him before the world.

The disciples prayed with intense earnestness to be fitted to meet people and speak words that would lead sinners to Christ. Putting away all differences, they came close together. And as they drew nearer to God, they realized what a privilege they had had to associate so closely with Christ.

The disciples did not ask for a blessing just for themselves. They felt a great burden for the salvation of others. In obedience to the Savior's word, they offered their requests for the gift of the Holy Spirit, and in heaven Christ claimed the gift so that He could pour it on His people.

How the Holy Spirit Came on the Apostles

"When the Day of Pentecost was fully come, they were all with one accord in one place. And suddenly there came a sound from heaven, as of a rushing mighty wind, and it filled the

---

* This chapter is based on Acts 2:1–41.

whole house where they were sitting." The Spirit came on the praying disciples with a fullness that reached every heart. Heaven rejoiced in being able to pour out the riches of the Spirit's grace. Words of repentance and confession mingled with songs of praise. Lost in awe, the apostles grasped the gift they had been given.

And what followed? The sword of the Spirit, newly edged with power and bathed in the lightnings of heaven, cut its way through unbelief. Thousands were converted in a day.

"When He, the Spirit of truth, has come," Christ had said, "He will guide you into all truth; for He will not speak on His own authority, but whatever He hears He will speak; and He will tell you things to come" (John 16:13).

When Christ entered the heavenly gates, He was made king amid the adoration of the angels. The Holy Spirit descended on the disciples, and Christ was truly glorified. The Spirit's outpouring on the Day of Pentecost was Heaven's announcement that the Redeemer had been inaugurated. The Holy Spirit was sent as a sign that as Priest and King, He had received all authority in heaven and on earth and was the Anointed One.

"Then there appeared to them divided tongues, as of fire, and one sat upon each of them. And they were all filled with the Holy Spirit and began to speak with other tongues, as the Spirit gave them utterance." The gift of the Holy Spirit enabled the disciples to speak fluently languages that they had not learned. The appearance of fire signified the power that would accompany their work.

What the Genuine Gift of Tongues Accomplished

"There were dwelling in Jerusalem Jews, devout men, from every nation under heaven." Scattered to almost every part of the world, they had learned to speak various languages. Many of these Jews were in Jerusalem, attending the religious festivals. Every known tongue was represented. This diversity of languages would have greatly hindered the preaching of the gospel. So God miraculously did for the apostles what they could not have accomplished for themselves in a lifetime. Now they could accurately speak the languages of those for whom they were working—a strong evidence that their calling came from Heaven. From this time onward the language of the disciples was pure, simple, and accurate, whether in their native tongue or in a foreign language.

The people were "amazed and marveled, saying to one another, 'Look, are not all these who speak Galileans? And how is it that we hear, each in our own language?'"

The priests and rulers were furious. They had put the Nazarene to death, but here were His servants telling the story of His life and ministry in all the languages then spoken. The priests claimed that they were drunk from the new wine prepared for the feast. But those who understood the different languages testified that the disciples spoke these languages accurately.

In answer to the accusation, Peter showed that this fulfilled Joel's prophecy. He said, "These are not drunk, as you suppose, since it is only the third hour of the day. But this is what was spoken by the prophet Joel:

'And it shall come to pass in the last days, says God,
That I will pour out of My Spirit on all flesh;
Your sons and your daughters shall prophesy,
Your young men shall see visions,
Your old men shall dream dreams.
And on My menservants and on My maidservants
I will pour out My Spirit in those days;
And they shall prophesy.' " (See Joel 2:28, 29.)

Conviction That Jesus Was the True Messiah

Peter bore a powerful witness to the death and resurrection of Christ: "Jesus of Nazareth . . . you have taken by lawless hands, have crucified, and put to death; whom God raised up, having loosed the pains of death, because it was not possible that He should be held by it."

Knowing that his hearers' prejudice was great, Peter spoke of David, whom the Jews thought of as one of the nation's greatest leaders. "David says concerning Him:

'I foresaw the Lord always before My face,
For He is at My right hand, that I may not be shaken. . . .
You will not leave My soul in Hades,
Nor will You allow Your Holy One to see corruption.' . . .

"Let me speak freely to you of the patriarch David, that he is both dead and buried, and his tomb is with us to this day." "He . . . spoke concerning the resurrection of the Christ, that His soul was not left in Hades, nor did His flesh see corruption. This Jesus God has raised up, of which we are all witnesses."

The people pressed in from all directions, crowding the temple. Priests and rulers were there, their hearts still filled with lasting hatred against Christ, their hands not cleansed from the blood they shed when they crucified the world's Redeemer. They found the apostles fearless and filled with the Spirit, proclaiming that Jesus of Nazareth is divine, declaring boldly that the One whom cruel hands had so recently humiliated and crucified is the Prince of life, exalted to the right hand of God.

Some who listened had taken part in Christ's condemnation and death, their voices having called for His crucifixion. When Pilate asked, "Whom do you want me to release to you?" they had shouted, "Not this Man, but Barabbas!" When Pilate delivered Christ to them, they had called out, "His blood be on us and on our children." (Matthew 27:17; John 18:40; Matthew 27:25.)

Now they heard the disciples proclaiming that it was the Son of God they had crucified. Priests and rulers trembled. Conviction and anguish seized the people. They said to Peter and the rest of the apostles, "Men and brethren, what shall we do?" The power that accompanied the speaker convinced them that Jesus was truly the Messiah.

"Repent, and let every one of you

be baptized in the name of Jesus Christ for the remission of sins; and you shall receive the gift of the Holy Spirit."

Thousands in Jerusalem Converted

Peter urged the guilt-stricken people to recognize that they had rejected Christ because the priests and rulers had deceived them, and that if they continued to look to these men, they would never accept Christ. These powerful men were ambitious for earthly glory. They were not willing to come to Christ to receive light.

The scriptures that Christ had explained to the disciples stood out in their minds with the luster of perfect truth. The veil was now removed, and they understood with perfect clarity the purpose of Christ's mission and the nature of His kingdom. As they opened the plan of salvation to their hearers, many were convicted and convinced. Traditions and superstitions were swept away, and they accepted the teachings of the Savior.

"Then those who gladly received his word were baptized; and that day about three thousand souls were added to them." In Jerusalem, the stronghold of Judaism, thousands of people openly declared their faith in Jesus as the Messiah.

The disciples were astonished and overjoyed. They did not think of this as the result of their own efforts; they realized that they were building on the work of others. Christ had sown the seed of truth and watered it with His blood. The conversions on the Day of Pentecost were the harvest of His work.

The apostles' arguments alone would not have removed prejudice. But the Holy Spirit sent the words of the apostles to their targets like sharp arrows of the Almighty, convicting the people of their terrible guilt in rejecting the Lord of glory.

The disciples were no longer ignorant and uncultured, a collection of independent, conflicting interests. They were of "one accord," "of one heart and one soul." They had become like their Master in mind and character, and others recognized that "they had been with Jesus." (Acts 2:46; 4:32, 13.) The truths they could not understand while Christ was with them now became clear. No longer was it only a matter of faith with them that Christ was the Son of God. They knew that He truly was the Messiah, and they told their experience with a confidence that carried with it the conviction that God was with them.

Brought into close fellowship with Christ, the disciples sat with Him "in heavenly places." A love that was full, deep, and far-reaching drove them to go to the ends of the earth, filled with an intense longing to carry forward the work He had begun. The Spirit gave them power and spoke through them. The peace of Christ radiated from their faces. They had devoted their lives to Him, and their faces themselves witnessed to the surrender they had made.

The Gift of the Spirit Is for Us

C hrist was standing in the shadow of the cross, fully aware of the load of guilt about to rest on Him as the Sin Bearer, when He instructed His disciples about a most essential gift He was going to give to His followers. "I will pray the Father," He said, "and He will give you another Helper, that He may abide with you forever—the Spirit of truth, . . . for He dwells with you and will be in you" (John 14:16, 17). By the divine power of the Holy Spirit they were to resist the evil that had been accumulating for centuries.

What was the result of the Spirit's outpouring on the Day of Pentecost? The good news of a risen Savior was carried to the farthest parts of the world. Converts flocked to the church from all directions. Some who had opposed the gospel the most bitterly became its champions. One focus rose above every other—to reveal the likeness of Christ's character and to work to enlarge His kingdom.

"With great power the apostles gave witness to the resurrection of the Lord Jesus. And great grace was upon them all" (Acts 4:33). Chosen men consecrated their lives to the work of giving to others the hope that filled their hearts with peace and joy. Nothing could restrain or intimidate them. As they went from place to place, the poor had the gospel preached to them, and miracles of divine grace took place.

From the Day of Pentecost to today, the Comforter has been sent to all who have yielded themselves to the Lord and His service. The Holy Spirit has come as a counselor, sanctifier, guide, and witness. Through the long centuries of persecution, the men and women who revealed the presence of the Spirit in their lives have stood as signs and wonders in the world. They have shown the transforming power of redeeming love.

Those who were filled with power at Pentecost were not freed from further temptation by this experience. The enemy repeatedly attacked them, trying to rob them of their Christian experience. They had to try with all their God-given powers to reach the full potential of men and women in Christ. Daily they prayed that God would help them to reach still higher toward perfection. Even the weakest ones learned to improve the powers God had given them and to become sanctified, refined, and noble. As they submitted in humility to the molding influence of the Holy Spirit, their lives more and more reflected the Divine.

God Has Not Restricted His Gift

The passing of time has made no change in Christ's promise to send the Holy Spirit. If we do not see the fulfillment, it is because we do not appreciate the promise as we should. Wherever Christians think little of the Holy Spirit, there we will find spiritual drought, spiritual darkness, and spiritual death. When minor matters occupy the attention, the divine power necessary for the church's growth and prosperity is missing.

Why don't we hunger and thirst for the Spirit? The Lord is more willing to give the Spirit than parents are to give good gifts to their children. Every worker should be asking God for the daily baptism of the Spirit. The presence of the Spirit with God's workers will give a power to our sharing of truth that not all the glory of the world could give.

The words Jesus spoke to the disciples are also spoken to us. The Comforter is ours as well as theirs. The Spirit furnishes the strength that sustains struggling Christians in every emergency, amid the hatred of the world and the awareness of their own failures. When the outlook seems dark and the future perplexing, and we feel helpless and alone, the Holy Spirit brings comfort to the heart.

Holiness is living by every word that proceeds from the mouth of God. It is trusting God in darkness as well as in the light, walking by faith and not by sight.

The nature of the Holy Spirit is a mystery. People may bring together passages of Scripture and put a human construction on them, but accepting fanciful ideas will not strengthen the church. Regarding mysteries that are too deep for human understanding, silence is golden.

The Holy Spirit convicts of sin (see John 16:8). The sinner who responds will be brought to repentance and awakened to the importance of obeying God's requirements. To the repentant sinner, the Holy Spirit reveals the Lamb of God that takes away the sin of the world. Christ said, "He will teach you all things, and bring to your remembrance all things that I said to you" (John 14:26).

The Spirit is given as a regenerating agency, to make real in our lives the salvation our Redeemer's death won for us. The Spirit is constantly working to draw attention to the cross of Calvary, to unfold the love of God, and to open to the convicted heart the precious things of the Scriptures. After He brings conviction of sin, the Holy Spirit withdraws the affections from the things of this earth and fills the soul with a desire for holiness. "He will guide you into all truth" (John 16:13). The Spirit will take the things of God and stamp them on the heart.

From the beginning, God has been working by His Holy Spirit through human beings. In the days of the apostles He worked powerfully for His church through the Holy Spirit. The same power that sustained the patriarchs, that gave Caleb and Joshua faith and courage, and that made the work of the church in the apostles' time effective has strengthened God's faithful children in every age since. Through the Holy Spirit during the Dark Ages the Waldensian Christians helped prepare the way for the Reformation. The same power gave success to the efforts of noble men and women who pioneered the way for modern missions and for the translation of the Bible into the languages of all nations.

And today those who proclaim the cross are going from land to land, preparing the way for the second advent of Christ. They are exalting God's law. The Spirit is moving on hearts, and those who respond become witnesses for God's truth. Consecrated men and women communicate the light that clearly shows the way of salvation through Christ. And as they continue to let their light shine, they receive still more of the Spirit's power. In this way the earth is to be lighted with the glory of God.

On the other hand, some Christians are idly waiting for some spiritual refreshing to greatly increase their ability to enlighten others. They allow their light to burn dim while they look to a time when they will be transformed and fitted for service without any effort on their part.

The Early Rain and the Latter Rain

It is true that when God's work on the earth is closing, special evidences of divine favor will accompany the earnest efforts of consecrated believers. Using the illustration of the early and latter rains that fall in Eastern lands at seedtime and harvest, the prophets foretold the outpouring of the Spirit. The outpouring in the days of the apostles was the early, or former, rain, and the result of it was glorious.

But near the close of earth's harvest a special measure of the Spirit is promised to prepare the church for the coming of the Son of man. This outpouring is the latter rain, and Christians are to send their prayers for this added power to the Lord of the harvest "in the time of the latter rain." In response, "the Lord . . . will give them showers of rain" (Zechariah 10:1).

"He will cause the rain to come down
     for you—
The former rain,
And the latter rain."

                              Joel 2:23

But only those who constantly receive fresh supplies of grace will have the ability to use that power. Daily they are improving the opportunities for service that lie within their reach, witnessing wherever they may be, at home or in a public sphere of usefulness.

Even Christ during His life on earth asked His Father daily for fresh supplies of grace. The Son of God bowed in prayer to His Father! He strengthened His faith by prayer and gathered to Himself power to resist evil and to minister to others.

The Elder Brother of our race knows the needs of those who live in a world of sin and temptation. The messengers whom He sees fit to send are weak and prone to make mistakes, but He promises divine aid to all who give themselves to His service. His own example assures us that faith and complete consecration to His work will bring the Holy Spirit's aid in the battle against sin.

Morning by morning, as those who carry the gospel renew their vows of consecration to the Lord, He will give them His Spirit, with its reviving, sanctifying power. As they go out to the day's duties, the unseen influence of the Holy Spirit enables them to be "God's fellow workers."

Peter and John Forbidden to Do Christ's Work*

A short time after the Holy Spirit came down, Peter and John were going up to the temple. At the gate Beautiful they saw a cripple, forty years of age, whose life from birth had been one of pain. For a long time this unfortunate man had wanted to be healed but was far away from where Jesus was working. His pleadings finally persuaded some friends to carry him to the gate of the temple, but he found that the One on whom he had centered his hopes had been put to death.

His friends knew how long he had eagerly hoped to be healed by Jesus, and they brought him to the temple daily so that passersby could give him small donations to relieve his needs. As Peter and John passed him, he asked for a little money from them. "Peter said, 'Look at us.' So he gave them his attention, expecting to receive something from them. Then Peter said, 'Silver and gold I do not have.'" The crippled man's face fell, but the apostle continued: "'But what I do have I give you: In the name of Jesus Christ of Nazareth, rise up and walk.'

"And he took him by the right hand and lifted him up, and immediately his feet and ankle bones received strength. So he, leaping up, stood and walked and entered the temple with them—walking, leaping, and praising God. And all the people saw him walking and praising God. Then they knew that it was he who sat begging alms at the Beautiful Gate of the temple."

And "all the people ran together to them in the porch which is called Solomon's, greatly amazed." Here was this man, a helpless cripple for forty years, rejoicing in the full use of his legs and happy in believing in Jesus.

Peter assured the people that the cure had happened through the merits of Jesus of Nazareth, whom God had raised from the dead. "His name, through faith in His name, has made this man strong, whom you see and know. Yes, the faith which comes through Him has given him this perfect soundness in the presence of you all."

The True Guilt of the Jews Revealed

The apostles spoke plainly of the Jews' great sin in putting to death the Prince of life, but they were careful not to drive their hearers to despair. "You

---

* This chapter is based on Acts 3; 4:1–31.

denied the Holy One and the Just," Peter said, "and asked for a murderer to be granted to you, and killed the Prince of life, whom God raised from the dead, of which we are witnesses." "Yet now, brethren, I know that you did it in ignorance, as did also your rulers." He told them that the Holy Spirit was calling them to repent. Only by faith in the One whom they had crucified could they have their sins forgiven.

"Repent therefore and be converted," Peter pleaded, "that your sins may be blotted out, so that times of refreshing may come from the presence of the Lord." "God, having raised up His Servant Jesus, sent Him to bless you, in turning away every one of you from your iniquities."

Many were waiting for this testimony, and when they heard it, they believed and joined forces with those who accepted the gospel.

While the disciples were speaking, "the priests, the captain of the temple, and the Sadducees came upon them, being greatly disturbed that they taught the people and preached in Jesus the resurrection from the dead."

The priests had spread the report that the disciples had stolen Christ's body while the Roman guard slept. It is not surprising that they were unhappy when they heard Peter and John preaching the resurrection of the One they had murdered. The Sadducees felt that their most cherished doctrine was in danger.

Pharisees and Sadducees agreed that if these new teachers were not stopped, their own influence would be in greater danger than when Jesus was on earth. So with the help of a number of Sadducees, the captain of the temple arrested Peter and John and put them in prison.

The Jewish rulers had received more than enough evidence that the apostles were speaking and acting under divine inspiration, but they firmly resisted the truth. Though at times they had been convinced that Christ was the Son of God, they had repressed that conviction and had crucified Him. Now God was giving them another opportunity to turn to Him. But the Jewish teachers refused to admit that the men charging them with crucifying Christ were speaking by the Holy Spirit's direction.

They became even more determined not to admit that they had been wrong. It was not that they could not yield. They could, but would not. They persistently rejected light and silenced the convictions of the Spirit, and their rebellion intensified with each new act of resistance against the message God had given His servants to proclaim.

A Sin Worse Than the Original Crucifixion of Christ

God does not declare His judgment against unrepentant sinners merely because of the sins they have committed, but because, when they are called to repent, they choose to continue to defy the light. If the Jewish leaders had submitted to the convicting power of the Holy Spirit, God would have pardoned them, but they were determined not to yield.

On the day following the crippled man's healing, Annas and Caiaphas met for the trial, and the prisoners were brought before them. In that very room, in front of some of those men, Peter had shamefully denied his Lord. Now he had an opportunity to redeem his cowardice. The Peter who denied Christ was impulsive and self-confident, but since his fall he had been converted. He was modest and self-distrustful, filled with the Holy Spirit, and was determined to remove the stain of his apostasy by honoring the name he had once disowned.

The priests were forced to ask the accused disciples how the cure of the crippled man had happened. With holy boldness Peter said, "Let it be known to you all, and to all the people of Israel, that by the name of Jesus Christ of Nazareth, whom you crucified, whom God raised from the dead, by Him this man stands here before you whole."

The Jewish leaders had thought the disciples would be overcome with fear and confusion when brought before the Sanhedrin. Instead, these witnesses spoke with a convincing power that silenced their opponents. There was no trace of fear in Peter's voice as he declared concerning Christ, "This is the 'stone that was rejected by you builders, which has become the chief cornerstone.'"

As the priests listened to the apostles' fearless words, "they realized that they had been with Jesus." When the disciples first heard the words of Christ, they felt that they needed Him. They searched for Him, they found Him, they followed Him, in the temple, at the table, on the mountainside, in the field. They were like students with a teacher, daily receiving lessons of eternal truth from Him.

Jesus, the Savior, who had walked and talked and prayed with them, had gone up to heaven in human form. They knew that He was standing before the throne of God, still their Friend and Savior, forever identified with suffering humanity. Their union with Him was stronger now than when He was with them in person. An indwelling Christ radiated out through them, so that people marveled when they saw it.

The man who had been miraculously healed stood close beside Peter as a convincing witness. The appearance of this man added weight to Peter's words. Priests and rulers were silent, unable to refute Peter's statement, but they were no less determined to put a stop to the disciples' teaching.

The priests had crucified Jesus, but here was convincing proof that they had not put a stop to the working of miracles in His name nor to the spreading of the truth He taught. The crippled man's healing and the apostles' preaching had filled Jerusalem with excitement!

The priests and rulers ordered the apostles to be taken away so that they could counsel among themselves. It would be useless to deny that the man had been healed. To cover up the miracle by falsehoods was impossible, since it had happened before a crowd of people. They felt that they must stop the work of the disciples, or their own disgrace would follow.

Calling them again before the Sanhedrin, the priests commanded them not to speak or teach in the name of Jesus. But Peter and John answered: "Whether it is right in the sight of God to listen to you more than to God, you judge. For we cannot but speak the things which we have seen and heard." So with repeated threats and warnings, the apostles were set free.

The Divine Gift of Holy Boldness

While Peter and John were prisoners, the other disciples prayed constantly for them, fearing that the leaders might repeat the cruelty they had shown to Christ. As soon as the two apostles were released, they reported the result of the hearing. The believers were overjoyed. "They raised their voices together to God and said, 'Sovereign Lord, . . . look at their threats, and grant to your servants to speak your word with all boldness, while you stretch out your hand to heal, and signs and wonders are performed through the name of your holy servant Jesus'" (NRSV).

The disciples saw that they would meet the same determined opposition that Christ had encountered. While their united prayers were going up to heaven in faith, the answer came. They were given a fresh outpouring of the Holy Spirit. Filled with courage, they went out again to proclaim the word of God. "With great power the apostles gave witness to the resurrection of the Lord Jesus." And God blessed their efforts.

The principle for which the disciples stood so fearlessly is the same that followers of the gospel clung to in the days of the Reformation. At the Diet of Spires, in 1529, the German princes heard the emperor's decree restricting religious liberty and prohibiting further spread of the reformed doctrines. Would the princes accept the decree? Should the light of the gospel be shut out from so many still in darkness? Those who had accepted the reformed faith met together, and their unanimous decision was, "Let us reject this decree. In matters of conscience the majority has no power."

The banner of religious liberty held high by the founders of the gospel church and by God's witnesses during the centuries since then has been committed to our hands in this last conflict. We are to recognize human government as divinely appointed, and we are to teach obedience to it as a sacred duty within its legitimate sphere. But when its claims conflict with the claims of God, we must obey God rather than men. A "Thus says the Lord" is not to be set aside for a "Thus says the church" or a "Thus says the state."

We are not to defy authorities. We should carefully consider our words, so that we do not appear antagonistic to law and order. We are not to say or do anything that would unnecessarily close up our opportunity to proclaim the truths committed to us. If the authorities forbid us to do this work, then we may say, as did the apostles, "Whether it is right in the sight of God to listen to you more than to God, you judge. For we cannot but speak the things which we have seen and heard."

A Dishonest Husband and Wife Punished*

As the disciples proclaimed the gospel, a great number of people believed. Many of these early believers were immediately cut off from family and friends, and it was necessary to provide them with food and shelter.

Those among the believers who had money and possessions cheerfully sacrificed to meet the emergency. Selling their houses or lands, they brought the money and laid it at the apostles' feet. Their love for their fellow believers and the cause they had embraced was greater than their love of money and possessions. They considered people to have higher value than earthly wealth.

In sharp contrast were the actions of Ananias and Sapphira. These professed disciples had heard the apostles preach the gospel. They had been present when "the place where they were assembled together was shaken; and they were all filled with the Holy Spirit" (Acts 4:31). Under the direct influence of the Spirit of God, Ananias and Sapphira had made a pledge to give to the Lord the proceeds from the sale of a certain piece of property.

Afterward, they began to regret their promise and harbored feelings of greed. They thought they had been too hasty and decided not to fulfill their pledge. Ashamed to have the others know that their selfish hearts grudged what they had solemnly dedicated to God, they deliberately decided to sell their property and pretend to give all the money into the general fund, but to keep a large share for themselves. In this way they would receive money to live on from the common fund and at the same time gain the admiration of their fellow believers. But God sees hypocrisy and falsehood. Ananias and Sapphira lied to the Holy Spirit, and God repaid their sin with swift judgment. When Ananias came with his offering, Peter said: "'Ananias, why has Satan filled your heart to lie to the Holy Spirit and keep back part of the price of the land for yourself? While it remained, was it not your own? And after it was sold, was it not in your own control? Why have you conceived this thing in your heart? You have not lied to men but to God.'

"Then Ananias, hearing these words, fell down and breathed his last. So great fear came upon all who heard these things."

No one had pressured Ananias,

---

* This chapter is based on Acts 4:32 to 5:11.

forcing him to sacrifice his possessions. He had acted from choice. But in attempting to deceive the disciples, he had lied to the Almighty.

"Now it was about three hours later when his wife came in, not knowing what had happened. And Peter answered her, 'Tell me whether you sold the land for so much?'

"She said, 'Yes, for so much.'

"Then Peter said to her, 'How is it that you have agreed together to test the Spirit of the Lord? Look, the feet of those who have buried your husband are at the door, and they will carry you out.' Then immediately she fell down at his feet and breathed her last. And the young men came in and found her dead, and carrying her out, buried her by her husband. So great fear came upon all the church and upon all who heard these things."

Why This Display of God's Wrath?

Infinite Wisdom saw that this display of God's wrath was necessary to guard the young church from becoming demoralized. The church would have been in danger if, when many converts were coming in, men and women had been added who were worshiping money. This judgment was a warning to the church to avoid falsehood and hypocrisy and to beware of robbing God.

God has made the preaching of the gospel dependent on the labors and gifts of His people—voluntary offerings and the tithe. God claims the tenth; He leaves everyone free to decide whether to give more than this. But when the Holy Spirit stirs someone's heart and that person makes a

vow to give a certain amount, the one who vows no longer has any right to the consecrated portion. Are promises we make to God less binding than written agreements with other people?

When divine light is shining into the heart with unusual clearness, habits of selfishness relax their grasp, and there is a desire to give to God. But Satan is not pleased to see the Redeemer's kingdom on earth built up. He suggests that the pledge was too much, that it may cripple their efforts to get property or gratify the desires of their families.

God blesses men and women with property so that they may be able to give to His cause. He gives them health and the ability to earn money. In turn, He invites them to show their gratitude by returning tithes and offerings. If funds would flow into the treasury in harmony with this divinely appointed plan, there would be plenty available to advance the Lord's work.

But hearts become hardened through selfishness. Like Ananias and Sapphira, many people spend money lavishly in gratifying self while they bring to God almost unwillingly a meager offering. They forget that God will no more accept the pittance they hand into the treasury than He accepted the offering of Ananias and Sapphira.

God wants us to learn how deep His hatred is for hypocrisy and deception. Ananias and Sapphira lied to the Holy Spirit and lost this life and the life that is to come. God declares that into the Holy City "there shall by no means enter . . . anything that defiles, or causes an abomination or a lie" (Revelation 21:27). Let telling the truth become a part of our lives! Playing fast and loose with truth means making shipwreck of faith. "Stand therefore, having girded your waist with truth" (Ephesians 6:14). Those who tell untruths sell their souls in a cheap market. They may seem to make business advancement that they could not gain by fair dealing; but finally they can trust no one. As liars themselves, they have no confidence in the word of others.

In the case of Ananias and Sapphira, fraud against God was quickly punished. Many in our own time commit the same sin. It is no less terrible in His sight now than in the apostles' time. God has given the warning: all who give themselves up to hypocrisy and covetousness are destroying their own souls.

Peter and John Freed From Prison*

In Christ's strength the disciples went out to tell the story of the manger and the cross and to triumph over all opposition. From their lips came words of divine eloquence that shook the world.

In Jerusalem, where deep prejudice and confused ideas prevailed about Him who had been crucified as a criminal, the disciples told the Jews of Christ's mission, His crucifixion, resurrection, and ascension. Priests and rulers were amazed to hear the bold testimony. The power of the risen Savior had truly fallen on the disciples. Along the streets where they were to walk, the people laid their sick "on cots and mats, in order that Peter's shadow might fall on some of them as he came by" (NRSV). Crowds gathered around them, and those who were healed glorified the name of the Redeemer.

As the Sadducees, who did not believe in a resurrection, heard the apostles declare that Christ had risen from the dead, they were enraged. If the apostles were allowed to preach a risen Savior, the sect of the Sadducees would soon become extinct. The Pharisees knew that the disciples'

teaching tended to undermine the Jewish ceremonies. Now both Sadducees and Pharisees determined that the disciples should be stopped. Filled with resentment, the priests put Peter and John in prison.

Those whom the Lord had entrusted with truth had proved unfaithful, and God chose others to do His work. The unfaithful leaders would not even admit the possibility that they did not rightly understand the Word or had misinterpreted the Scriptures. What right do these teachers have, they said, some of them just fishermen, to present ideas contrary to the doctrines that we have taught the people?

The disciples were not frightened. The Holy Spirit brought to their minds the words Christ had spoken: "If they persecuted Me, they will also persecute you." "The time is coming that whoever kills you will think that he offers God service." "These things I have told you, that when the time comes, you may remember that I told you of them." (John 15:20; 16:2, 4.)

God's Command Comes First

The mighty Ruler of the universe took the disciples' imprisonment into

* This chapter is based on Acts 5:12–42.

His own hands, for men were warring against His work. That night the angel of the Lord opened the prison doors and said to the disciples, "Go, stand in the temple and speak to the people all the words of this life." Did the apostles say, "We cannot do this until we have received permission from the magistrates?" No. God had said, "Go," and they obeyed. "They entered the temple early in the morning and taught."

When Peter and John appeared among the believers and told how the angel had led them through the group of soldiers guarding the prison, commanding them to resume the work that had been interrupted, the believers were filled with joy.

In the meantime the high priest had "called the council together." The priests and rulers had decided to charge the disciples with insurrection, to accuse them of murdering Ananias and Sapphira and of conspiring to deprive the priests of their authority. They hoped to stir up the mob to deal with the disciples as it had with Jesus. The priests feared that if people came to recognize Jesus as the Messiah, they would become angry with the religious leaders, who would then have to answer for the murder of Christ. They decided to take strong measures to prevent this.

When they sent for the prisoners, they were amazed at the word brought back: the prison doors were securely bolted and the guard stationed in front of them, but the prisoners were nowhere to be found.

Soon the report came, " 'The men whom you put in prison are standing in the temple and teaching the people!'

"Then the captain went with the officers and brought them without violence, for they feared the people, lest they should be stoned."

Although the apostles were delivered from prison, they were not safe from punishment. By sending an angel to deliver them, God had given them a sign of His presence. But now they were to suffer for the One whose gospel they were preaching.

Peter's Amazing Boldness

The record left by Peter and John is heroic. As they stood for the second time before the men who intended to destroy them, no fear or hesitation showed in their words or attitude. And when the high priest said, "Did we not strictly command you not to teach in this name? And look, you have filled Jerusalem with your doctrine, and intend to bring this Man's blood on us!" Peter answered, "We ought to obey God rather than men." It was an angel from heaven who delivered them from prison, and in following his directions they were obeying the divine command.

Then the Spirit came upon the disciples, and the accused became the accusers, charging the murder of Christ on those who composed the council. "The God of our fathers raised up Jesus whom you murdered by hanging on a tree. Him God has exalted to His right hand to be Prince and Savior, to give repentance to Israel and forgiveness of sins. And we are His witnesses to these things; and so also is the Holy Spirit whom God has given to those who obey Him."

The Jews were so enraged at these words that they decided to put the prisoners to death without further trial and without authority from the Roman officers. Already guilty of the blood of Christ, they were now eager to stain their hands with the blood of His disciples.

But in the council one man recognized the voice of God in the words the disciples had spoken. Gamaliel, a Pharisee with learning and high position, saw clearly that the violent step the priests were planning would lead to terrible consequences. Before addressing the council, he asked that the prisoners be removed. He knew very well that the murderers of Christ would stop at nothing to carry out their intentions.

He then spoke with great deliberation: "Fellow Israelites, consider carefully what you propose to do to these men. . . . I tell you, keep away from these men and let them alone; because if this plan or this undertaking is of human origin, it will fail; but if it is of God, you will not be able to overthrow them—in that case you may even be found fighting against God!" (NRSV).

The priests realized that they had to agree with Gamaliel. Very reluctantly, after beating the disciples and again commanding them not to preach in the name of Jesus any more, they released them. "So they departed from the presence of the council, rejoicing that they were counted worthy to suffer shame for His name. And daily in the temple, and in every house, they did not cease teaching and preaching Jesus as the Christ."

In the World We Have Trouble

Christ said about Himself, "Do not think that I came to bring peace on earth: I did not come to bring peace but a sword" (Matthew 10:34). He was the Prince of Peace, yet He was the cause of division. He who came to proclaim good news opened a controversy that burns deep and stirs intense passion in the human heart. And He warns His followers, "You will be betrayed even by parents and brothers, relatives and friends; and they will put some of you to death" (Luke 21:16).

Every insult and cruelty that Satan could persuade human hearts to devise has been inflicted on the followers of Jesus. The carnal heart still bitterly opposes the law of God. The world is no more in harmony with the principles of Christ today than in the days of the apostles. The same hatred that prompted the cry, "Crucify Him, crucify Him!" still works in those who rebel against God. The same spirit that consigned men and women to prison, to exile, and to death in the Dark Ages, that invented the torture of the Inquisition, that planned and executed the Massacre of St. Bartholomew, and that lit the fires of Smithfield, is still at work. Those who proclaim the gospel have always done so in the face of opposition, danger, and suffering.

Scorn and persecution have separated many from earthly friends, but never from the love of Christ. Never are Christ's followers more dearly loved by the Savior than when they are blamed and misunderstood for the truth's sake. Christ stands by their side. When they are confined within prison walls, Christ cheers their hearts with His love. When they suffer death for Christ's sake, the Savior says to them, They may kill the body, but they cannot hurt the soul.

"Fear not; for I am with you;
Be not dismayed, for I am your God.
I will strengthen you,
Yes, I will help you,
I will uphold you with My righteous right hand."

Isaiah 41:10

"He will redeem their life from oppression and violence;
And precious shall be their blood in His sight."

Psalm 72:14

Why the Seven Deacons Were Chosen*

In those days, when the number of the disciples was multiplying, there arose a complaint against the Hebrews by the Hellenists, because their widows were neglected in the daily distribution."

The early church was made up of many classes of people, of different nationalities. At the time of Pentecost, "there were dwelling in Jerusalem Jews, devout men, from every nation under heaven" (Acts 2:5). Among those of the Hebrew faith were Greek-speaking Jews known as Hellenists. Distrust had existed between them and the Jews of Palestine for a long time.

Those who had been converted were united by Christian love. Despite their former prejudices, all were in harmony with one another. But Satan tried to take advantage of former habits of thought, using them to introduce disunion into the church.

The enemy succeeded in stirring up the suspicions of some whose habit had been to find fault with their spiritual leaders, and so "there arose a complaint against the Hebrews by the Hellenists." The cause of complaint was an alleged neglect of the Greek widows in the daily distribution of help to the poor. The apostles had to act quickly to remove all opportunity for dissatisfaction, to prevent the enemy from bringing division among the believers.

Under the wise leadership of the apostles, the church was continually enlarging, and this growth increased the burdens on those in charge. They needed to distribute the responsibilities that a few had carried faithfully during the earlier days. The apostles must lay on others some of the burdens they had borne by themselves up to that time.

Calling the believers together, the apostles stated that the spiritual leaders should be relieved from the task of distributing to the poor and from similar burdens. They must be free to preach the gospel. "Therefore, brethren, seek out from among you seven men of good reputation, full of the Holy Spirit and wisdom, whom we may appoint over this business; but we will give ourselves continually to prayer and to the ministry of the word." The believers followed this advice, and by prayer and laying on of hands they set apart seven chosen men as deacons.

The Results of This New Plan

The appointment of the seven was

---

* This chapter is based on Acts 6:1–7.

a great blessing to the church. These officers gave careful consideration to individual needs as well as to the general financial interests of the church, and they were an important help in binding together the various interests of the church.

"Then the word of God spread, and the number of the disciples multiplied greatly in Jerusalem, and a great many of the priests were obedient to the faith." This was due both to the greater freedom the apostles now had and the zeal that the seven deacons showed. These men, ordained to look after the needs of the poor, were also fully qualified to instruct others in the truth, and they earnestly engaged in the work.

The proclamation of the gospel was to be worldwide, and the messengers of the cross should remain united, in this way revealing to the world that they were one with Christ in God. (See John 17:11, 14, 21, 23.) Their power was dependent on their keeping a close connection with the One who had commissioned them to preach the gospel.

If they would continue to work in unity, heavenly messengers would open the way for them, hearts would be prepared for the truth, and many would be won to Christ. The church would go forward

"Fair as the moon,
Clear as the sun,
Awesome as an army with banners"
    (Song of Solomon 6:10),

gloriously fulfilling her divine mission.

The church at Jerusalem was to serve as a model for the organization of churches everywhere. Those carrying the responsibility of overseeing the church were, as wise shepherds, to "tend the flock of God" and "be examples to the flock" (1 Peter 5:2, 3, NRSV), and the deacons were to be "men of good reputation, full of the Holy Spirit and wisdom."

When many believers had been formed into churches in various parts of the world, the organization was further perfected. All the members were to make a wise use of the talents entrusted to them. Some were given special gifts—"first apostles, second prophets, third teachers, after that miracles, then gifts of healings, helps, administrations, varieties of tongues" (1 Corinthians 12:28). But all were to work in harmony.

Each Believer Has a Special Gift of the Spirit

"To each is given the manifestation of the Spirit for the common good. To one is given through the Spirit the utterance of wisdom, and to another the utterance of knowledge according to the same Spirit, to another faith by the same Spirit, to another gifts of healing by the one Spirit, to another the working of miracles, to another prophecy, to another the discernment of spirits, to another various kinds of tongues, to another the interpretation of tongues. All these are activated by one and the same Spirit, who allots to each one individually just as the Spirit chooses.

"For just as the body is one and has many members, and all the members of the body, though many, are one body, so it is with Christ" (verses 7–12, NRSV).

Stephen, the First Martyr for Christ*

Stephen, the most prominent of the seven deacons, spoke the Greek language and was familiar with the customs of the Greeks. Because of this, he found opportunity to preach the gospel in the synagogues of the Greek Jews and boldly spoke of his faith. Educated rabbis and doctors of the law engaged him in public discussion, but "they were not able to resist the wisdom and the Spirit by which he spoke." He completely defeated his opponents. To him the promise was fulfilled, "I will give you a mouth and wisdom which all your adversaries will not be able to contradict or resist" (Luke 21:15).

The priests and rulers were filled with bitter hatred. They determined to silence his voice. Several times they had bribed the Roman authorities to overlook situations where the Jews had tried, condemned, and executed prisoners. The enemies of Stephen did not doubt that they could do this again, so they brought him before the Sanhedrin council for trial.

Well-educated Jews were called in to refute the arguments of the prisoner. Saul of Tarsus was there and used eloquence and logic to convince the people that Stephen was preaching dangerous doctrines. But in Stephen he met someone who had a full understanding of God's purpose in spreading the gospel to other nations.

The priests and rulers determined to make an example of Stephen. It would satisfy their revengeful hatred, and they would prevent others from adopting his belief. They hired witnesses to give false testimony. "We have heard him say," they declared, "that this Jesus of Nazareth will destroy this place and change the customs which Moses delivered to us."

A Holy Radiance Shines on Stephen's Face

As Stephen stood to answer the charges, "all who sat in the council . . . saw his face as the face of an angel." Many trembled and shaded their faces, but the rulers' stubborn unbelief and prejudice did not waver.

Stephen began his defense in a clear, thrilling voice that rang through the council hall. In words that held the assembly spellbound, he reviewed the history of the chosen people. He showed a thorough knowledge of the Jewish religious system and the spiritual interpretation of it now evident in

---

* This chapter is based on Acts 6:5–15; 7.

Christ. He made plain his loyalty to God and to the Jewish faith, while he connected Jesus Christ with all the Jewish history.

When Stephen connected Christ with the prophecies, the priest, pretending to be horror-stricken, tore his robe. To Stephen this was a signal that he was giving his last testimony. He abruptly ended his sermon.

Turning on his enraged judges, he called out: "You stiff-necked and uncircumcised in heart and ears! You always resist the Holy Spirit; as your fathers did, so do you. Which of the prophets did your fathers not persecute? And they killed those who foretold the coming of the Just One, of whom you now have become the betrayers and murderers, who have received the law by the direction of angels and have not kept it."

Priests and rulers were beside themselves with anger. In their cruel faces the prisoner read his fate, but he did not waver. For him the fear of death was gone. The scene before him faded from his vision. The gates of heaven seemed open to him, and, looking in, he saw Christ, as if just risen from His throne, standing ready to sustain His servant. Stephen exclaimed, "I see the heavens opened and the Son of Man standing at the right hand of God!"

As he described the glorious scene, it was more than his persecutors could endure. Covering their ears, they ran furiously at him in one united action and "cast him out of the city." "While they were stoning Stephen, he prayed, 'Lord Jesus, receive my spirit.' Then he knelt down and cried in a loud voice, 'Lord, do not hold this sin against them.' When he had said this, he died" (NRSV).

The Roman authorities accepted bribes of large sums of money to make no investigation.

Stephen's Martyrdom Makes a Deep Impression

The memory of Stephen's face and his words, which touched the hearts of those who heard them, remained in the minds of the onlookers and testified to the truth of what he had preached. His death was a bitter trial to the church, but it resulted in the conviction of Saul, who could not erase from his memory the glory that had rested on the martyr's face.

Saul's secret conviction—that Stephen had been honored by God when dishonored by men—made him angry. He continued to persecute the followers of Christ, arresting them in their houses and delivering them to the priests and rulers for imprisonment and death. His zeal brought terror to the Christians at Jerusalem. The Roman authorities secretly helped the Jews in order to make peace with them and win their favor.

After Stephen's death, Saul was elected a member of the Sanhedrin council in recognition of the part he had acted. He was a mighty instrument in the hands of Satan to carry out his rebellion against the Son of God. But Someone mightier than Satan had chosen Saul to take the place of the martyred Stephen, to spread far and wide the news of salvation through His blood.

The Gospel Reaches Samaria and Ethiopia*

After the death of Stephen a relentless persecution arose against the believers in Jerusalem. "They were all scattered throughout the regions of Judea and Samaria." Saul "made havoc of the church, entering every house, and dragging off men and women, committing them to prison." Later he said about this cruel work: "I myself was convinced that I ought to do many things against the name of Jesus of Nazareth. . . . I not only locked up many of the saints in prison, . . . by punishing them often in all the synagogues I tried to force them to blaspheme." "I also cast my vote against them when they were being condemned to death." (Acts 26:9–11, NRSV.)

At this time of danger Nicodemus came forward and fearlessly declared his faith in the Savior. Nicodemus was a member of the Sanhedrin. As he had witnessed Christ's wonderful works, the conviction had fastened on his mind that this was the One sent by God. Too proud to acknowledge his sympathy with the Galilean Teacher openly, he had gone to Jesus for a secret interview. Jesus unfolded to him His mission to the world, yet Nicode-

mus had still hesitated. For three years there was little apparent fruit. But in the Sanhedrin council he had repeatedly defeated schemes to destroy Christ. When Christ had finally been lifted up on the cross, Nicodemus remembered the words spoken to him in the night interview. "As Moses lifted up the serpent in the wilderness, even so must the Son of Man be lifted up" (John 3:14); and he saw in Jesus the world's Redeemer.

With Joseph of Arimathea, Nicodemus had borne the expense of Jesus' burial. The disciples had been afraid to show themselves openly as Christ's followers, but Nicodemus and Joseph, rich and honored men, had come boldly to do for their dead Master what the poor disciples would have found impossible to do. Their wealth and influence had protected them, to a great extent, from the evil intentions of the priests and rulers.

Nicodemus No Longer Cautious and Questioning

Now Nicodemus came forward to defend the infant church. He encouraged the faith of the disciples and used his wealth to help sustain the church

---

* *This chapter is based on Acts 8.*

at Jerusalem and advance the work. Those who had treated him with reverence now scorned him, and he became poor, yet he never wavered in defending his faith.

The persecution gave a great push to the work of the gospel. The ministry in Jerusalem had been successful, and there was danger that the disciples would linger there too long, forgetting the Savior's instruction to go to all the world. Instead of educating new converts to carry the gospel to those who had not heard it, they were in danger of taking a course that would lead the believers to be satisfied with what they had already accomplished. God permitted persecution to come to scatter His representatives where they could work for others. Driven from Jerusalem, the believers "went everywhere preaching the word."

When persecution scattered them, they went out filled with missionary zeal. They knew they held in their hands the bread of life for a starving world, and the love of Christ impelled them to break this bread to all who were in need. Wherever they went, they healed the sick and preached the gospel to the poor.

Philip, one of the seven deacons, was among those driven from Jerusalem. He "went down to the city of Samaria and preached Christ to them. And the multitudes with one accord heeded the things spoken by Philip, hearing and seeing the miracles which he did. . . . There was great joy in that city."

Christ's message to the Samaritan woman at Jacob's well had borne fruit. The woman had gone to the men of the city, saying, "Could this be the Christ?" They went with her, heard Jesus, and believed on Him. For two days Jesus stayed with them, "and many more believed because of His own word." (John 4:29, 41.)

When His disciples were driven from Jerusalem, the Samaritans welcomed them, and the Jewish converts gathered a precious harvest from among those who had once been their bitterest enemies.

While Philip was in Samaria, a heavenly messenger directed him to " 'go toward the south along the road which goes down from Jerusalem to Gaza.' . . . So he arose and went." He did not hesitate to obey, because he had learned the lesson of conforming to God's will.

The Baptism of the First Person From Africa

"And behold, a man of Ethiopia, a eunuch of great authority under Candace the queen of the Ethiopians, who had charge of all her treasury, and had come to Jerusalem to worship, was returning. And sitting in his chariot, he was reading Isaiah the prophet." God saw that this Ethiopian of good reputation and wide influence would give others the light he had received and would exert a strong influence for the gospel. Angels were with this seeker for light, and the Holy Spirit brought him in touch with someone who could lead him to the Savior.

The Holy Spirit directed Philip to go to the Ethiopian and explain the prophecy he was reading. "Go near," the Spirit said, "and overtake this chariot." Philip asked the official, " 'Do you understand what you are reading?' And he said, 'How can I, unless someone guides me?' And he asked Philip to come up and sit with him." The scripture he was reading was the prophecy of Isaiah relating to Christ:

"He was led as a sheep to the
    slaughter;
And as a lamb before its shearer is
    silent,
So He opened not His mouth.
In His humiliation His justice was
    taken away,
And who will declare His generation?
For His life is taken from the earth."

"Of whom does the prophet say this," the official asked, "of himself or of some other man?" Then Philip, beginning at the same scripture, "preached Jesus to him."

The man's heart was thrilled, and he was ready to accept the light. He did not make his high position an excuse for refusing the gospel. "As they went down the road, they came to some water. And the eunuch said, 'See, here is water. What hinders me from being baptized?'

"Then Philip said, 'If you believe with all your heart, you may.'

"And he answered and said, 'I believe that Jesus Christ is the son of God.'

"So he commanded the chariot to stand still. And both Philip and the eunuch went down into the water, and he baptized him. Now when they came up out of the water, the Spirit of the Lord caught Philip away, so that the eunuch saw him no more; and he went on his way rejoicing."

Angels Still Guide the Footsteps of People

This Ethiopian represented a large class who need to be taught by such missionaries as Philip—people who will hear the voice of God and go where He sends them. Many who are reading the Scriptures cannot understand their true meaning. All over the world men and women are looking longingly to heaven. Prayers and tears and inquiries go up from hearts hungering for light. Many are on the brink of the kingdom, waiting only to be gathered in.

An angel guided Philip to a man who was seeking light, and today angels will guide workers who will allow the Holy Spirit to sanctify their tongues and ennoble their hearts. The angel could have done the work himself for the Ethiopian, but this is not God's way of working. It is His plan that we are to work for our fellow human beings.

In every age everyone who has received the gospel has been given sacred truth to share with the world. God's faithful people have always been aggressive, wisely using their talents in His service.

The members of God's church are to be zealous, separating from worldly ambition and walking in the footsteps of Him who went about doing good. They are to minister to those in need of help, bringing to sinners a knowledge of the Savior's love. Such work brings a rich reward. Those who engage in it will see people won to the Savior. Everyone who has received Christ is called to work for the salvation of others. "The Spirit and the bride say, 'Come!' And let him who hears say, 'Come!'" (Revelation 22:17). The call to give this invitation includes everyone who has heard the invitation!

Thousands who have heard the message are still sitting idly in the marketplace, when they could engage in active service. To these Christ is saying, "Why have you been standing here idle all day?" And He adds, "You also go into the vineyard" (Matthew 20:6, 7).

God has waited a long time for the spirit of service to take possession of the whole church. When the members do their appointed work in fulfilling the gospel commission, the whole world will be warned and the Lord Jesus will return to this earth with power and great glory. "This gospel of the kingdom will be preached in all the world as a witness to all the nations, and then the end will come" (Matthew 24:14).

From Saul to Paul: Persecutor to Disciple*

Saul of Tarsus, a Roman citizen by birth, was a Jew by heritage and had been educated by the finest rabbis. He was "a Hebrew of the Hebrews; concerning the law, a Pharisee; concerning zeal, persecuting the church; concerning the righteousness which is in the law, blameless" (Philippians 3:5, 6). He inspired high hopes that he would be an able and zealous defender of the ancient faith. His elevation to the Sanhedrin council placed him in a position of power.

Saul had taken part in condemning Stephen, and the striking evidence of God's presence with the martyr had led him to doubt the cause he had taken up against the followers of Jesus. But the arguments of the priests finally convinced him that Stephen was a blasphemer, that Christ was a fraud, and that the religious leaders must be right.

Saul's education and prejudice, his respect for his teachers, and his pride braced him to rebel against the voice of conscience. And having decided that the priests and scribes were right, he became a bitter opponent of the disciples of Jesus. His activity in causing holy men and women to be condemned to imprisonment and even to death brought gloom to the newly organized church and caused many to seek safety by fleeing.

Those who were driven from Jerusalem "went everywhere preaching the word" (Acts 8:4). In Damascus the new faith gained many converts.

The priests and rulers had hoped that by stern persecution they could suppress the heresy. Now they must carry forward in other places the firm measures they had taken in Jerusalem against the new teaching. Saul offered his services for the special work at Damascus. "Breathing threats and murder against the disciples of the Lord," he "went to the high priest and asked letters from him to the synagogues of Damascus, so that if he found any who were of the Way, whether men or women, he might bring them bound to Jerusalem." So "with authority and commission from the chief priests" (Acts 26:12), Saul of Tarsus, in the vigor of manhood and burning with mistaken zeal, set out on that memorable journey.

A Light Too Glorious for Mortal Eyes to Bear

As the weary travelers neared

---

* This chapter is based on Acts 9:1–18.

Damascus, "at midday" they came within view of fertile lands, beautiful gardens, and fruitful orchards, watered by cool streams from the mountains. While Saul gazed with admiration on the attractive city below, suddenly, as he said later, there shone "around me and those who journeyed with me" "a light from heaven, brighter than the sun." Blinded, Saul fell on his face to the ground. He heard "a voice speaking . . . in the Hebrew language, 'Saul, Saul, why are you persecuting Me?' . . . 'I am Jesus, whom you are persecuting.' " (Acts 22:6; 26:13–15.)

Almost blinded by the light, Saul's companions heard a voice but saw no one. But Saul understood the words spoken, and in the glorious Being who stood before him he saw the Crucified One. The image of the Savior's face was imprinted forever on the heart of the stricken Jew. A flood of light poured into the darkened chambers of his mind, revealing the error of his former life and his need of the Holy Spirit.

Saul now saw that he had been doing the work of Satan. He had believed the priests and rulers when they told him that the story of the resurrection was a clever lie by the disciples. Now that Jesus Himself stood revealed, he was convinced of the disciples' claims.

In that hour the prophetic records were opened to Saul's understanding. He saw that the prophets had foretold the crucifixion, resurrection, and ascension of Jesus, and these proved that He was the Messiah. God brought Stephen's sermon forcibly to his mind, and he realized that the martyr really had seen "the glory of God, and Jesus standing at the right hand of God" (Acts 7:55)!

Saul Under Conviction

In that moment of divine revelation Saul remembered with terror that he had consented to Stephen's sacrifice, and that many other followers of Jesus had met death through his efforts. There were no valid arguments against Stephen's clear reasoning. The scholarly Jew had seen the face of the martyr as if it had been "the face of an angel" (Acts 6:15). He had seen Stephen forgive his enemies. He also had witnessed the strength and cheerful acceptance of their fate of many whom he had caused to be tormented. He had seen some even yield up their lives with rejoicing for their faith.

All these things had sometimes forced on Saul's mind an almost overwhelming conviction that Jesus was the promised Messiah. At such times he had struggled for entire nights against this conviction. Now Christ had spoken with His own voice, saying, "Saul, Saul, why are you persecuting Me?" And the question, "Who are You, Lord?" was answered by the same voice, "I am Jesus, whom you are persecuting." Christ here identifies Himself with His people. In persecuting the followers of Jesus, Saul had struck directly against the Lord of heaven.

"Trembling and astonished," he inquired, " 'Lord, what do You want me to do?'

"Then the Lord said to him, 'Arise and go into the city, and you will be told what you must do.' " When Saul arose from the ground, he found himself totally without sight. He believed that this blindness was a punishment from God. In terrible darkness he groped around, and in fear his companions "led him by the hand and brought him into Damascus."

On the morning of that day, Saul had approached Damascus with feelings of self-satisfaction because of the confidence the chief priest had placed in him. He was to stop the spread of the new faith in Damascus and had looked forward eagerly to the experiences before him.

But how different was his entrance into the city from what he had expected! Blind, tortured by remorse, not knowing what judgment might be in store for him, he sought out the home of the disciple Judas, where, left alone, he had much opportunity to reflect and pray.

For three days Saul was "without sight, and neither ate nor drank." Again and again with anguish he recalled his guilt in allowing himself to be controlled by the hatred of the priests and rulers, even when the face of Stephen had been lighted up with the radiance of heaven. He reviewed the many times he had closed his eyes against evidence and had urged the persecution of believers in Jesus.

In Lonely Seclusion

Saul spent these days of self-examination and humiliation in lonely seclusion. The believers feared that he might be putting on an act in order to deceive them, and they refused him sympathy. He had no desire to appeal to the unconverted Jews, for he knew they would not even listen to his story.

So his only hope of help was in a merciful God, and to Him he appealed with a broken heart. Shut in with God alone, Saul recalled many passages of Scripture referring to the first advent of Christ. As he reflected on the meaning of these prophecies, he was astonished at his former blindness and the blindness of the Jews in general. Prejudice and unbelief had prevented him from recognizing Jesus as the Messiah of prophecy.

As Saul yielded to the Holy Spirit, he saw the mistakes of his life and recognized the far-reaching claims of the law of God. He had been a proud Pharisee, confident that he was justified by his good works, but now he bowed before God with humility, confessing his unworthiness and pleading the merits of a crucified Savior. Saul longed to come into full harmony with the Father and the Son, and in intensity he offered fervent prayers to the throne of grace.

His prayers were not in vain. The inmost thoughts of his heart were transformed, and his mind came into harmony with God's purposes. Christ and His righteousness became more to Saul than the whole world.

He had believed that Jesus had disregarded the law of God and taught His disciples that it was of no effect, but after conversion Saul recognized Jesus as the one who had come into the world for the purpose of upholding His Father's law. He was convinced that Jesus was the originator of the Jewish system of sacrifices and that symbol had met fulfillment at the Crucifixion.

Saul was one whom Christ chose

for a most important work, yet the Lord did not immediately tell him of the work he was assigned. When Saul asked, "What do You want me to do?" the Savior placed him in connection with His church, to learn God's will for him. Christ had performed the work of revelation and conviction. Now the repentant Saul was to learn from those whom God had designated to teach His truth.

While Saul continued alone in prayer, the Lord appeared in vision to "a certain disciple at Damascus named Ananias." "Arise and go to the street called Straight, and inquire at the house of Judas for one called Saul of Tarsus, for behold, he is praying. And in a vision he has seen a man named Ananias coming in and putting his hand on him, so that he might receive his sight."

Ananias could scarcely believe the words of the angel. "Lord, I have heard from many about this man, how much harm he has done to Your saints in Jerusalem. And here he has authority from the chief priests to bind all who call on Your name." But the command was firm: "Go, for he is a chosen vessel of Mine to bear My name before Gentiles, kings, and the children of Israel."

Obediently, Ananias sought out the man who had breathed out threatenings against all who believed in Jesus. Putting his hands on the head of the repentant sufferer, he said, "'Brother Saul, the Lord Jesus . . . has sent me that you may receive your sight and be filled with the Holy Spirit.' Immediately there fell from his eyes something like scales, and he received his sight at once; and he arose and was baptized."

Thus Jesus placed Saul in connection with His appointed agencies on earth. The work of directing the repentant sinner in the way of life belonged to the organized church.

Many have an idea that they are responsible to Christ alone, independent of His recognized followers on earth. Jesus is the friend of sinners and has all power, but He respects the means He has chosen for our salvation. He directs sinners to the church, which He has made a channel of light to the world.

When Saul was given a revelation of Christ, he was placed in direct communication with the church. In this case Ananias represented Christ and also Christ's ministers, who are appointed to act in His place. In Christ's place Ananias touched the eyes of Saul. Representing Christ, he placed his hands on him, and as he prayed in Christ's name, Saul received the Holy Spirit. Ananias did all this in the name of Christ and by Christ's authority. Christ is the fountain; the church is the channel of communication.

How God Educated Paul*

Paul remained "some days with the disciples at Damascus. Immediately he preached the Christ in the synagogues, that He is the Son of God," who "died for our sins according to the Scriptures, . . . was buried, and . . . rose again the third day" (1 Corinthians 15:3, 4). His arguments from prophecy were so persuasive that the Jews were defeated and unable to answer him.

He who had journeyed to Damascus to persecute the believers was now preaching the gospel, strengthening its disciples, and bringing in new converts! Formerly known as a zealous defender of the Jewish religion, Paul could reason with extraordinary clearness, and by his withering sarcasm he could place an opponent in an unflattering light. Now the Jews saw this young man of unusual promise fearlessly preaching in the name of Jesus.

A general killed in battle is lost to his army, but his death gives no strength to the enemy. But when a prominent man joins the opposing forces, they gain a distinct advantage. The Lord could easily have struck Saul dead, and the persecuting power would have lost much strength. But

God not only spared Saul's life but converted him, transferring a champion from the enemy's side to the side of Christ. Paul was an eloquent speaker and a severe critic. With stern purpose and unflinching courage, he possessed the very qualifications that the early church needed.

All who heard him in Damascus were amazed. He declared that his change of faith resulted not from impulse, but from overwhelming evidence. He showed that the prophecies relating to the first advent of Christ had been literally fulfilled in Jesus of Nazareth.

Paul "increased all the more in strength, and confounded the Jews who dwelt in Damascus, proving that Jesus is the Christ." But many hardened their hearts, and soon their astonishment at his conversion changed into intense hatred.

The opposition grew so fierce that Paul was not allowed to continue at Damascus. He "went to Arabia" (Galatians 1:17), where he found a safe refuge.

Paul's "University" in the Desert

In the solitude of the desert Paul had opportunity to study and meditate.

---

* *This chapter is based on Acts 9:19–30.*

He calmly reviewed his past experience and turned to God with all his heart, not resting until he knew for certain that God had accepted his repentance and pardoned his sin. Jesus communed with him and established him in the faith, granting him an abundance of wisdom and grace. When the mind is brought into close communication with the mind of God, the effect on body, mind, and soul is beyond measure.

Under the inspiration of the Holy Spirit, Ananias had said to Paul: "The God of our fathers has chosen you that you should know His will, and see the Just One, and hear the voice of His mouth. For you will be His witness to all men of what you have seen and heard. And now why are you waiting? Arise and be baptized, and wash away your sins, calling on the name of the Lord" (Acts 22:14–16).

Jesus Himself, when He confronted Saul on the journey to Damascus, declared: "I have appeared to you for this purpose, to make you a minister and a witness both of the things which you have seen and of the things which I will yet reveal to you. I will deliver you from the Jewish people, as well as from the Gentiles, to whom I now send you, to open their eyes, in order to turn them from darkness to light, and from the power of Satan to God, that they may receive forgiveness of sins and inheritance among those who are sanctified by faith in Me" (Acts 26:16–18).

As he pondered these things, Paul understood more clearly his call "to be an apostle of Jesus Christ" (1 Corinthians 1:1). His call had come "not

from men nor through man, but through Jesus Christ and God the Father" (Galatians 1:1). He gave much study to the Scriptures, in order that he could preach "not with eloquent wisdom, so that the cross of Christ might not be emptied of its power," "but in demonstration of the Spirit and of power," that the faith of all who heard "should not be in the wisdom of men but in the power of God." (1 Corinthians 1:17, NRSV; 2:4, 5.) Viewing the wisdom of the world in the light of the cross, Paul "decided to know nothing among you except Jesus Christ and him crucified" (1 Corinthians 2:2, NRSV).

Paul never lost sight of the Source of wisdom and strength. Hear him say, "For to me, to live is Christ" (Philippians 1:21). "I regard everything as loss because of the surpassing value of knowing Christ Jesus my Lord. For his sake I have suffered the loss of all things" (Philippians 3:8, NRSV).

The Former Persecutor Is Persecuted

From Arabia Paul "returned again to Damascus" (Galatians 1:17), and "preached boldly . . . in the name of Jesus." Unable to counter his arguments, "the Jews plotted to kill him." They had the gates of the city guarded day and night to cut off his escape. Finally, the disciples "took him by night and let him down through an opening in the wall, lowering him in a basket" (NRSV).

After his escape he went to Jerusalem, about three years having passed since his conversion. His chief purpose was to visit Peter (Galatians 1:18). Upon arriving "he tried to join the disciples; but they were all afraid of him, and did not believe that he was a disciple." Could so bigoted a Pharisee become a sincere follower of Jesus? "But Barnabas took him and brought him to the apostles. And he declared to them how he had seen the Lord on the road, and that He had spoken to him, and how he had preached boldly at Damascus in the name of Jesus."

Soon the disciples had abundant evidence that his experience was genuine. The future apostle to the Gentiles was now back where his former associates lived, and he longed to make plain to these leaders the prophecies concerning the Messiah. Paul felt sure that these teachers in Israel were as sincere and honest as he had been. But he had miscalculated. Those at the head of the Jewish church refused to believe, but "attempted to kill him."

Sorrow filled his heart. With shame he thought of the part he had taken in Stephen's martyrdom, and now he worked to show the validity of the truth for which Stephen had given his life.

Burdened for those who refused to believe, Paul was praying in the temple when a heavenly messenger appeared and said, "Make haste and get out of Jerusalem quickly, for they will not receive your testimony concerning Me" (Acts 22:18). To Paul it seemed cowardly to run away. And so he answered: "Lord, they know that in every synagogue I imprisoned and beat those who believe on You. And when the blood of Your martyr Stephen was shed, I also was standing by consenting to his death, and guarding the clothes of those who were killing him." But God did not intend for His servant to expose his life needlessly, and the heavenly messenger replied, "Depart; for I will send you far from here to the Gentiles." (Verses 19–21.)

Learning of this vision, the believers quickly helped Paul's secret escape. They "brought him down to Caesarea and sent him out to Tarsus." Paul's departure suspended the violent opposition of the Jews for a while, and many people joined the believers.

The Gospel Goes to the Gentiles*

In his ministry at Lydda, Peter healed Aeneas, who had been paralyzed and confined to his bed for eight years. "Aeneas, Jesus the Christ heals you," the apostle said. "Arise and make your bed." "He arose immediately. So all who dwelt at Lydda and Sharon saw him and turned to the Lord."

At Joppa, near Lydda, lived a woman named Dorcas, a worthy disciple of Jesus. She filled her life with acts of kindness. She knew who needed comfortable clothing and who needed sympathy, and she ministered freely to the poor and sorrowful. Her skillful fingers were more active than her tongue.

"But it happened in those days that she became sick and died." Hearing that Peter was at Lydda, the believers sent messengers to him, "imploring him not to delay in coming to them. . . . When he had come, they brought him to the upper room. And all the widows stood by him weeping, showing the tunics and garments which Dorcas made while she was with them."

The apostle's heart was touched with sympathy. Then, directing that the weeping friends leave the room,

he knelt down and prayed for God to restore Dorcas to life. Turning to the body, he said, "'Tabitha, arise.' And she opened her eyes, and when she saw Peter she sat up." God saw fit to bring her back from the land of the enemy so that her skill and energy could still be a blessing to others.

While Peter was still at Joppa, he was called by God to take the gospel to Cornelius in Caesarea. This Roman centurion had been born to a noble family, and he held a position of honor. He had gained a knowledge of God from the Jews, and he worshiped Him with a true heart. He was widely known for his good deeds and righteous life. The Bible describes him as "a devout man and one who feared God with all his household, who gave alms generously to the people, and prayed to God always." He worshiped God and prayed in his home, for he did not dare to attempt to carry out his plans or to bear his responsibilities without God's help.

Though Cornelius believed the prophecies, he had no knowledge of the gospel as revealed in the life and death of Christ. But the same Holy Watcher who said about Abraham, "I

---

* This chapter is based on Acts 9:32 to 11:18.

know him," knew Cornelius and sent a message direct from heaven to him.

The angel appeared to him while he was praying. As the centurion heard himself addressed by name, he said, "What is it, lord?" The angel answered, "Send men to Joppa, and send for Simon whose surname is Peter. He is lodging with Simon, a tanner, whose house is by the sea." The angel even gave the occupation of the man with whom Peter was staying! Heaven knows all about the history and business of human beings, with the experience and work of the humble laborer as well as with that of the king on his throne.

Frail, Tempted Humans Are the Messengers

The angel was not instructed to tell Cornelius the story of the cross. A man subject to human weaknesses and temptations was to tell him of the crucified and risen Savior. God does not choose angels as His representatives, but human beings, people of like passions with those they are trying to save. Christ took humanity so that He could reach humanity. We needed a divine-human Savior to bring salvation to the world. And to men and women God has committed the sacred trust of making known "the unsearchable riches of Christ" (Ephesians 3:8). The Lord brings those who are seeking for truth into contact with fellow beings who know the truth. Those who have received light are to share it with those in darkness. God has made humanity the working agency through which the gospel exercises its transforming power.

Cornelius gladly obeyed. When

the angel had gone, he "called two of his household servants and a devout soldier from among those who waited on him continually. So when he had explained all these things to them, he sent them to Joppa."

After speaking with Cornelius, the angel went to Peter. At the time, he was praying on the roof of the house where he was staying, and "became very hungry and wanted to eat; but while they made ready, he fell into a trance." It was not just for physical food that Peter was hungry. He hungered for the salvation of his fellow Jews. He had an intense desire to show them the prophecies relating to Christ.

In the vision Peter saw "a great sheet. . . . In it were all kinds of four-footed animals of the earth, wild beasts, creeping things, and birds of the air. And a voice came to him, 'Rise, Peter; kill and eat.'

"But Peter said, 'Not so, Lord! For I have never eaten anything common or unclean.'

"And a voice spoke to him again the second time, 'What God has cleansed you must not call common.' This was done three times. And the object was taken up into heaven again."

This vision revealed to Peter God's plan—that the Gentiles should be heirs to the blessings of salvation along with the Jews. None of the disciples had yet preached the gospel to Gentiles. In their minds the Gentiles were excluded from the blessings of the gospel. Now the Lord was trying to teach Peter the worldwide extent of God's plan.

Many Gentiles had listened to the

preaching of Peter and the other apostles, and many Greek Jews had become believers in Christ. Cornelius, however, was to be the first important convert among the Gentiles. The door that many Jewish converts had closed against Gentiles was now to be thrown open. Gentiles who accepted the gospel were to be equal with Jewish disciples, without needing circumcision.

How carefully the Lord worked to overcome the prejudice in Peter's mind! By the vision He intended to teach that in heaven there are no racial distinctions. Through Christ the heathen may receive the privileges of the gospel.

While Peter was thinking about the vision, the men Cornelius had sent arrived and stood in front of the home where he was staying. Then the Spirit said to him, "Three men are searching for you. Now get up, go down, and go with them without hesitation; for I have sent them" (NRSV).

Peter Finds This a Difficult Command

Peter was reluctant to carry out the duty given him, but he dared not disobey. He went down and said, "I am he whom you seek. For what reason have you come?" They told him, "Cornelius the centurion, a just man, one who fears God and has a good reputation among all the nation of the Jews, was divinely instructed by a holy angel to summon you to his house, and to hear words from you."

In obedience to God, on the following morning the apostle set out, accompanied by six other Christians. These would be witnesses to everything that he would say or do, for Peter knew that he would have to answer for such a direct violation of Jewish teachings.

As Peter entered the Gentile's house, Cornelius greeted him as someone that Heaven honored. Overwhelmed with reverence for the one God had sent to teach him, he fell at the apostle's feet and worshiped him. Peter was horror-stricken and lifted the centurion up, saying, "Stand up; I myself am also a man."

To the large company of Cornelius's "relatives and close friends," Peter said: "You know how unlawful it is for a Jewish man to keep company with or go to one of another nation. But God has shown me that I should not call any man common or unclean. Therefore I came . . . as soon as I was sent for. I ask, then, for what reason have you sent for me?"

Cornelius then told his experience, saying in conclusion: We are "all present before God, to hear all the things commanded you by God."

Peter said, "I perceive that God shows no partiality. But in every nation whoever fears Him and works righteousness is accepted by Him."

Then the apostle preached Christ to that group of attentive hearers. As Peter pointed them to Jesus as the sinner's only hope, he himself understood more fully the vision he had seen, and his heart glowed with the spirit of the truth he was presenting.

Suddenly, "While Peter was still speaking these words, the Holy Spirit fell on all those who heard the word. And those of the circumcision who believed were astonished, as many as came with Peter, because the gift of the Holy Spirit had been poured out on the Gentiles also. For they heard them speak with tongues and magnify God.

"Then Peter answered, 'Can anyone forbid water, that these should not be baptized who have received the Holy Spirit just as we have?' And he commanded them to be baptized in the name of the Lord."

This is how the gospel came to those who had been "strangers and foreigners," making them members of the household of God. From the household of Cornelius a widespread work of grace went forward in that heathen city.

Today there are many like Cornelius whom the Lord wants to connect with His work. Their sympathies are with the Lord's people, but ties binding them to the world hold them firmly. We should make special efforts for these people.

God calls for earnest, humble workers who will take the gospel to the higher classes. The greatest people of this earth are not beyond the power of a wonder-working God. If workers will do their duty, God will convert people who occupy responsible positions, people of intellect and influence. Converted, they will have a special burden for other members of this neglected class. They will consecrate time and money to the work, and new efficiency and power will be added to the church.

Many in the world are nearer the kingdom than we suppose. Every-

where are people who will take their stand for Christ. Urged by love, they will urge others to come to Him.

Peter Places the Matter Before His Associates

When the believers in Judea heard that Peter had preached to Gentiles, they were surprised and offended. The next time they saw Peter, they strongly condemned him: "You went in to uncircumcised men and ate with them!"

Peter related his experience—the vision, the command to go to the Gentiles, the coming of the messengers, his journey to Caesarea, and the meeting with Cornelius. He told about talking with the centurion, who had told him of the vision by which God had directed him to send for Peter.

"As I began to speak," he said, "the Holy Spirit fell upon them, as upon us at the beginning. Then I remembered the word of the Lord, how He said, 'John indeed baptized with water, but you shall be baptized with the Holy Spirit.' If therefore God gave them the same gift as He gave us when we believed on the Lord Jesus Christ, who was I that I could withstand God?"

The brethren were silenced. Convinced that their prejudice and exclusiveness were completely contrary to the gospel, they said, "Then God has also granted to the Gentiles repentance to life."

In this way prejudice was broken down, exclusiveness abandoned, and the way opened for the gospel to be preached to the Gentiles.

An Angel Delivers Peter From Prison*

About that time Herod the king laid violent hands upon some who belonged to the church" (NRSV). Herod Agrippa, who ruled under Claudius the Roman emperor, professed to be a convert to the Jewish faith. Wanting to gain the favor of the Jews and hoping that this would protect his position and honors, he proceeded to persecute the church of Christ. He threw James, the brother of John, into prison and sent an executioner to kill him. When he saw that this greatly pleased the Jews, he imprisoned Peter also.

The death of James brought the believers great distress. When Peter was also imprisoned, the entire church fasted and prayed.

The Jews praised Herod's act in putting James to death, though some held that a public execution would have more thoroughly intimidated the believers. So Herod meant to gratify the Jews even more by making a public spectacle of Peter's death, but not in front of all the people then assembled in Jerusalem. He was afraid that the sight of Peter being led out to die might excite the pity of the crowds.

The priests and elders also were afraid that Peter might make one of those powerful appeals to study the life and character of Jesus—appeals that they had been unable to counter. Peter's zeal had led many to take their stand for the gospel, and the rulers feared that if he were given an opportunity to defend his faith, the crowds who had come to the city to worship would demand his release.

While Peter's execution was being delayed on various pretexts until after Passover, the church had time for heart-searching. They prayed for Peter without stopping, for they felt that the work of Christ could not afford to lose him.

Meanwhile worshipers from every nation came to the temple, a glittering vision of beauty and grandeur. But Jehovah was no longer to be found in that lovely place. When Christ looked on the interior of the temple for the last time, He said, "See, your house is left to you, desolate" (Matthew 23:38, NRSV). God had withdrawn His presence forever.

God Answers the Constant Prayers of His People

Herod finally set the day of Peter's

---

* This chapter is based on Acts 12:1–23.

execution, but the prayers of the believers still went up to heaven. Angels were watching over the imprisoned apostle.

To prevent any possibility of escape, Peter had been put under the charge of sixteen soldiers who guarded him day and night. In a rock-hewn cell he was placed between two soldiers and bound by two chains, each fastened to one of the soldiers. He was unable to move without their knowledge. With the prison doors fastened and a guard stationed at them, there was no chance of rescue or escape. But man's extremity is God's opportunity. The bolts and bars and the Roman guard would only make God's triumph complete when He delivered Peter. Herod, lifting his hand against Omnipotence, was to be utterly defeated.

The last night before the execution God sent a mighty angel from heaven. The strong gates opened without the aid of human hands. The angel passed through, and the gates closed noiselessly behind him. He entered the cell, and there lay Peter, sleeping the peaceful sleep of perfect trust.

Not until the apostle felt the touch of the angel's hand and heard a voice saying, "Get up quickly" (NRSV), did he wake up enough to see his cell illuminated by an angel of glory standing before him. Mechanically he obeyed, and when he got up he lifted his hands, dimly conscious that the chains had fallen from his wrists.

Again the voice told him, "Fasten your belt and put on your sandals" (NRSV). Peter mechanically obeyed, believing that he was dreaming.

Once more the angel commanded, "Wrap your cloak around you and follow me" (NRSV). He moved toward the door. The usually talkative Peter was now speechless from amazement. They stepped over the guard. All by itself the heavily bolted door swung open and closed again immediately, while the guards were motionless at their post.

The second door opened like the first, with no creaking of hinges or rattling of bolts. They passed through, and it closed again just as silently. In the same way they passed through the third gate and found themselves in the open street. Neither one spoke a word. The angel went on in front, encircled by dazzling brightness, and Peter followed, still believing that he was dreaming. They passed through one street, and then the angel disappeared, his mission accomplished.

Peter Finally Realizes He Is Free

Peter found himself in deep darkness, but as his eyes gradually became accustomed to it, it seemed to lessen, and he discovered that he was alone in the silent street, the cool night air blowing on his face. He was free, in a familiar part of the city. He recognized the place as one where he had often been and had expected to pass by in the morning for the last time.

He remembered falling asleep, chained between two soldiers, with his sandals and outer garments removed. He looked at himself and found that he was fully dressed. His swollen wrists were free from the restraints. He realized that his freedom was no dream or vision, but a reality. An angel had delivered him from prison and death!

"Then Peter came to himself and said, 'Now I am sure that the Lord has sent his angel and rescued me from the hands of Herod'" (NRSV).

The apostle made his way quickly to the house where at that moment his fellow Christians were praying earnestly for him. "When he knocked at the outer gate, a maid named Rhoda came to answer. On recognizing Peter's voice, she was so overjoyed that, instead of opening the gate, she ran in and announced that Peter was standing at the gate. They said to her, 'You are out of your mind!' But she insisted that it was so. They said, 'It is his angel.' Meanwhile Peter continued knocking; and when they opened the gate, they saw him and were amazed. He motioned to them with his hand to be silent, and described for them how the Lord had brought him out of the prison." And Peter "left and went to another place" (NRSV). God had heard their prayers and delivered him from the hands of Herod.

In the morning, a large gathering of people assembled to witness the apostles' execution. Herod sent officers to the prison for Peter to bring him with a great display of arms, not only to be sure he did not escape but to intimidate all who sympathized with him.

When the keepers found that Peter had escaped, they were terrified. They had been clearly warned that their lives would be required for the life of their prisoner, and they had been especially vigilant. When the officers came for Peter at the prison, the bolts and bars were still fastened, the chains were still secured to the wrists of the two soldiers, but the prisoner was gone.

When the report of Peter's escape came to Herod, he was enraged. He ordered the prison guard to be put to death. Herod was determined not to acknowledge that divine power had overruled his plans, and he set himself boldly to defy God.

Not long after this, Herod went to a great festival in Caesarea designed to gain the praise of the people. There was much feasting and wine drinking. With pomp and ceremony he addressed the people in an eloquent oration. Dressed in a robe sparkling with silver and gold, which caught the rays of the sun in its glittering folds, he was a stunning sight. The majesty of his appearance and the force of his well-chosen language swayed the crowd. Wild with enthusiasm, they showered flattery on him, declaring that no mortal could look as great as that or speak with such eloquence. They declared that from then on they would worship him as a god.

Some whose voices were now glorifying a vile sinner had a few years before raised the frenzied cry, Away with Jesus! Crucify Him! Under His humble exterior, the Jews could not recognize the Lord of life and glory. But they were ready to worship as a god the king whose splendid garments of silver and gold covered a corrupt, cruel heart.

King Herod Struck Down by an Angel

Herod accepted the idolatry of the people as his right. A glow of gratified pride spread over his face as he heard the shout, "The voice of a god, and not of a mortal!" (NRSV).

But suddenly his face became pale

When Moses was trying to carry burdens so heavy that he would have soon worn away, Jethro counseled him to plan for a wise distribution of responsibilities. "You should represent the people before God," Jethro advised, "and you should bring their cases before God." Jethro further advised that men be appointed to act as "officers over thousands, hundreds, fifties, and tens," relieving Moses of many minor matters that consecrated helpers could handle. (Exodus 18:19, 21, NRSV.)

Those in leading positions of responsibility in the church should deal with the more serious matters demanding special wisdom and compassion. Such people should not adjust minor matters that others are well qualified to manage.

"Moses chose able men from all Israel. . . . Hard cases they brought to Moses, but any minor case they decided themselves" (verses 25, 26, NRSV). Moses was careful to select men possessing dignity, sound judgment, and experience.

Solomon was called to fill a position of leading responsibility, and David gave him a special command: "You, my son Solomon, know the God of your father, and serve Him with a loyal heart and with a willing mind; for the Lord searches all hearts and understands all the intent of the thoughts. If you seek Him, He will be found by you" (1 Chronicles 28:9).

A Beautiful Plan of Organization

The same principles of piety and justice that were to guide God's people in the time of Moses and David were also for those given the care of the newly organized church in the gospel era. In setting things in order and ordaining certain men to act as officers, the apostles held to the standards of leadership outlined in the Old Testament. He who is called to leading responsibility in the church "must be blameless; he must not be arrogant or quick-tempered or addicted to wine or violent or greedy for gain; but he must be hospitable, a lover of goodness, prudent, upright, devout, and self-controlled. He must have a firm grasp of the word that is trustworthy in accordance with the teaching, so that he may be able both to preach with sound doctrine and to refute those who contradict it" (Titus 1:7–9, NRSV).

The order that the early Christian church maintained made it possible for them to move forward as a well-disciplined army. Though scattered over a large territory, believers were all one body; all moved in agreement and in harmony. When dissension arose in a local church, they did not permit matters to create division, but referred them to a general council of appointed delegates from the various churches, with the apostles and elders in positions of leading responsibility. In this way they thwarted the plans of the enemy to disrupt and destroy.

"God is not the author of confusion but of peace" (1 Corinthians 14:33). He requires us to observe order and system today. Christian is to be united with Christian, church with church, every agency subordinate to the Holy Spirit, and all combined in giving the world the good news of God's grace.

as death and twisted with agony. Great drops of sweat came from his pores. For a moment he stood motionless with pain and terror. Then turning his purple face to his horror-stricken friends, he cried out in hollow tones, He whom you have exalted as a god is stricken with death.

Suffering excruciating anguish, he was carried from the festive scene. A moment before, he had proudly received the worship of that vast crowd. Now he realized he was in the hands of a Ruler who was mightier than himself.

He remembered his persecution of Christ's followers, his command to execute James, his plan to put the apostle Peter to death. He remembered how in humiliation and rage he had taken revenge on the prison guards. He felt that God was now dealing with him. He found no relief from pain of body or anguish of mind, and he expected none. Herod knew that in accepting the worship of the people he had filled up his cup of iniquity.

The same angel who had come to rescue Peter was the messenger of judgment to Herod, laying his pride in the dust and bringing the punishment of the Almighty on him. Herod died in great agony of mind and body.

The news that the apostle of Christ had been delivered from prison and death while his persecutor had been struck down by the curse of God went to all lands, leading many to believe in Christ.

What Angels Are Doing Today

As in the days of the apostles, heavenly messengers today are working to comfort the sorrowing, protect the unrepentant, and win hearts to Christ. Angels are constantly carrying the prayers of the needy and distressed to the Father above and bringing hope and courage to human hearts. These angels create a heavenly atmosphere around us, lifting us toward the unseen and the eternal.

Only by spiritual vision can we recognize heavenly things. Only the spiritual ear can hear the harmony of heavenly voices. "The angel of the Lord encamps all around those who fear Him, and delivers them" (Psalm 34:7). God commissions angels to guard His chosen ones from "the pestilence that walks in darkness" and "the destruction that lays waste at noonday" (Psalm 91:6).

Angels have talked with human beings as someone might speak with a friend and have led them to places of safety. Again and again the encouraging words of angels have renewed the drooping spirits of the faithful.

Angels work tirelessly to help those for whom Christ died. "There will be more joy in heaven over one sinner who repents than over ninety-nine just persons who need no repentance" (Luke 15:7). Angels carry to heaven a report of every effort to dispel darkness and spread the knowledge of Christ.

The powers of heaven are watching the warfare that God's servants are carrying on. All the heavenly angels are at the service of the humble, believing people of God.

Remember that every true child of God has the cooperation of heavenly beings. Invisible armies surround the meek and lowly ones who believe and claim the promises of God. Angels that excel in strength stand at God's right hand, "all ministering spirits sent forth to minister for those who will inherit salvation" (Hebrews 1:14).

Dramatic Success at Antioch[*]

After persecution had driven the disciples from Jerusalem, the gospel message spread rapidly. Many small gatherings of believers formed in important centers. Some disciples "traveled as far as Phoenicia, Cyprus, and Antioch, preaching the word," usually just to the Hebrew and Greek Jews found in nearly all the cities of the world.

In Antioch, the major city of Syria, the people received the gospel gladly. Extensive commerce brought many people of various nationalities to the city. People thought well of Antioch because of its healthful location, beautiful surroundings, wealth, culture, and refinement. It had become a city of luxury and vice.

In Antioch disciples from Cyprus and Cyrene taught the gospel publicly. Their earnest labors bore fruit. "A great number believed and turned to the Lord."

News of this came to the church in Jerusalem, and "they sent out Barnabas to go as far as Antioch." Barnabas saw the work that had already been accomplished, and he "was glad, and encouraged them all that with purpose of heart they should continue with the Lord." Many were added to the believers there. As the work developed, Barnabas felt the need of help. He went to Tarsus to seek for Paul, who had been working in "the regions of Syria and Cilicia," preaching "the faith which he once tried to destroy" (Galatians 1:21, 23). Barnabas persuaded him to return with him.

In the populous city of Antioch, Paul's learning and zeal exerted a powerful influence, and he proved to be just the help that Barnabas needed. For a year the two worked together, bringing a knowledge of the world's Redeemer to many people.

The disciples were first called Christians in Antioch. People called them that because Christ was the theme of their preaching and their conversation. They never stopped telling people about His teachings and miracles of healing. With quivering lips and tearful eyes they spoke of His betrayal, trial, and execution, the torture His enemies inflicted on Him, and the Godlike pity with which He prayed for those who persecuted Him. His resurrection, ascension, and work as Mediator for fallen humanity were topics on which they loved to dwell. Well

---

* This chapter is based on Acts 11:19–26; 13:1–3.

might the heathen call them Christians!

The Beautiful Name God Gave the Believers

God gave them the name of Christian, a royal name given to all who join themselves to Christ. Of this name James wrote later, "Do not the rich . . . blaspheme that noble name by which you are called?" (James 2:6, 7). And Peter declared, "If you are reproached for the name of Christ, blessed are you" (1 Peter 4:14).

Living among a people who seemed not to care much about things of eternal value, the believers at Antioch tried to get the attention of the honest in heart. In their humble ministry in the various walks of life, they bore testimony every day to their faith in Christ.

Today God intends that chosen, talented workers be stationed in important centers of population. It is also His purpose that church members living in these cities use their God-given talents in working to draw others to Christ. Such workers will find that many who never could have been reached in any other way are ready to respond to intelligent personal effort.

God is calling on ministers, physicians, nurses, literature workers, and other consecrated, talented church members who know the Word of God and the power of His grace to consider the needs of the unwarned cities. We must use every possible means to put today's opportunities to wise use.

Working with Barnabas strengthened Paul's conviction that the Lord had called him to work for the Gentile world. When he was converted, the Lord told him that he was to minister to the Gentiles, "to open their eyes, in order to turn them from darkness to light, and from the power of Satan to God, that they may receive forgiveness of sins and an inheritance among those who are sanctified by faith in Me" (Acts 26:18). The angel had said to Ananias, "He is a chosen vessel of Mine to bear My name before Gentiles, kings, and the children of Israel" (Acts 9:15).

So the Lord had given Paul his commission to enter the mission field of the Gentile world, to make known "the mystery" that had been "kept secret since the world began" (Romans 16:25), "that the Gentiles should be fellow heirs, of the same body, and partakers of His promise in Christ through the gospel, of which," says Paul, "I became a minister. . . . To me, who am less than the least of all the saints, this grace was given, that I should preach among the Gentiles the unsearchable riches of Christ" (Ephesians 3:6–8).

Neither Paul nor Barnabas had yet been formally ordained to gospel ministry, but God was about to entrust them with a difficult task for which they would need every advantage that the church could provide them.

The Meaning of Gospel Ordination

"Now in the church at Antioch there were prophets and teachers: Barnabas, Simeon who was called Niger, Lucius of Cyrene, Manaen . . . , and Saul. While they were worshiping the Lord and fasting, the Holy Spirit said, 'Set apart for me Barnabas and Saul for the work to which I have called them'" (Acts 13:1, 2, NRSV). These apostles, whom the church solemnly dedicated to God by fasting and prayer and laying on of hands, were authorized not only to teach the truth but to perform the rite of baptism and to organize churches.

They were now to proclaim the gospel among the Gentiles with vigor, and the church was to be strengthened by a great harvest of new Christians. The apostles taught that "the middle wall of separation" (Ephesians 2:14) that had separated the Jewish and the Gentile world was broken down in Christ. This would naturally subject them to the charge of heresy, and many believing Jews would question their authority as ministers of the gospel. In order to put their work above challenge, God instructed the church to set them apart publicly to the work of the ministry, recognizing their divine appointment to carry the good news of the gospel to the Gentiles.

Both Paul and Barnabas had already received their commission from God Himself, and laying on of hands gave them no new qualification. It was understood as a form of designation to an appointed office. By this means the church set its seal of approval on the work of God.

To the Jew this form was significant. When a father blessed his children, he laid his hands reverently on their heads. When an animal was devoted to sacrifice, the priest laid his hand on the head of the victim. When the ministers in Antioch laid their hands on Paul and Barnabas, by that action they asked God to pour His blessing on the chosen apostles in their appointed work.

In later years, people attached too much importance to laying on of hands, as if a power came instantly on those who received such ordination. But in the setting apart of these two apostles, there is no record that virtue came on them merely by laying on of hands.

Years before, when God first revealed to Paul His plans concerning Him, He brought him into contact with the newly organized church. Furthermore, God did not leave the church at Damascus in darkness regarding the converted Pharisee. And now the Holy Spirit again gave the church the work of ordaining Paul and his fellow worker.

God Recognizes and Honors Church Organization

God has made His church a channel of light. He does not give an experience to one of His servants that is contrary to the experience of the church itself. Neither does He give one individual a knowledge of His will for the entire church while leaving the church in darkness. He puts His servants in close connection with His church so that they may have less confidence in themselves and greater confidence in others whom He is leading.

Those who constantly lean toward individual independence seem unable to realize that independence of spirit will likely lead people to have too much confidence in themselves rather than to respect the counsel and judgment of their fellow church members, especially of those in the offices God has appointed for leadership. God has granted His church special authority that no one can rightly disregard, for anyone who does this despises the voice of God.

Satan tries to separate such people from those God has used to build up and extend His work. Any worker in the Lord's cause who passes these by and thinks that his light must come through no other channel than directly from God is in danger of being deceived by the enemy and overthrown. The Lord intends that all believers should maintain a close relationship—Christian should be united to Christian and church to church, every agency under the Holy Spirit. All believers will be united in an organized effort to give to the world the good news of God's grace.

Paul believed that his ordination marked a new epoch in his life. He would later date the beginning of his apostleship to this time.

While the light was shining brightly at Antioch, the apostles were carrying on important work in Jerusalem. Every year, many Jews from all lands came to worship at the temple. Some of these devout pilgrims were earnest students of the prophecies, longing for the Messiah to come. The apostles preached Christ with unflinching courage, though they knew they were placing their lives in danger. Many people became converts to the faith, and when they returned home, they scattered seeds of truth through all nations and among all classes of people.

Peter, James, and John felt confident that God had appointed them to preach Christ among their countrymen at home. Faithfully and wisely they testified about what they had seen and heard, appealing to the "more sure word of prophecy" (2 Peter 1:19, KJV) to persuade "the house of Israel . . . that God has made this Jesus . . . both Lord and Christ" (Acts 2:36).

Heralds of the Gospel *

After their ordination Paul and Barnabas "went down to Seleucia, and from there they sailed to Cyprus." Barnabas was "a native of Cyprus" (Acts 4:36, NRSV), and now he and Paul visited this island, accompanied by John Mark, a relative of Barnabas. Cyprus was one of the places where believers had gone because of persecution after Stephen's death.

Mark's mother had become a Christian, and the apostles were always sure of a welcome and rest in her home at Jerusalem. During one of these visits to his mother's home, Mark suggested to Paul and Barnabas that he go with them on their missionary tour. He longed to devote himself to the work of the gospel.

When the apostles "had gone through the island to Paphos, they found a certain sorcerer, a false prophet, a Jew whose name was Bar-Jesus, who was with the proconsul, Sergius Paulus, an intelligent man. This man called for Barnabas and Saul and sought to hear the word of God. But Elymas the sorcerer (for so his name is translated) withstood them, seeking to turn the proconsul away from the faith."

When Sergius Paulus was listening to the apostles, the forces of evil worked through the sorcerer Elymas to try to turn him from the faith and so defeat God's plans. The fallen enemy works in this way to keep people of influence on his side and prevent them from giving effective service in God's cause.

Paul had the courage to rebuke the one through whom the enemy was working. "Filled with the Holy Spirit," he "said, 'You son of the devil, you enemy of all righteousness, full of all deceit and villainy, will you not stop making crooked the straight paths of the Lord? And now listen—the hand of the Lord is against you, and you will be blind for a while, unable to see the sun.' Immediately mist and darkness came over him, and he went about groping for someone to lead him by the hand" (NRSV).

The sorcerer had closed his eyes to gospel truth, and in righteous anger the Lord caused his natural eyes to be closed. This blindness was only for a time, so that he could repent and seek pardon from the God he had offended. The fact that he had to grope about in blindness proved to everyone that the

---

This chapter is based on Acts 13:4–52.

apostles' miracles, which Elymas had denounced as skillful tricks, were done by the power of God. The deputy was convinced, and he accepted the gospel.

Those who preach the truth will meet Satan in many forms. It is the duty of Christ's ministers to stand faithful at their posts, in the fear of God. In this way they may put the forces of Satan into confusion, triumphing in the name of the Lord.

Paul and his companions continued their journey, going to Perga in Pamphylia. They met hardships and did not have everything they needed, and in the towns and cities and along lonely highways they were surrounded by dangers seen and unseen. But Paul and Barnabas had learned to trust God's power. As faithful shepherds in search of lost sheep, forgetful of themselves, they did not turn away from weariness, hunger, and cold.

Here Mark became overwhelmed with fear and discouragement. He was not used to hardships, and he lost heart when opposition and danger came. He failed to endure hardship as a good soldier of the cross. He still had to learn to face danger, persecution, and trouble with a brave heart. Losing all courage, he returned to Jerusalem.

This caused Paul to judge Mark harshly for a while. Barnabas was inclined to excuse him. He saw qualifications in him that would fit him to be a useful worker. In later years the young man gave himself completely to proclaiming the gospel in difficult fields. Under the wise training of Barnabas, he developed into a valuable worker.

Paul and Mark Later Reconciled

Afterward Paul was reconciled to Mark. He recommended him to the Colossians as a fellow worker "for the kingdom of God" and "a comfort to me." He spoke of Mark as profitable, "useful to me for ministry." (Colossians 4:11; 2 Timothy 4:11.)

At Antioch in Pisidia Paul and Barnabas went to the Jewish synagogue on the Sabbath. "After the reading of the law and the prophets, the officials of the synagogue sent them a message, saying, 'Brothers, if you have any word of exhortation for the people, give it'" (NRSV). Being invited to speak, "Paul stood up and with a gesture began to speak:

"'You Israelites, and others who fear God, listen.'" Then he proceeded to give a history of how the Lord had dealt with the Jews and how He had promised a Savior. He boldly declared that "God has brought to Israel a Savior, Jesus, as he promised; before his coming John had already proclaimed a baptism of repentance to all the people of Israel. And as John was finishing his work, he said, 'What do you suppose that I am? I am not he. No, but one is coming after me; I am not worthy to untie the thong of the sandals on his feet'" (NRSV). Powerfully he preached Jesus as the Messiah of prophecy.

Paul Speaks Plainly

Paul said, "My brothers, . . . because the residents of Jerusalem and their leaders did not recognize him or understand the words of the prophets that are read every sabbath, they fulfilled those words [the prophecies] by condemning him" (NRSV).

Paul did not hesitate to speak the truth about the Jewish leaders. "Though they found no cause for death in Him," the apostle said, "they asked Pilate that He should be put to death. Now when they had fulfilled all that was written concerning Him, they took Him down from the tree and laid Him in a tomb. But God raised Him from the dead. He was seen for many days by those who came up with Him from Galilee to Jerusalem, who are His witnesses to the people. And we declare to you glad tidings," the apostle continued. "God has . . . raised up Jesus."

And now Paul preached repentance and forgiveness of sin through the merits of Jesus their Savior: "By Him everyone who believes is justified from all things from which you could not be justified by the law of Moses."

The apostle's appeal to Old Testament prophecies and his declaration that these had been fulfilled in Jesus of Nazareth were convincing. And his assurance that the "glad tidings" were for both Jews and Gentiles brought hope and joy.

"So when the Jews went out of the synagogue, the Gentiles begged that these words might be preached to them the next Sabbath." "Many Jews and devout converts to Judaism" (NRSV) accepted the good news that day. Paul and Barnabas "persuaded them to continue in the grace of God."

The next Sabbath, the interest that Paul's words had stirred up brought together "almost the whole city . . . to hear the word of God. But when the

Jews saw the multitudes, they were filled with envy; and contradicting and blaspheming, they opposed the things spoken by Paul. Then Paul and Barnabas grew bold and said, 'It was necessary that the word of God should be spoken to you first; but since you reject it, and judge yourselves unworthy of everlasting life, behold, we turn to the Gentiles.' "

"When the Gentiles heard this, they were glad and glorified the word of the Lord. And as many as had been appointed to eternal life believed." Thus "the word of the Lord was being spread throughout all the region."

Centuries before, prophecy had predicted this ingathering of the Gentiles. (See Hosea 1:10; 2:23.) The Savior Himself foretold the spread of the gospel among them. (See Matthew 21:43.) And after His resurrection He commissioned His disciples to go "into all the world" and "make disciples of all the nations." (Mark 16:15; Matthew 28:19.)

The Gentiles See the Light

Later, in important centers, Paul and his companions preached the gospel to both Jews and Gentiles. But from this time on their chief energies were directed toward heathen peoples who had little or no knowledge of the true God and of His Son. Through the untiring efforts of the apostles to the Gentiles, those "without Christ" who "once were far off" learned that they had been "brought near by the blood of Christ" and that through faith they could become "members of the household of God" (Ephesians 2:12, 13, 19).

To those who believe, Christ is a

dependable foundation. This living stone is broad enough and strong enough to support the weight and burden of the whole world. The apostle wrote: "You are . . . built on the foundation of the apostles and prophets, Jesus Christ Himself being the chief cornerstone" (Ephesians 2:19, 20).

As the gospel spread in Pisidia, in blind prejudice the unbelieving Jews "stirred up the devout and prominent women and the chief men of the city, raised up persecution against Paul and Barnabas, and expelled them" from that district.

The apostles were not discouraged. They remembered the words of their Master: "Rejoice and be exceedingly glad, for great is your reward in heaven, for so they persecuted the prophets who were before you" (Matthew 5:12).

The gospel message was advancing!

The Apostles Are Both Persecuted and Adored*

In Iconium as at Antioch, Paul and Barnabas began their work in the synagogue of their own people. "A great multitude both of the Jews and of the Greeks believed." But as in other places, "the unbelieving Jews stirred up the Gentiles and poisoned their minds against the brethren."

However, despite the opposition and prejudice, the apostles went on, "speaking boldly in the Lord," and God "was bearing witness to the word of His grace, granting signs and wonders to be done by their hands." Converts multiplied.

The message's popularity filled the unbelieving Jews with envy, and they made up their minds to stop Paul and Barnabas. By false reports they led the authorities to fear that the city would be stirred up to revolt. They suggested that it was for secret and dangerous plans that large numbers were becoming followers of the apostles.

The disciples were repeatedly brought before the authorities, but their defense was so clear and sensible that the magistrates did not dare to condemn them. They could not help but acknowledge that if people accepted the teachings of Paul and Barnabas, it would improve the morals and order of the city.

Opposition brought the message of truth publicity. The Jews' efforts to hinder the work only resulted in adding greater numbers to the new faith. The people of the city were "divided; part sided with the Jews, and part with the apostles."

The Jews were so enraged that they decided to resort to violence. Stirring up the ignorant, noisy mob, they created a riot, which they blamed on the disciples. They determined to have the mob stone Paul and Barnabas.

Friends of the apostles, though unbelievers, urged them not to expose themselves needlessly to the mob, but to escape. So Paul and Barnabas left secretly from Iconium, leaving the believers to carry on alone. But they made up their minds to return after the excitement had died down.

In every age and land, God's messengers have met opposition from those who reject light. By misrepresentation and falsehood, enemies of the gospel have often seemed to triumph,

---

* This chapter is based on Acts 14:1–26.

closing doors by which God's messengers might reach the people. But these doors cannot remain closed forever!

Excitement at Lystra

Driven from Iconium, the apostles went to Lystra and Derbe, in Lycaonia. Among these mostly heathen, superstitious people were some who were willing to accept the gospel. The apostles decided to work in these places.

There was no synagogue in Lystra, though a few Jews were living in the town. Many of the inhabitants worshiped Zeus. When Paul and Barnabas explained the simple truths of the gospel, many wanted to connect these doctrines with the worship of Zeus.

The apostles tried to give the people a knowledge of the Creator and His Son. They first directed attention to the works of God—the sun, moon, and stars, the order of the recurring seasons, the mighty snow-capped mountains, and other wonders of nature, which showed a skill beyond human understanding. Through these, the apostles led the minds of the heathen to think about the Ruler of the universe.

After making plain these fundamental truths, the apostles told the Lystrians of the Son of God, who came from heaven because He loved the human race. They spoke of His life, His rejection, His trial and crucifixion, His resurrection, and His ascension to heaven to act as humanity's representative.

While Paul was telling of Christ's work as a healer, he saw a cripple looking intently at him and who believed his words. Paul's heart went out in sympathy toward the afflicted man, whom he now saw "had faith to be healed." Paul commanded the cripple to stand. The sufferer had only been able to sit, but now he obeyed instantly, and for the first time in his life stood on his feet. Strength came with faith, and he "leaped and walked. Now when the people saw what Paul had done, they raised their voices, saying in the Lycaonian language, 'The gods have come down to us in the likeness of men!'" Their tradition said that the gods occasionally visited the earth. Barnabas they called Zeus, the father of gods, because of his stately, dignified bearing, even temper, and kindness. Paul they believed to be Hermes, "because he was the chief speaker," active and eloquent.

The Lystrians persuaded the priest of Zeus to honor the apostles, and he "brought oxen and garlands to the gates, intending to sacrifice with the multitudes." Unaware of these preparations, Paul and Barnabas had been resting. Soon, however, they became aware of music and the shouting of a large crowd who had come where they were staying.

The apostles "tore their clothes and ran in among the multitude" in the hope of preventing anything further. In a loud voice that rose above the shouting, Paul said: "Men, why are you doing these things? We also are men with the same nature as you, and preach to you that you should turn from these useless things to the living God, who made the heaven, the earth, the sea, and all things that are in them."

In spite of Paul's efforts to direct

the people to God as the only object worthy of worship, their belief was so firm that these men were indeed gods, and their enthusiasm was so great, that Paul and Barnabas could "scarcely restrain" them. The Lystrians had seen a cripple who had never been able to walk rejoice in perfect health and strength. Only after Paul and Barnabas had carefully explained their mission as representatives of the God of heaven and of His Son, the great Healer, did the people give up their plans.

Jews Incite the Crowd to Stone Paul

The work of Paul and Barnabas was suddenly blocked. "Jews from Antioch and Iconium came there," and when they learned of the apostles' success, they determined to persecute them. These Jews inspired the people of Lystra with the same bitterness that filled their own minds. Those who had recently thought of Paul and Barnabas as divine were persuaded that the apostles actually deserved to die.

The Lystrians turned against Paul and Barnabas with an enthusiasm nearly as great as when they had honored them as gods. They planned to attack the apostles by force. The Jews warned them not to allow Paul to speak, claiming that he would bewitch the people.

The Lystrians became possessed with a satanic fury, and, taking hold of Paul, they stoned him. The apostle thought his end had come. The cruel part he himself had acted at Stephen's martyrdom came vividly to his mind. Covered with bruises and faint with pain, he fell to the ground, and the infuriated mob "dragged him out of the city, supposing him to be dead."

In this difficult time the Lystrian believers who had been converted to the faith of Jesus remained loyal and true. Cruel persecution by their enemies only confirmed the faith of these devoted people, and now, in the face of danger, they showed their loyalty by gathering around the body of Paul, whom they believed was dead.

As they were weeping, the apostle suddenly rose to his feet with the praise of God on his lips. This unexpected miracle seemed to be a sign from Heaven validating their change of belief. They praised God with renewed faith.

Among those who had been converted at Lystra was one who would share with the apostle the trials and joys of pioneer service in difficult places. This was Timothy. This youth was among the number who took their stand beside Paul's apparently lifeless body and saw him stand up, bruised and covered with blood, but with praises on his lips because he had been permitted to suffer for Christ.

The day following, the apostles left for Derbe, where many accepted the Savior. But neither Paul nor Barnabas was content to take up work elsewhere without confirming the faith of the converts where they had recently labored. So, despite the danger, "they returned to Lystra, Iconium, and Antioch, strengthening the souls of the disciples, exhorting them to continue in the faith." Many had accepted the gospel, and the apostles worked to establish them in the faith.

Instruction and Organization Essential to Success

The apostles were careful to surround the new converts with the safeguards of gospel organization. Churches were organized wherever there were believers. They appointed officers and established proper order and system for the believers' spiritual welfare.

Throughout his ministry, Paul was careful to follow the gospel plan of uniting all believers in Christ into one body. Even when believers were very few in number, at the proper time they were organized into a church and taught to help one another, remembering the promise, "Where two or three are gathered together in My name, I am there in the midst of them" (Matthew 18:20).

The care of these churches remained an ever-increasing burden on Paul's mind. No matter how small a company of believers might be, it was the object of his constant care. He watched over the smaller churches tenderly, so that the members could be established in the truth and taught to exert unselfish efforts for those around them.

Paul and Barnabas tried to follow Christ's example of willing sacrifice. Wide-awake, untiring, they did not consider their personal ease, but with prayerful anxiety they sowed the seed of truth and gave practical instruction of immense value to all who took their stand for the gospel. This spirit of earnestness made a lasting impression on the minds of the new disciples.

When people of ability were converted, as in the case of Timothy, Paul and Barnabas made sure to show them the need for workers to spread the gospel. When the apostles left, the faith of these people did not fail, but increased. They had been faithfully instructed how to work unselfishly, untiringly, for their fellow human beings. This careful training of new converts was an important factor in the remarkable success that Paul and Barnabas had.

The first missionary journey was coming to a close. Committing the newly organized churches to the Lord, the apostles "went down to Attalia. From there they sailed to Antioch."

Thorny Problems Settled by the Holy Spirit*

When they arrived at Antioch in Syria, Paul and Barnabas called the believers together and reported "all that God had done with them, and that He had opened the door of faith to the Gentiles" (Acts 14:27). The large, growing church at Antioch was a center of missionary activity and was made up of both Jews and Gentiles.

While the apostles united with lay members to win people to the Lord, certain Jewish believers from Judea "of the sect of the Pharisees" succeeded in introducing a question that confused and troubled the believing Gentiles. These Judaizing teachers claimed that in order to be saved, one must be circumcised and keep the ceremonial law.

Paul and Barnabas opposed this false doctrine, but many of the believing Jews of Antioch thought the brethren who had recently come from Judea were right. Many of the Jews who had been converted to Christ still felt that since God had once outlined the Hebrew way of worship, it was unlikely that He would ever authorize a change in it. They insisted that the Jewish cere-

monies become a part of the Christian religion. They were slow to realize that the sacrificial offerings had prefigured the death of the Son of God, in which symbol met fulfillment, and were no longer binding.

Paul had gained a clear understanding of the Savior's mission as the Redeemer of Gentiles as well as Jews and had learned the difference between a living faith and a dead formalism. In the light of the gospel, the ceremonies committed to Israel took on a new significance. What they foreshadowed had now happened, and those who were living under the gospel system had been freed from observing them. God's unchangeable law of Ten Commandments, however, Paul still kept in spirit as well as in the letter of the law.

The question of circumcision brought much discussion and contention. Finally, the members of the church decided to send Paul and Barnabas, with some responsible men from the church, to Jerusalem to present the matter before the apostles and elders. A final decision given in general council was to be accepted universally by the different churches.

---

* This chapter is based on Acts 15:1-35.

The First General Church Council

At Jerusalem the delegates from Antioch told of the success that had come from their ministry among the Gentiles. They then gave a clear outline of the confusion that arose when certain converted Pharisees had declared that the Gentile converts must be circumcised and keep the law of Moses.

The assembly warmly discussed this question and also the problem of foods offered to idols. Many Gentile converts were living among superstitious people who made frequent sacrifices and offerings to idols. The Jews were afraid that Gentile converts would bring a stain on Christianity by buying things that had been offered to idols, making it appear that they approved of the customs of idol worshipers.

Again, the Gentiles routinely ate the flesh of animals that had been strangled, but God had instructed the Jews that when animals were killed for food, the blood should flow from the body. God had given these directions for preserving health. The Jews believed it was sinful to use blood as something to eat. The Gentiles, though, made a practice of catching the blood from the sacrificial victim and using it in preparing food. Therefore, if Jew and Gentile were to eat at the same table, the Jew would be shocked and outraged by the Gentile.

The Gentiles, especially Greeks, were immoral, and there was danger that some would profess Christianity without turning away from their evil practices. The Jewish Christians could not tolerate the immorality that the heathen did not even consider as crimi-

nal. So the Jews held that circumcision and the observance of the ceremonial law should be required of Gentile converts as a test of their sincerity. This, they believed, would prevent the church from receiving as members those who might later bring dishonor on God's church by immorality.

The various points of concern seemed to present the council with difficulties too great to resolve. "When there had been much dispute, Peter rose up and said to them: 'Men and brethren, you know that a good while ago God chose among us, that by my mouth the Gentiles should hear the word of the gospel and believe.'" He reasoned that the Holy Spirit had already decided the matter they were disputing by descending with equal power on Gentiles and Jews. He told about his vision and the call to go to the centurion and instruct him in the faith of Christ. This message showed that God accepted all who respected and honored Him. Peter told how astonished he was when he witnessed the Holy Spirit taking possession of Gentiles as well as Jews. Light and glory also lit up the faces of the uncircumcised Gentiles. This was God's warning that Peter was not to consider one as inferior to the other, for the blood of Christ could cleanse from all impurity.

Once before, Peter had told how the Holy Spirit fell on the Gentiles. He had said, "If therefore God gave them the same gift as He gave us when we believed on the Lord Jesus Christ, who was I that I could withstand God?" (Acts 11:17). Now, with equal force, he said: "So God, who knows the heart, acknowledged them by giving them the Holy Spirit, just as He did to us, and made no distinction between us and them, purifying their hearts by faith. Now therefore, why do you test God by putting a yoke on the neck of the disciples which neither our fathers nor we were able to bear?" This yoke was not the Ten Commandments. Peter was referring here to the law of ceremonies, which was made void by Christ's crucifixion.

"The whole assembly kept silence, and listened to Barnabas and Paul as they told of all the signs and wonders that God had done through them among the Gentiles" (NRSV).

How the Holy Spirit Led the Council

The Holy Spirit saw fit not to impose the ceremonial law on Gentile converts, and the mind of the apostles on this was the same as the mind of the Spirit of God. James presided at the council, and his decision was, "We should not trouble those from among the Gentiles who are turning to God."

This ended the discussion. These events refute the doctrine that Peter was the head of the church. Those who have claimed to be his successors have no Scriptural foundation for their claim that Peter was elevated above the others as the deputy of the Most High. If those who are called the successors of Peter had followed Peter's example, they would always have remained on an equality with their brothers and sisters in the church.

James tried to impress the other leaders that the Gentiles had made a great change in their lives and should not be troubled with questions of mi-

nor importance, or they might become discouraged in following Christ.

The Gentile converts, however, were to give up customs inconsistent with Christianity. They were to stay away from foods offered to idols, from sexual immorality, from the meat of strangled animals, and from blood. They were to keep the commandments and lead holy lives.

Judas and Silas were sent with Paul and Barnabas to tell the Gentiles the decision of the council. The message that was to put an end to all the controversy was the voice of the highest authority on earth.

The council that decided this case was composed of apostles and teachers who had been prominent in raising up Jewish and Gentile Christian churches, along with delegates from various places. The most influential churches were represented. The council moved with the dignity of a church established by the divine will. As a result of their deliberations, they all saw that God Himself had answered the question at issue by giving the Gentiles the Holy Spirit. It was their part to follow the guidance of the Spirit.

The entire body of Christians was not called to vote on the question. The "apostles and elders" framed and issued the decree, which the churches then generally accepted. Not all, however, were pleased. A dissenting group of self-confident members indulged in complaining and faultfinding, trying to pull down the work of the men God had ordained to teach the gospel. The church will have such obstacles to meet till the close of time.

Trouble in Jerusalem

The greatest exclusiveness and bigotry were found at Jerusalem. When Jewish Christians living within sight of the temple saw the Christian church no longer keeping the ceremonies of Judaism and perceived that Jewish customs would soon be lost sight of in the new faith, many became angry at Paul. Even the disciples were not all prepared to accept the council's decision willingly. Some, zealous for the ceremonial law, began to be suspicious of Paul. They thought his principles were lax in regard to the Jewish law.

The far-reaching decisions of the general council brought confidence to the Gentile believers, and the cause of God prospered. In Antioch Judas and Silas "exhorted and strengthened the brethren with many words."

Later, when Peter visited Antioch, he won confidence by his careful, wise conduct toward the Gentile converts. In harmony with the light from heaven, he ate with the Gentile converts. But when certain Jews who were zealous for the ceremonial law came from Jerusalem, Peter unwisely changed. A number of the Jews "played the hypocrite with him, so that even Barnabas was carried away with their hypocrisy." This weakness on the part of those who had been respected as leaders left a painful impression on tne Gentile believers. It threatened to divide the church. But Paul, who saw how Peter's two-faced course was undermining the church, openly rebuked him. In the presence of the church, Paul asked Peter, "If you, being a Jew, live in the manner of Gentiles and not as the Jews, why do you compel Gentiles to live as Jews?" (Galatians 2:13, 14).

Peter saw his error and immediately set about to repair the evil, as much as he could. God permitted Peter to reveal this weakness in order for him to see that there was nothing in himself to boast about. Even the best people, if left to themselves, will make mistakes. God also saw that in later times some would claim for Peter and his pretended successors the exalted rights, titles, and privileges that belong to God alone. This record of the apostle's weakness was proof of his human frailties and that in no way did he stand above the other apostles.

The greater the responsibilities placed on us as human beings and the larger our opportunities to dictate and control, the more harm we are sure to do if we do not carefully follow the way of the Lord and work in harmony with decisions that come from the general body of believers in united council.

In light of Peter's fall and restoration, his close acquaintance with Christ, and all the knowledge and influence he had gained by teaching the Word, is it not strange that he would pretend to be what he was not and evade the principles of the gospel in order to have certain people think well of him? May God give each of us a realization of our helplessness, our inability to steer our own ship straight and safe into the harbor.

Paul often had to stand alone. He did not dare to make any concessions that would involve principle. At times the burden was heavy. Human traditions must not take the place of revealed truth. He realized that the church must never be brought under the control of human power.

Paul had received the gospel direct from heaven, and he maintained a vital connection with heaven. God had taught him not to bind unnecessary burdens on the Gentile Christians. He knew the mind of the Spirit and took a firm, unyielding position that brought the churches freedom from Jewish rites.

Even though Paul was personally taught by God, he was always ready to recognize the authority God had placed in the body of believers united in church fellowship. When important matters arose, he was glad to unite with his fellow Christians in seeking God for wisdom to make right decisions. "God is not the author of confusion but of peace, as in all the churches of the saints" (1 Corinthians 14:33). All united in church capacity should be "submissive to one another" (1 Peter 5:5).

Paul's Secret: Exalt the Cross*

After spending some time at Antioch, Paul suggested to Barnabas, his fellow worker, "Let us now go back and visit our brethren in every city where we have preached the word of the Lord, and see how they are doing."

Both Paul and Barnabas had a special interest in those who had accepted the gospel under their ministry, and they longed to see them once more. Even when he was far away from the scene of his earlier labors, Paul tried to help these converts become strong in faith and wholehearted in their consecration to God.

Barnabas was ready to go, but he wanted to take Mark with them. Paul objected. He "insisted that they should not take with them" someone who had left them for the safety and comforts of home during their first missionary journey. He argued that anyone with so little stamina was not fit for a work that required self-denial, bravery, faith, and a willingness to sacrifice even life itself. Their disagreement was so sharp that "Barnabas took Mark and sailed to Cyprus; but Paul chose Silas and departed."

Paul and Silas finally reached Derbe and Lystra. A mob had stoned Paul at Lystra, yet he was anxious to see how those who had accepted the gospel were enduring difficulty. He was not disappointed, for the Lystrian believers had remained firm in the face of violent opposition.

Here Paul again met Timothy, who was convinced that it was his duty to give himself fully to the work of the ministry. He longed to share the apostle's labors. Silas, Paul's companion, was an experienced worker, gifted with the spirit of prophecy, but the work was so great that they needed more laborers. In Timothy Paul saw someone who appreciated the sacredness of the work and was not afraid to meet persecution. Yet the apostle did not dare to take Timothy, an inexperienced youth, without fully satisfying himself about his character and past life.

How Two Women Trained a Man of God

Timothy had known the Scriptures since his childhood. The faith of his mother and grandmother constantly reminded him of the blessing in doing God's will. The lessons he had received from them kept him pure in speech and free from the evil influ-

---

* This chapter is based on Acts 15:36–41; 16:1–6.

ences that surrounded him. In this way his home instructors had cooperated with God in preparing him to work for the Lord.

Paul saw that Timothy was firm in his faith, and he chose him as a companion in labor and travel. Timothy's mother and grandmother, who had taught him in childhood, were rewarded by seeing him linked with the great apostle. Even though Timothy was only a youth, he was prepared to take his place as Paul's helper. He was young, but he carried his responsibilities with Christian meekness.

Paul wisely advised Timothy to be circumcised in order to remove from the minds of the Jews a possible objection to Timothy's ministry. If it became known that one of Paul's companions was uncircumcised, prejudice and bigotry might stand in the way of his work. He wanted to bring a knowledge of the gospel to the Jews as well as to Gentiles, so he tried to remove every excuse for opposition. Yet while he yielded this much to Jewish prejudice, he believed and taught that circumcision or uncircumcision was nothing, and the gospel of Christ everything.

Paul loved Timothy, his "own son in the faith" (1 Timothy 1:2, KJV). As they traveled, he carefully taught him how to do successful work, to deepen his sense of the sacred nature of the gospel minister's work.

Timothy constantly turned to Paul for advice and instruction. He exercised sound judgment and calm thought, asking at every step, Is this the way of the Lord? The Holy Spirit recognized him as someone who could be molded and fashioned into a temple for the divine Presence to dwell in.

Timothy had no especially brilliant talents, but his genuine walk with God gave him influence. Those who try to win others for Christ must throw all their energies into the work. They must take firm hold of God, daily receiving grace and power.

Before moving on into new territory, Paul and his companions visited the churches in Pisidia and the surrounding regions. "They delivered to them the decrees to keep, which were determined by the apostles and elders at Jerusalem. So the churches were strengthened in the faith, and increased in number daily."

The apostle Paul felt a deep responsibility for those converted through his work. He knew that preaching alone was not enough to educate the believers to share the word of life. He knew that bit by bit, here a little and there a little, they must be taught to move forward in the work of Christ.

Whenever people refuse to use their God-given powers, these powers decay. Truth that is not lived, that is not shared, loses its life-giving power, its healing vitality. Paul's knowledge, his eloquence, his miracles, would all mean nothing if those for whom he labored failed to receive the grace of God because he had not been faithful in his work. And so he pleaded with those who had accepted Christ to be "blameless and innocent, children of God without blemish in the midst of a crooked and perverse generation, . . . holding fast to the word of life" (Philippians 2:15, 16, NRSV).

Every true minister feels a heavy responsibility for the believers entrusted to his care, to help them become laborers together with God. To a large degree, the well-being of the church depends on his work. Earnestly he tries to inspire believers to win others to Christ, remembering that every person added to the church should be one more agency for carrying out the plan of redemption.

The Cross and Righteousness by Faith

Having visited the chuches in Pisidia, Paul and Silas, with Timothy, continued on into Phrygia and Galatia, where they proclaimed the good news of the gospel. The Galatians were strong in the worship of idols, but they rejoiced in the message that promised freedom from the slavery of sin. Paul and his fellow workers proclaimed the doctrine of righteousness by faith in Christ's atoning sacrifice. Seeing how helpless the human race was, Christ came to redeem men and women by living a life of obedience to God's law and by paying the penalty for disobedience. In the light of the cross many began to understand the greatness of the Father's love. "By the hearing of faith" they received the Spirit of God and became "the children of God by faith in Christ." (Galatians 3:2, 26, KJV.)

Paul lived the kind of life among the Galatians that he could later say, "I urge you to become like me" (Galatians 4:12). God enabled him to rise above his physical ailments and present Jesus as the sinner's only hope. Those who heard him knew he had been with Jesus. He was able to tear down the fortresses of Satan. Hearts were broken by his presentation of God's love revealed in the sacrifice of His only Son.

All through his ministry among the Gentiles, the apostle kept presenting to them the cross of Calvary. The devoted messengers who carried the good news of salvation to a perishing world allowed no self-exaltation to mar their presentation of Christ and Him crucified. They did not covet authority or high position. Christ, the same yesterday, today, and forever, was the theme of their teaching.

If those who teach the Word of God today would lift the cross of Christ higher, their ministry would be far more successful. Christ's death proves God's love for us. It is our pledge of salvation. To remove the cross from the Christian would be like blotting out the sun from the sky. The cross brings us near to God, reconciling us to Him.

The light of the Savior's love shines from the cross, and when the sinner looks up to the One who died to save him, he may rejoice, for his sins are pardoned. Kneeling in faith at the cross, he has arrived at the highest place that anyone can reach.

Is it any wonder that Paul exclaimed, "God forbid that I should glory, save in the cross of our Lord Jesus Christ" (Galatians 6:14, KJV)? It is our privilege also to glory in the cross. Then with the light that streams from Calvary shining in our faces, we may go out to reveal this light to those in darkness.

Angels Open a Philippian Prison*

The time had come for the gospel to be preached in Europe. At Troas "a vision appeared to Paul in the night. A man of Macedonia stood and pleaded with him, saying, 'Come over to Macedonia and help us.'"

The call was imperative. According to Luke, who accompanied Paul, Silas, and Timothy to Europe, "After he had seen the vision, immediately we sought to go to Macdeonia, concluding that the Lord had called us to preach the gospel to them.

"Therefore . . . we . . . came . . . to Philippi. . . . On the Sabbath day," Luke continued, "we went out of the city to the riverside, where prayer was customarily made; and we sat down and spoke to the women who met there. Now a certain woman named Lydia heard us. She was a seller of purple from the city of Thyatira, who worshiped God. The Lord opened her heart." Lydia and her household received the truth gladly and were baptized.

As the messengers of the cross went about their work, a woman followed them, calling out, " 'These men are the servants of the Most High God, who proclaim to us the way of salvation.' And this she did for many days." This woman was a special agent of Satan and had made a lot of money for her masters by fortune-telling. Satan knew that his kingdom was being invaded, and he hoped to mingle his deceptions with the truths taught by those who were spreading the gospel. This woman's words of recommendation were an injury to the cause of truth, giving the gospel a bad name; her words led many to believe that the apostles were controlled by the same spirit as this emissary of Satan was.

The apostles endured this for quite a while. Then Paul commanded the evil spirit to leave the woman. Her immediate silence showed that the demon recognized the apostles as the servants of God. Freed from the evil spirit and restored to her right mind, the woman chose to follow Christ. Then her masters were alarmed. All hope of receiving money from her fortune-telling was gone. Their income would soon be completely cut off if the apostles were allowed to continue.

Many others in the city were interested in getting money through Satan's trickery, and these people brought the servants of God into court

---

* *This chapter is based on Acts 16:7-40.*

with the accusation, "These men, being Jews, exceedingly trouble our city; and they teach customs which are not lawful for us, being Romans, to receive or observe."

A Frenzied Multitude

A mob spirit took over, and the authorities gave the command to beat the apostles with whips. "They threw them into prison, commanding the jailer to keep them securely. Having received such a charge, he put them into the inner prison and fastened their feet in the stocks."

The apostles suffered extreme torture, but they did not complain. Instead, in the darkness of the dungeon, they encouraged each other and sang praises to God. A deep love for their Redeemer cheered their hearts. Paul thought of the persecution he had brought on the disciples of Christ and rejoiced that his heart had been opened to feel the power of the wonderful truths he had once despised.

The other prisoners were astonished to hear the sound of prayer and singing from the inner prison. They usually had heard shrieks, moans, and swearing, but never words of prayer and praise from the gloomy cell. Guards and prisoners marveled. Who were these men who could rejoice while enduring cold, hunger, and torture?

On the way to their homes the court officials heard more details about the men they had sentenced to beating and imprisonment. They saw the woman who had been freed from Satan's influence and were struck by the change in her face and behavior. Now she was quiet and peaceable. They regretted what they had done and decided that in the morning they would command that the apostles be privately released and escorted from the city, beyond danger from the mob.

But while these men were criminally negligent in their solemn responsibilities, God had not forgotten His servants who were suffering for Christ's sake. He sent angels to the prison, and the earth trembled at their steps. They threw open the heavily bolted prison doors, the chains and fetters fell from the prisoners, and a bright light flooded the prison.

The keeper of the jail had heard the prayers and songs of the imprisoned apostles. He had seen their swollen, bleeding wounds, and he himself had fastened their feet in the stocks. He had expected to hear bitter groans and curses, but instead he heard songs of joy. With these sounds in his ears the jailer had fallen asleep.

He was awakened by the earthquake and the shaking of prison walls. In alarm he saw that all the prison doors were open, and the fear flashed through him that the prisoners had escaped. Paul and Silas had been entrusted to his care the night before, and he was certain that his apparent unfaithfulness would bring him the death penalty. It was better to die by his own hand than submit to a disgraceful execution.

He was about to kill himself when he heard Paul's voice, "Do yourself no harm, for we are all here." Every prisoner was in place, restrained by the power of God. The apostles had not resented the severe treatment the jailer had given them. Filled with the love of the Savior, they had no room for hatred.

A Cruel Jailer Is Converted

The jailer called for lights and hurried into the inner dungeon. What kind of men were these who repaid cruelty with kindness? Kneeling before the apostles, he asked their forgiveness. Then, bringing them out into the open courtyard, he inquired, "Sirs, what must I do to be saved?"

Everything else seemed unimportant compared with his desire to have the peace and cheerfulness that the apostles showed under abuse. He saw the light of heaven in their faces, and with renewed force the words of the woman came to his mind: "These men are the servants of the Most High God, who proclaim to us the way of salvation." He asked the disciples to show him the way of life.

"Believe on the Lord Jesus Christ, and you will be saved, you and your household," the apostles answered. And "they spoke the word of the Lord to him and to all who were in his house." The jailer then washed the wounds of the apostles, and they baptized him, with all his household. The minds of the prison's inmates were opened to listen to the apostles. The God whom these men served had miraculously released them from their captivity.

The Authorities Apologize

The earthquake had terrified the citizens of Philippi, and when in the morning the officers of the prison told the court officials what had happened during the night, they sent the sergeants to set the apostles free. But Paul declared, "They have beaten us in public, uncondemned, men who are Roman citizens, and have thrown us into prison; and now they are going to discharge us in secret? Certainly not! Let them come and take us out themselves" (NRSV).

It was unlawful to whip a Roman except for bold, shocking crimes or to put him in prison without a trial. Paul and Silas, having been publicly imprisoned, now refused to be released privately without a proper explanation on the part of the officials.

The authorities were alarmed. Would the apostles complain to the emperor? Going immediately to the prison, they apologized to Paul and Silas and personally brought them out of the prison. They feared the apostles' influence over the people, and they also feared the Power that had intervened to help them.

The apostles would not insist on staying where they were not wanted. "They went out of the prison and entered the house of Lydia; and when they had seen the brethren, they encouraged them and departed."

The apostles had experienced opposition and persecution in Philippi, but the conversion of the jailer and his household more than made up for the disgrace and suffering they had endured. The news of their unjust imprisonment and miraculous deliverance became known through all that region and brought the work of the apostles to the attention of a large number who otherwise would not have been reached.

Paul's Example Became a Lasting Influence

Paul's work at Philippi resulted in a church whose membership steadily increased. His willingness to suffer for Christ had a lasting influence on the converts. They gave themselves to the cause of their Redeemer with wholehearted devotion. They were so firm in the faith that Paul wrote, "I thank my God upon every remembrance of you, always in every prayer of mine making request for you all with joy, for your fellowship in the gospel from the first day until now" (Philippians 1:3–5).

A terrible struggle takes place between the forces of good and evil. "We do not wrestle against flesh and blood," Paul says, "but against principalities, against powers, against the rulers of the darkness of this age" (Ephesians 6:12). Till the close of time there will be conflict between the church and those who are under the control of evil angels.

The early Christians often had to meet the powers of darkness face to face. Today, when this world's end is rapidly approaching, Satan is making many plans to occupy minds and divert attention from the truths that are essential to salvation. In every city he has agents who are busily organizing those opposed to the law of God. The archdeceiver is at work to introduce elements of confusion and rebellion.

Wickedness is reaching a new height, and yet many ministers of the gospel are saying, "Peace and safety." But clothed with the armor of heaven, God's faithful messengers are to go forward fearlessly and victoriously, never stopping their warfare until every person within their reach has received the message of truth for this time.

A Revival and a Riot at Thessalonica*

After leaving Philippi, Paul and Silas made their way to Thessalonica. Here they spoke to large congregations in the Jewish synagogue. Their appearance showed that they had been treated shamefully, and this required an explanation. Without exalting themselves, they magnified the One who had brought about their deliverance.

In preaching, Paul appealed to the Old Testament prophecies foretelling Christ's birth, sufferings, death, resurrection, and ascension. He clearly proved that Jesus of Nazareth was the Messiah and showed that it was the voice of Christ that had been speaking through patriarchs and prophets:

1. The sentence pronounced on Satan,

"I will put enmity
Between you and the woman,
And between your seed and her
    Seed;
He shall bruise your head,
And you shall bruise His heel"
    (Genesis 3:15),

was a promise to our first parents of redemption through Christ.

2. To Abraham God gave the promise that the Savior would come: "In your seed all the nations of the earth shall be blessed." " 'Your Seed,' who is Christ." (Genesis 22:18; Galatians 3:16.)

3. Moses prophesied of the Messiah to come: "The Lord your God will raise up for you a Prophet like me from your midst, from your brethren. Him you shall hear" (Deuteronomy 18:15).

4. The Messiah was to be from the royal line, for Jacob said,

"The scepter shall not depart from
    Judah,
Nor a lawgiver from between his feet,
Until Shiloh comes;
And to Him shall be the obedience of
    the people."

Genesis 49:10

5. Isaiah prophesied,

"A shoot shall come out from the
    stump of Jesse,
And a branch shall grow out of his
    roots."

Isaiah 11:1, NRSV

6. Jeremiah also bore witness of the

---

* This chapter is based on Acts 17:1–10.

coming Redeemer: "The days are surely coming, says the Lord, when I will raise up for David a righteous Branch, and he shall reign as king and deal wisely, and shall execute justice and righteousness in the land. . . . And this is the name by which he will be called: 'The Lord is our righteousness'" (Jeremiah 23:5, 6, NRSV).

7. Even the birthplace of the Messiah was foretold:

"You, Bethlehem Ephrathah,
Though you are little among the
     thousands of Judah,
Yet out of you shall come forth to Me
The One to be Ruler in Israel;
Whose goings forth are from of old,
From everlasting."

Micah 5:2

8. The work the Savior was to do had been fully outlined:

"To preach good tidings to the poor;
. . . to heal the brokenhearted,
To proclaim liberty to the captives,
And the opening of the prison to
     those who are bound;
To proclaim the acceptable year of
     the Lord,
And the day of vengeance of our
     God;
To comfort all who mourn."

Isaiah 61:1, 2

"Behold! My Servant whom I uphold,
My Elect One in whom My soul
     delights!
I have put My Spirit upon Him;
He will bring forth justice to the
     Gentiles. . . .
He will not fail nor be discouraged,

Till He has established justice in the
     earth."

Isaiah 42:1, 4

9. With convincing power Paul reasoned from the Scriptures that "the Christ had to suffer and rise again from the dead." Through Isaiah, the Promised One had prophesied of Himself:

"I gave My back to those who struck
     Me,
And My cheeks to those who plucked
     out the beard;
I did not hide My face from shame
     and spitting."

Isaiah 50:6

Through the psalmist Christ had foretold the treatment He would receive from humanity:

"I am . . . a reproach of men, and
     despised by the people.
All those who see Me ridicule Me;
They shoot out the lip, they shake the
     head, saying,
'He trusted in the Lord, let Him
     rescue Him;
Let Him deliver Him, since He
     delights in Him!' . . .
I can count all My bones.
They look and stare at Me.
They divide My garments among
     them,
And for My clothing they cast lots."

Psalm 22:6–8, 17, 18

10. Isaiah's prophecies of Christ's sufferings and death were unmistakably plain:

"Who has believed our report?

And to whom has the arm of the
Lord been revealed? . . .
He has . . . no beauty that we should
desire Him.
He is despised and rejected by men,
A Man of sorrows and acquainted
with grief.
And we hid, as it were, our faces
from Him;
He was despised, and we did not
esteem Him. . . .
But He was wounded for our
transgressions,
He was bruised for our iniquities;
The chastisement for our peace was
upon Him,
And by His stripes we are healed.
All we like sheep have gone astray;
We have turned, every one, to his
own way;
And the Lord has laid on Him the
iniquity of us all.
He was oppressed and He was
afflicted,
Yet He opened not His mouth. . . .
For the transgression of My people
He was stricken."

Isaiah 53:1–8

11. The Old Testament even gave indications of how He would die. As the bronze serpent had been lifted up in the wilderness, so was the Redeemer to be "lifted up" (John 3:14). If "one shall say unto Him, What are these wounds in Thine hands? then He shall answer, Those with which I was wounded in the house of my friends" (Zechariah 13:6, KJV).

12. But He who was to die at the hands of evil men was to rise again as a conqueror:

"My flesh also will rest in hope.
For You will not leave My soul in
Sheol [the grave],
Nor will You allow Your Holy One to
see corruption."

Psalm 16:9, 10

13. Paul showed how closely God had linked the sacrificial service with the prophecies relating to the One "led as a lamb to the slaughter." The Messiah was to give His life as "an offering for sin" (Isaiah 53:7, 10.) Isaiah had testified that the Lamb of God

"poured out His soul unto death, . . .
And He bore the sin of many,
And made intercession for the
transgressors."

Isaiah 53:12

So the Savior was not to come as an earthly king to deliver the Jewish nation from earthly oppressors, but to live a life of poverty and humility and finally to be despised, rejected, and killed. The Savior would offer Himself as a sacrifice for the fallen race, fulfilling every requirement of the broken law. In Him the sacrificial symbols were to meet their fulfillment. His death on the cross would show the true meaning of the entire Jewish system.

Paul Relates the Story of His Conversion

Paul told the Thessalonian Jews of his amazing experience at the gate of Damascus. Before conversion his faith had not been anchored in Christ; he had trusted in forms and ceremonies. While boasting that he was blameless in performing the deeds of the law, he had refused the One who gave value to the law.

But at his conversion, everything had changed. The persecutor saw Jesus as the Son of God, the One who had met every specification of the Sacred Writings.

As Paul proclaimed the gospel with holy boldness at Thessalonica, a flood of light opened up the true meaning of the tabernacle service. He carried the minds of his hearers beyond the ministry of Christ in the heavenly sanctuary to the time when He would come in power and great glory and establish His kingdom. Paul was a believer in the Second Coming. He presented the truths concerning this event so clearly that the minds of many received an impression that never faded away.

For three Sabbaths in a row Paul preached, reasoning from the Scriptures about the "Lamb slain from the foundation of the world" (Revelation 13:8). He lifted up Christ, whose ministry, when properly understood, is the key that gives us access to the rich treasures of the Old Testament Scriptures.

Paul's words gripped the attention of large congregations. "Some of them were persuaded; and a great multitude of the devout Greeks, and not a few of the leading women, joined Paul and Silas." But as in other places they had already entered, the apostles met with opposition. By uniting with "some of the evil men from the marketplace," the Jews succeeded in setting "the city in an uproar." They "attacked the house of Jason," but they could not find either Paul or Silas. In their disappointed rage the mob "dragged Jason and some brethren to the rulers of the city, crying out, 'These who have turned the world upside down have come here too. Jason has harbored them, and these are all acting contrary to the decrees of Caesar, saying there is another king—Jesus.' "

The officials took a security bond from the accused believers to help assure the peace. Fearing further violence, "the brethren immediately sent Paul and Silas away by night to Berea."

Those who teach unpopular truths today sometimes meet with better reception, even from those who claim to be Christians, than Paul and his fellow workers did. But the messengers of the cross must move forward with faith and courage, in the name of Jesus. They must lift up Christ as our mediator in the heavenly sanctuary, the One in whom those who have broken God's law may find peace and pardon.

Paul Preaches in Berea and Athens*

At Berea Paul found Jews who were willing to investigate the truth. "These were more fair-minded than those in Thessalonica, in that they received the word with all readiness, and searched the Scriptures daily to find out whether these things were so. Therefore many of them believed, and also not a few of the Greeks, prominent women as well as men."

The Bereans studied the Bible—not from curiosity, but to learn what was written there about the promised Messiah. As they compared scripture with scripture each day, heavenly angels enlightened their minds.

Today, if those who hear unpopular Bible truths proclaimed would follow the example of the Bereans, there would be a large number loyal to God's law. But when these truths are presented, many are reluctant to study the evidences offered. Some assume that even if these doctrines are true, it is not important whether they accept the new light. In this way they become separated from heaven. Those who are sincerely seeking for truth will, in the light of God's Word, carefully investigate the doctrines presented to them.

Filled with hatred, the unbeliev-ing Jews of Thessalonica followed the apostles to Berea and stirred up the rabble's excitable passions against them. The believers were afraid there would be violence, so they sent Paul to Athens, accompanied by some Bereans who had recently accepted the faith. The enemies of Christ could not prevent the gospel from going forward, but they made the work of the apostles very hard. Yet Paul pressed steadily onward.

When Paul arrived in Athens, he sent the Berean believers back with a message to Silas and Timothy to join him immediately. Timothy had come to Berea before Paul left there, and he had remained with Silas to teach the new converts.

The Great City of Paganism

Athens was the capital city of heathenism. Here Paul met with a people famous for their intelligence and culture. Statues of gods and deified heroes met the eye everywhere, while magnificent architecture and paintings represented national glory and the worship of heathen gods. The senses of the people were charmed by splendid works of art. Massive sanctuaries and temples

---

* *This chapter is based on Acts 17:11–34.*

involving immense expense were everywhere. Sculptures and shrines commemorated victories in war and the deeds of celebrated men.

As Paul looked at the beauty and saw the city completely engrossed in idolatry, his spirit was stirred, and his heart went out in pity to the people who, despite their culture, were ignorant of the true God. Paul's spiritual nature was so much alive to the beauty of heavenly things that the glory of the riches that will never perish made the splendor surrounding him look valueless in his eyes. As he saw the magnificence of Athens, he was deeply impressed with the importance of the work before him.

While he waited for Silas and Timothy, Paul was not idle. He "reasoned in the synagogue with the Jews and with the Gentile worshipers, and in the marketplace daily with those who happened to be there." But the apostle was soon to meet paganism in its most subtle, alluring form.

As an unusual teacher, Paul was setting new and strange doctrines before the people. Some of the great men of Athens found Paul and started talking with him. Soon a crowd gathered. Some ridiculed the apostle as someone far beneath them socially and intellectually. They jeered, "'What does this babbler want to say?'

"Others said, 'He seems to be a proclaimer of foreign gods.'"

The Epicurean and Stoic philosophers and others who came in contact with him soon saw that Paul had a store of knowledge greater than their own. His intellectual power commanded the respect of the educated, while his earnest, logical reasoning held the attention of all in the audience. He was able to meet all classes with convincing arguments. So the apostle stood unflinching, matching logic with logic, philosophy with philosophy.

His heathen opponents reminded him about the fate of Socrates, who introduced strange gods and had been condemned to death. They counseled Paul not to endanger his life in the same way. But when they saw that he was determined to accomplish his errand among them and to tell his story no matter the cost, they decided to give him a fair hearing on Mars' Hill.

Paul's Impressive Oration on Mars' Hill

This was one of the most sacred spots in Athens, regarded with a superstitious reverence. In this place men who acted as judges on moral as well as civil questions often carefully considered matters connected with religion. Here, away from the noise and bustle of crowded streets, they could hear the apostle without interruption. Poets, artists, philosophers—the scholars and sages of Athens—addressed him: "May we know what this new doctrine is of which you speak? For you are bringing some strange things to our ears. Therefore we want to know what these things mean."

The apostle was calm and self-possessed, and his words convinced his hearers that he was no shallow babbler. "Men of Athens," he said, "I perceive that in all things you are very religious; for as I was passing through and considering the objects of your worship, I even found an altar with this inscription:

TO THE UNKNOWN GOD.

Therefore, the One whom you worship without knowing, Him I proclaim to you." With all their general knowledge, they were ignorant of the God who created the universe. Yet some were longing for greater light.

With his hand outstretched toward the temple crowded with idols, Paul exposed the errors of the Athenians' religion. His hearers were astonished. He showed that he was familiar with their art, their literature, and their religion. Pointing to their statues and idols, he declared that God could not be compared to these graven images. These images had no life, moving only when human hands moved them, and those who worshiped them were superior in every way to the things they worshiped.

Paul drew the minds of his hearers to the Deity whom they had called the "Unknown God." This Being needed nothing from human efforts to add to His power and glory.

The people were carried away with admiration for Paul's logical presentation of the attributes of the true God. Eloquently the apostle declared: "God who made the world and everything in it, since He is Lord of heaven and earth, does not dwell in temples made with hands. Nor is He worshiped with men's hands, as though He needed anything, since He gives to all life, breath, and all things."

In that age when human rights were often unrecognized, Paul proclaimed that God "made from one blood every nation of men to dwell on all the face of the earth." All are equal, and every human being owes supreme allegiance to the Creator. Then the apostle showed how, through all God's dealings with humanity, His purpose of grace and mercy runs like a thread of gold. He "determined their preappointed times and the boundaries of their dwellings, so that they should seek the Lord, in the hope that they might grope for Him and find Him, though He is not far from each one of us."

With words borrowed from one of their own poets he pictured God as a Father, whose children they were. " 'In Him we live and move and have our being,' " he declared; "as also some of your own poets have said, 'For we are also His offspring.' Therefore, since we are the offspring of God, we ought not to think that the Divine Nature is like gold or silver or stone, something shaped by art and man's devising."

The Great Philosophers Rejected the Gospel

In the ages of darkness before the birth of Christ, the divine Ruler had not held the heathen fully responsible for their idol worship. But now He expected repentance, not only from the poor and humble, but from the proud philosophers and princes. "He has appointed a day on which He will judge the world in righteousness by the Man whom He has ordained. He has given assurance of this to all by raising Him from the dead." As Paul spoke of the resurrection from the dead, "some mocked, while others said, 'We will hear you again on this matter.' "

So the Athenians, clinging to their idols, turned from the light. Boasting of their learning and refinement, they were becoming more corrupt and more content with the vague mysteries of idol worship.

Some who listened to Paul were convicted, but they would not humble themselves to accept the plan of salvation. No eloquence, no argument, can convert the sinner. The power of God alone can make the truth go straight to the heart. The Greeks sought after wisdom, yet to them the message of the cross was foolishness.

In their pride of intellect we can find the reason why the gospel met with little success among the Athenians. Worldly wise people who come to Christ as lost sinners will become wise unto salvation, but those who boast of their own wisdom will fail to receive the light and knowledge that He alone can give.

In this way Paul met the paganism of his day. His labors in Athens were not entirely fruitless. Dionysius, one of the most prominent citizens, and some others accepted the gospel.

The Athenians, with all their knowledge, refinement, and art, still were sunken in vice. Through His servant, God rebuked the sins of a proud, self-sufficient people. The words of the apostle, as recorded by the inspired writer, bear witness to his courage in loneliness and opposition and to the victory he gained for Christianity in the very heart of paganism.

Truth to Be Taught Tactfully

If Paul's stirring speech had been a direct attack on the gods and the great men of the city, he would have been in danger of being executed like Socrates. But with a tact that came from divine love, he carefully drew their minds away from heathen gods by revealing the true God to them.

Today the truths of Scripture are to be brought to the attention of the great men of the world, so that they can choose between obedience to God's law and allegiance to the prince of evil. God does not force them to accept truth, but if they turn from it, He leaves them to be filled with the fruit of their own choices.

"The message of the cross is foolishness to those who are perishing, but to us who are being saved it is the power of God." "God has chosen the foolish things of the world to put to shame the wise, and God has chosen the weak things of the world to put to shame the things which are mighty." (1 Corinthians 1:18, 27.) Many great scholars and statesmen, the world's most eminent people, will turn from the light in these last days. Yet God's servants are to communicate the truth to these men and women. Some will take their places as humble learners at the feet of Jesus, the Master Teacher.

In the darkest hour there is light above. Day by day God will renew the strength of those who love and serve Him. He places His own infinite understanding at their service, so that they will not go wrong. The light of God's truth is to shine amid the darkness that enfolds our world.

There is to be no discouragement in God's service. God is able and willing to give His servants the strength they need, and He will more than fulfill the highest expectations of those who put their trust in Him.

Preaching the Power of the Cross in Corinth*

Corinth was one of the leading cities of the world. Travelers from every land filled its streets, intent on business and pleasure. It was an important place in which to establish a presence for God and His truth.

Among the Jews living in Corinth were Aquila and Priscilla, earnest workers for Christ. Paul became acquainted with them, recognized their good qualities, and stayed and worked with them.

In this place filled with travelers, Venus was the favorite goddess, and many demoralizing rites accompanied her worship. Even among the heathen, the Corinthians had become famous for their gross immorality.

In Corinth the apostle followed a different course from how he had worked in Athens, where he met logic with logic, philosophy with philosophy. He realized that his teaching in Athens had borne little fruit. In his efforts to attract the attention of the careless and indifferent in Corinth he determined to avoid elaborate arguments, and "not to know anything among you except Jesus Christ and Him crucified." He would not preach "with persuasive words of human wisdom, but in dem-

onstration of the Spirit and of power." (1 Corinthians 2:2, 4.)

Jesus, whom Paul was about to present as the Christ, came from a town widely known for its wickedness. He had been rejected by His own nation and finally crucified as a criminal. The Greeks considered philosophy and science as the only way to reach true elevation and honor. Could Paul lead them to believe that faith in this obscure Jew would uplift and ennoble every power of the being?

To many people living today, the cross of Calvary stirs up sacred memories. But in Paul's day people regarded the cross with horror. To uphold as the Savior someone who had met death on the cross would naturally result in ridicule and opposition.

Paul knew very well how people would receive his message. It would make his Jewish hearers angry. In the opinion of the Greeks his words would be absurd. How could the cross have anything to do with elevating the race or saving mankind?

The One Object of Supreme Interest

But ever since Paul's career of persecuting the followers of the crucified

---

* This chapter is based on Acts 18:1–18.

Nazarene had been cut short, he had never stopped glorying in the cross. He had received a revelation of the infinite love of God as revealed in the death of Christ. This had worked a marvelous transformation in his life, bringing all his plans and purposes into harmony with heaven. He knew by experience that when a sinner yields to the love of the Father as seen in the sacrifice of His Son, a change of heart takes place, and Christ becomes everything to the believer.

From then on Paul devoted his life to trying to portray the love and power of the Crucified One. "I am a debtor," he wrote, "both to Greeks and to barbarians, both to wise and to unwise" (Romans 1:14). If his zeal ever weakened, one glance at the cross and the amazing love it revealed was enough to cause him to push ahead in the path of self-denial.

See the apostle in the synagogue at Corinth, reasoning from the writings of Moses and the prophets and bringing his hearers right to the advent of the promised Messiah. Listen as he makes plain the work of the One who by sacrificing His own life was to make atonement for sin and then begin His ministry in the heavenly sanctuary. The Messiah for whom Paul's hearers had been longing had already come. His death was the fulfillment of all the sacrificial offerings. His ministry in the sanctuary in heaven was the great reality that cast its shadow backward and revealed the meaning of the ministry of the Jewish priesthood.

From the Old Testament Scriptures Paul traced the ancestry of Jesus from Abraham through David, the royal psalmist. He read the testimony of the prophets concerning the character and work of the promised Messiah and showed that all these predictions had been fulfilled in Jesus of Nazareth.

Christ had come to offer salvation first of all to the nation that was looking for the Messiah's coming, but that nation had rejected Him and had chosen another leader, whose reign would end in death. Only repentance could save the Jewish nation from the approaching ruin.

Paul told the story of his own miraculous conversion. His listeners could not help but see that he loved the crucified and risen Savior with all his heart. They saw that his whole life was bound up with his Lord. Only those who were filled with the bitterest hatred could remain unmoved by his words.

Again the Jews Reject the Gospel

But the Jews of Corinth closed their eyes to the evidence the apostle presented and refused to listen to his appeals. The same spirit that had led them to reject Christ filled them with fury against His servant, and, if God had not especially protected him, they would have killed him.

"But when they opposed him and blasphemed, he shook his garments and said to them, 'Your blood be upon your own heads; I am clean. From now on I will go to the Gentiles.' And he departed from there and entered the house of a certain man named Justus, one who worshiped God."

Silas and Timothy had come to help Paul, and together they preached

Christ as the Savior. Avoiding complicated, far-fetched reasoning, the messengers of the cross appealed to the heathen to look at the infinite sacrifice Jesus made in mankind's behalf. If those groping in the darkness of heathenism could see the light streaming from Calvary's cross, they would be drawn, the Savior had declared, "to Myself" (John 12:32).

Their message was clear, plain, and forceful. And not only in their words, but in their daily life, the gospel was revealed. Angels cooperated with them, and many people were converted, showing the grace and power of God. "Crispus, the ruler of the synagogue, believed on the Lord with all his household. And many of the Corinthians, hearing, believed and were baptized."

Paul Bitterly Attacked

The Jews' hatred now intensified. The baptism of Crispus exasperated these stubborn opposers. They slandered the gospel and the name of Jesus. No words were too bitter, no device too low, for them to use. They boldly affirmed that Paul accomplished his wonderful works through the power of Satan.

The wickedness that Paul saw in corrupt Corinth almost took his courage away. The moral corruption among the Gentiles and the insults he received from the Jews caused him great distress. He doubted the wisdom of trying to build up a church from the material he found there.

As he was planning to leave for a more promising field, the Lord appeared to him in a vision and said, "Do not be afraid, but speak, and do not keep silent; for I am with you . . . ; for I have many people in this city." Paul understood this to be a guarantee that the Lord would give a harvest for the seed sown in Corinth. Encouraged, he continued to work there with zeal.

Paul spent much time in house-to-house effort. He visited the sick and the grieving, comforted the afflicted, and lifted up the oppressed. He was greatly concerned that his teaching bear the stamp of the divine rather than the human.

"We speak wisdom among those who are mature, yet not the wisdom of this age, nor of the rulers of this age, who are coming to nothing. But we speak the wisdom of God in a mystery, the hidden wisdom which God ordained before the ages for our glory, which none of the rulers of this age knew; for had they known, they would not have crucified the Lord of glory."

"These things we also speak, not in words which man's wisdom teaches but which the Holy Spirit teaches" (1 Corinthians 2:6–8, 13.)

Paul spoke of himself as "always carrying about in the body the dying of the Lord Jesus, that the life of Jesus also may be manifested in our body" (2 Corinthians 4:10). In the apostle's teachings, Christ was the central figure. "It is no longer I who live," he wrote, "but Christ lives in me" (Galatians 2:20).

Paul was an eloquent speaker. But now he set all soaring oratory aside. Instead of indulging in poetic but empty expressions that might please the senses but not touch the daily experience, with simple language he tried to bring to the heart the truths of vital importance. The present trials that people struggle with—these he wanted to meet with practical instruction in the fundamental principles of Christianity.

Many in Corinth turned from idols to serve the living God, and a large church was established under the banner of Christ. Some of the most shameless sinners among the Gentiles became towering examples of the power of Christ's blood to cleanse from sin.

Roman Proconsul Refuses to Be a Dupe of the Jews

Paul's increased success led the unbelieving Jews to oppose him even more fiercely. They "made a united attack on Paul and brought him before the tribunal" of Gallio, proconsul of Achaia (NRSV). With loud, angry voices they complained: "This fellow persuades men to worship God contrary to the law."

Paul's accusers thought that if they could fasten on him the charge of violating the Jewish religion, which was under the protection of the Roman power, he would probably be handed over to them for trial and sentence. But Gallio, a man of integrity, refused. Disgusted with their prejudice and self-righteousness, he would not allow the charge to stand. As Paul prepared to speak in self-defense, Gallio told him it was not necessary. Then turning to the angry accusers, he said: " 'If it were a matter of wrongdoing or wicked crimes, O Jews, there would be reason why I should bear with you. But if it is a question of words and names and your own law, look to it yourselves; for I do not want to be a judge of such matters.' And he drove them from the judgment seat."

Gallio's immediate dismissal of the case was the signal for the Jews to leave, frustrated and angry. The proconsul's decisive course opened the eyes of the noisy crowd who had been helping the Jews. For the first time during Paul's work in Europe, the mob turned to his side. "Then all the Greeks took Sosthenes, the ruler of the synagogue, and beat him before the judgment seat. But Gallio took no notice of these things."

"So Paul remained a good while" with the believers in Corinth. If the apostle had been forced to leave Corinth at this time, the converts would have been in a dangerous position. The Jews would have tried to follow up on the advantage they had gained, even to exterminate Christianity from that region.

Two Important Letters to the Thessalonians*

S ilas and Timothy's arrival in Corinth had greatly cheered Paul. They brought him "good news" of the "faith and love" of those who had accepted the gospel at Thessalonica. These believers had remained true, even through trial and hardship. He longed to visit them, but since this was not possible just then, he wrote them:

"Therefore, brethren, in all our affliction and distress we were comforted concerning you by your faith. For now we live, if you stand fast in the Lord.

"For what thanks can we render to God for you, for all the joy with which we rejoice for your sake before our God?"

Many people in Thessalonica had turned from idols and had "received the word in much affliction," and their hearts were filled with "joy of the Holy Spirit." In their faithfulness they were "examples to all in Macedonia and Achaia who believe." The apostle declared, "For from you the word of the Lord has sounded forth, not only in Macedonia and Achaia, but also in every place."

The hearts of the Thessalonian believers burned with zeal for their Savior. A wonderful transformation had taken place in their lives, and the truths they presented won other hearts to the Lord.

In this first letter Paul stated that he had not tried to win converts among the Thessalonians through deception or misleading. "For neither at any time did we use flattering words, as you know, nor a cloak for covetousness— God is witness. . . . But we were gentle among you, just as a nursing mother cherishes her own children. So . . . we were well pleased to impart to you not only the gospel of God, but also our own lives, because you had become dear to us."

"You know how we exhorted, and comforted, and charged every one of you, as a father does his own children, that you would walk worthy of God who calls you."

"What is our hope, or joy, or crown of rejoicing? Is it not even you in the presence of our Lord Jesus Christ at His coming? For you are our glory and joy."

Where Are the Dead?

Paul did his best to instruct the Thessalonian believers about the true condition of the dead. He spoke of

---

* This chapter is based on 1 and 2 Thessalonians.

those who die as being asleep—in a state of unconsciousness: "I do not want you to be ignorant, brethren, concerning those who have fallen asleep, lest you sorrow as others who have no hope. For if we believe that Jesus died and rose again, even so God will bring with Him those who sleep in Jesus. . . .

"For the Lord Himself will descend from heaven with a shout, with the voice of an archangel, and with the trumpet of God. And the dead in Christ will rise first. Then we who are alive and remain shall be caught up together with them in the clouds to meet the Lord in the air. And thus we shall always be with the Lord."

The Thessalonians had grasped the idea that Christ was coming to change the faithful who were alive and to take them to Himself. But one after another of their loved ones had been taken from them, and the Thessalonians hardly dared to hope to meet them in a future life.

As the believers opened and read Paul's letter, the words revealing the true condition of the dead brought them great joy and comfort. Those living when Christ comes would not go to meet their Lord ahead of those who had fallen asleep in Jesus. The dead in Christ will rise first, before the touch of immortality will be given to the living. "Therefore comfort one another with these words."

We can scarcely appreciate the hope and joy that this assurance brought the young church at Thessalonica. They cherished the letter that their father in the gospel sent them, and their hearts went out in love to him. He had told them these things before, but at that time their minds were trying to grasp doctrines that seemed new and strange. Paul's letter gave them new hope and a deeper affection for Jesus, who through His death had brought life and immortality to light. Their friends who believed in Jesus would be raised from the grave to live forever in God's kingdom. Paul's message dispelled the darkness that had shrouded the resting place of the dead. A new splendor crowned the Christian faith.

"God will bring with Him those who sleep in Jesus," Paul wrote. Many interpret this to mean that Jesus will bring the sleeping ones from heaven, but Paul meant that as Christ was raised from the dead, so God will call the sleeping redeemed from their graves.

Signs of Christ's Coming

At Thessalonica, Paul had so fully presented the signs of the times that would happen before the Son of man returns in the clouds of heaven that he did not write very much on this subject. However, he pointedly referred to his earlier teachings: "Concerning the times and the seasons, brethren, you have no need that I should write to you. For you yourselves know perfectly that the day of the Lord so comes as a thief in the night. For when they say, 'Peace and safety!' then sudden destruction comes upon them."

Today the signs of the end are quickly being fulfilled. Paul teaches that it is sinful to be careless about the signs that will precede the second coming of Christ. He calls people who are guilty of this children of darkness: "But you, brethren, are not in darkness, so that this Day should overtake you as a thief. You are all sons of light and sons of the day. We are not of the night nor of darkness."

To those living so near the great day of Jesus' coming, the words of Paul should be all the more important: "Let us who are of the day be sober, putting on the breastplate of faith and love, and as a helmet the hope of salvation. For God did not appoint us to wrath, but to obtain salvation through our Lord Jesus Christ, who died for us, that whether we wake or sleep, we should live together with Him."

Watchful Christians try to do all in their power to advance the gospel. They have severe trials, but they do not allow hard experiences to sour their outlook or destroy their peace of mind. They know that if they bear their trials well, the trials will purify them and bring them into closer fellowship with Christ.

The believers in Thessalonica were annoyed by people who came among them with fanatical ideas. Some were living "in a disorderly manner, not working at all, but are busybodies." Some, self-willed and rash, refused to follow the instruction of those who held authority in the church. They claimed the right to urge their views on the church publicly. Paul called the attention of the Thessalonians to their obligation to show respect to those who had been chosen to fill positions of authority in the church.

The apostle pleaded with them to reveal practical godliness in their daily life: "You know what instructions we gave you through the Lord Jesus. For this is the will of God, your sanctification: that you abstain from fornication. . . . For God did not call us to impurity but in holiness" (NRSV).

Paul wanted them to increase in their knowledge of Jesus Christ. He would often meet with little groups of men and women who loved Jesus, and bow with them in prayer, asking God to teach them how to maintain a living connection with Him. And he often pleaded with God to keep them from evil and help them to be earnest, active missionaries.

One of the strongest evidences of true conversion is love to God and to others. "Concerning brotherly love," the apostle wrote, "you have no need that I should write to you, for you yourselves are taught by God to love one another. . . . Aspire to lead a quiet life, to mind your own business, and to work with your own hands, as we commanded you, that you may walk properly toward those who are outside, and that you may lack nothing."

"And may the Lord make you increase and abound in love to one another and to all, just as we do to you, so that He may establish your hearts blameless in holiness before our God and Father at the coming of our Lord Jesus Christ with all His saints."

Paul cautioned the Thessalonians not to despise the gift of prophecy: "Do not quench the Spirit. Do not despise prophecies. Test all things; hold fast what is good." He urged them to pay careful attention to distinguishing the false from the true, and he closed his letter with the prayer that God would sanctify them fully, that in "spirit, soul, and body" they might "be preserved blameless at the coming of our Lord Jesus Christ." He added, "He . . . will do it."

Did Paul Expect to Live to See Christ Return?

Some of the Thessalonian believers understood Paul to be expressing the hope that he himself would live to witness the Savior's coming. This served to increase their enthusiasm and excitement. Those who had neglected their duties became more persistent in urging their mistaken views.

In his second letter Paul set about to correct their misunderstanding. Before the coming of Christ, important developments would take place that prophecy had foretold: "We ask you, not to be soon shaken in mind or troubled, either by spirit or by word or by letter, as if from us, as though the day of Christ had come. Let no one deceive you by any means; for that Day will not come unless the falling away comes first, and the man of sin is revealed, the son of perdition, who opposes and exalts himself above all that is called God or that is worshiped, so that he sits as God in the temple of God, showing himself that he is God."

No one was to teach that Paul had warned the Thessalonians that Christ would come immediately. The apostle cautioned the believers not to receive any such message as coming from him. He emphasized the fact that the papal power that the prophet Daniel described had not yet risen against God's people. Until this power performed its blasphemous work, it would be fruitless for the church to look for the coming of their Lord.

Terrible trials were going to oppress the true church. The "mystery of iniquity" (KVJ) had already begun to work. Future developments "according to the working of Satan" will be "with all power, signs, and lying wonders, and with all unrighteous deception among those who perish." Paul wrote about those who would deliberately reject the truth, "God will send them strong delusion, that they should believe the lie." God withdraws His Spirit, leaving them to the deceptions they love.

In this way Paul outlined the work of that evil power that was to continue through long centuries of darkness and persecution before the second coming of Christ. He advised the Thessalonian believers to take up bravely the work before them and not to neglect their duties or to sit back in idle waiting. After their glowing expectation of being delivered immediately, the routine of daily life would seem unbearable. So he urged them:

"Stand fast and hold the traditions which you were taught, whether by word or by our epistle.

"Now may our Lord Jesus Christ Himself, and our God and Father, who has loved us and given us everlasting consolation and good hope by grace, comfort your hearts and establish you in every good word and work." "May the Lord direct your hearts into the love of God and into the patience of Christ."

The apostle pointed them to his own example of diligence in earthly matters while he worked in the cause of Christ. He rebuked those who had yielded to laziness and aimless excitement, and directed that they "do their work quietly and . . . earn their own living" (NRSV).

Paul concluded this letter with a prayer that in all of life's toils and trials the peace of God and the grace of the Lord Jesus Christ would be their comfort and support.

Church Politics at Corinth*

After he left Corinth, Paul's place to work was Ephesus. He was on his way to Jerusalem to attend a festival, so he could stay only a short time. He made such a good impression on the Jews in the synagogue that they begged him to stay with them. He promised to return, "God willing," and left Aquila and Priscilla to carry on the work.

At this time "a certain Jew named Apollos, born at Alexandria, an eloquent man and mighty in the Scriptures, came to Ephesus." He had heard the preaching of John the Baptist and was living proof that the work of the prophet had not been in vain. Apollos "had been instructed in the way of the Lord; and being fervent in spirit, he spoke and taught accurately the things of the Lord, though he knew only the baptism of John."

In Ephesus, Apollos "began to speak boldly in the synagogue." Aquila and Priscilla, recognizing that he had not yet received the full light of the gospel, "took him aside and explained to him the way of God more accurately." He became one of the most effective spokesmen for the Christian faith.

Apollos went to Corinth, where "he vigorously refuted the Jews publicly, showing from the Scriptures that Jesus is the Christ." Paul had planted the seed of truth, and Apollos watered it. His success led some of the believers to value his efforts more than Paul's work. This brought a spirit of rivalry that threatened to weaken the spreading of the gospel.

During the year and a half that Paul spent in Corinth, he had purposely presented the gospel simply. "In demonstration of the Spirit and of power" he had declared "the testimony of God," that their "faith should not be in the wisdom of men but in the power of God" (1 Corinthians 2:4, 1, 5).

"I fed you with milk and not with solid food," he explained later, "for until now you were not able to receive it, and even now you are still not able" (1 Corinthians 3:2). Many Corinthian believers had been slow to learn. Their growth in spiritual knowledge had not measured up to their opportunities. When they should have been able to understand the deeper truths, they were no more advanced than the disciples had been when Christ said, "I still have many things to say to you,

---

* This chapter is based on Acts 18:18–28.

but you cannot bear them now" (John 16:12). Jealousy and evil suspicions had closed the hearts of many against the full working of the Holy Spirit. They were infants in the knowledge of Christ.

Paul had instructed the Corinthians in the alphabet of faith, as people who were ignorant of divine power on the heart. Those who followed him must carry forward the work, giving spiritual light as the church was able to bear it.

How Paul Handled Sexual Immorality

The apostle knew that among his hearers in Corinth there would be proud believers in human theories who would hope to find theories in nature that would contradict the Scriptures. He also knew that critics would argue against the Christian interpretation of God's Word and that skeptics would treat the gospel of Christ with scorn.

As he worked to lead people to the cross, Paul did not try to rebuke directly those who were living immoral lives or to show how hateful their sin was in the sight of a holy God. Instead, he talked especially about practical godliness and the holiness people must have if they will be counted worthy of a place in God's kingdom. In the light of the gospel of Christ they might see how offensive their immoral practices were in the sight of God. And so the theme of his teaching was Christ and Him crucified.

The philosopher turns aside from the light because it puts his proud theories to shame. The worldly person refuses it because it would separate him from his idols. Paul saw that people must understand the character of Christ before they could love Him or view the cross with the eye of faith. Only in the light of the cross can anyone begin to grasp the true value of a human being.

The refining influence of the grace of God changes a person's natural attitudes. Unconverted people would not find heaven desirable, and if it were possible for them to enter, they would find nothing attractive there. The impulses that control the natural heart must be subdued by the grace of Christ before anyone is able to enjoy the society of the pure, holy angels.

Paul had tried to impress the Corinthian believers that he and the ministers with him were all doing the same work, and all of them were dependent on God for success. The discussion in the church over the strengths of different ministers resulted from cherishing the traits of the natural heart. "For when one says, 'I am of Paul,' and another, 'I am of Apollos,' are you not carnal? . . .

"I planted, Apollos watered, but God gave the increase. So then neither he who plants is anything, nor he who waters, but God who gives the increase" (1 Corinthians 3:4–7).

It was Paul who had first preached the gospel in Corinth and organized the church. The seed he sowed must be watered, and this is what Apollos did. He gave further instruction, but it was God who gave the increase. Those who plant and those who water do not cause the growth of the seed. The honor and glory that comes with success belongs to the Master Worker.

God has given to each of His messengers an individual work. They are all to blend in harmony, controlled by the Holy Spirit. As they make the gospel known, the human instrument is hid, and Christ appears as the Chief among ten thousand, the One altogether lovely.

"We are God's fellow workers; you are God's field, you are God's building" (1 Corinthians 3:9). The apostle compares the church to a cultivated field and also to a building, which is to grow into a temple for the Lord. He gives His workmen wisdom and skill, and if they follow His instruction, He crowns their efforts with success.

God's servants are to work together, blending in a kindly, courteous way, "in honor giving preference to one another" (Romans 12:10). No one is to pull another's work to pieces, and there are to be no separate factions. Each person is to do his appointed work, respected, loved, and encouraged by the others. Together they are to carry the work forward to completion.

The Letter to the Corinthians Is Timely Today

In Paul's first letter to the Corinthian church, he referred to the comparisons made between his efforts and those of Apollos: "I have applied all this to Apollos and myself for your benefit, brothers and sisters, so that you may learn through us the meaning of the saying, 'Nothing beyond what is written,' so that none of you will be puffed up in favor of one against another. For who sees anything different in you? What do you have that you did not receive? And if you received it, why do you boast as if it were not a gift?" (1 Corinthians 4:6, 7, NRSV).

Paul told the church about the hardships that he and those working with him had endured. "To the present hour we both hunger and thirst, and we are poorly clothed, and beaten, and homeless. And we labor, working with our own hands. Being reviled, we bless; being persecuted, we endure; being defamed, we entreat. We have been made as the filth of the world, the offscouring of all things until now.

"I do not write these things to shame you, but as my beloved children I warn you. For though you might have ten thousand instructors in Christ, yet you do not have many fathers; for in Christ Jesus I have begotten you through the gospel" (1 Corinthians 4:11–15).

He who sends out gospel workers is dishonored when church members develop so strong an attachment to some favorite minister that they are unwilling to accept some other teacher. The Lord sends help to His people, not always what they might choose, but what they need, for people cannot recognize what is for their highest good. Not very often does one minister have all the qualifications necessary to develop a church perfectly, so God often sends others, each one possessing some qualifications that the others did not have.

The church should gratefully accept these servants of Christ. They should seek to gain all the benefit possible from each minister. In humility they should accept the truths that the servants of God bring, but no minister is to be idolized.

As God's ministers obtain the empowerment of the Holy Spirit to extend the triumphs of the cross, they will see results—they will accomplish a work that will withstand the attacks of Satan. Many people will turn from darkness to light, converted not to the human messenger but to Christ. Jesus only, the Man of Calvary, will appear. And God is just as ready to give power to His servants today as He was to give it to Paul and Apollos, to Silas and Timothy, to Peter, James, and John.

The Peril of Trying to Go It Alone

In Paul's day some misguided people claimed to believe in Christ, yet refused to show respect to His ambassadors. They claimed that Christ taught them directly without the aid of the ministers of the gospel. They were unwilling to submit to the voice of the church. People like this were in danger of being deceived.

God has placed people with different talents in the church, so that through the combined wisdom of many we may do what the Spirit wants. Workers who refuse to team up with others who have had long experience in the work of God will be unable to tell the difference between the false and the true. If they were chosen as leaders in the church, they would follow their own judgment regardless of the judgment of their fellow Christians. It is easy for the enemy to work through them. Impressions alone are not a safe guide to duty. The enemy persuades such people that God is guiding them, when in reality they are only following their human impulses. But if we take counsel with others in the church, God will give us an understanding of His will.

In the early church some refused to accept either Paul or Apollos, saying that Peter, also known as Cephas, was their leader. They affirmed that Peter had been one of Christ's closest associates, while Paul had been a persecutor of the believers. Controlled by prejudice, they did not show the generosity, the tenderness, that reveals that Christ is living in the heart.

The Lord instructed Paul to speak up in protest. Addressing those who were saying, " 'I am of Paul,' or 'I am of Apollos,' or 'I am of Cephas,' or 'I am of Christ,' " he asked, "Is Christ divided? Was Paul crucified for you? Or were you baptized in the name of Paul?" "Let no one boast in men," he pleaded. "Whether Paul or Apollos or Cephas, or the world or life or death, or things present or things to come—all are yours. And you are Christ's, and Christ is God's." (1 Corinthians 1:12, 13; 3:21–23.)

Apollos was sad because of the conflict at Corinth. He did not encourage it, but quickly left the scene of strife. Later, when Paul urged him to visit Corinth again, he declined until many years later when the church had reached a better spiritual condition.

Witchcraft Books Burned[*]

In the time of the apostles, Ephesus was the capital of the Roman province of Asia. Its harbor was crowded with ships, and its streets were thronged with people from every country. Like Corinth, it was a promising field for missionary work.

The Jews, widely scattered in all civilized lands, were generally expecting the Messiah. When John the Baptist was preaching, many who visited Jerusalem had gone out to the Jordan to listen to him. There they had heard him proclaim Jesus as the Promised One, and they had carried the news to all parts of the world. In this way God had prepared the way for the apostles.

At Ephesus, Paul found twelve believers who had been disciples of John the Baptist and who had gained some knowledge of Christ's mission. But when Paul asked them if they had received the Holy Spirit, they answered, "We have not so much as heard whether there is a Holy Spirit."

"Into what then were you baptized?" Paul inquired.

They said, "Into John's baptism."

Then the apostle told them of Christ's life and of His cruel and shameful death, and how He had risen triumphant over death. He repeated the Savior's commission: "All authority has been given to Me in heaven and on earth. Go therefore and make disciples of all the nations, baptizing them in the name of the Father and of the Son and of the Holy Spirit" (Matthew 28:18, 19). He also told them of Christ's promise to send the Comforter and described how gloriously the Lord had fulfilled this promise on the Day of Pentecost.

The men listened with amazement and joy. They grasped the truth of Christ's atoning sacrifice and received Him as their Redeemer. They were then baptized in the name of Jesus, and as Paul "laid hands on them," they received the Holy Spirit and were enabled to speak the languages of other nations and to prophesy. In this way God qualified them to preach the gospel in Asia Minor.

By cherishing a humble, teachable spirit, these men gained the experience that enabled them to go as workers into the harvest field. Their example presents a valuable lesson. Many make very little progress in their spiritual life because they are too self-

---

[*] This chapter is based on Acts 19:1–20.

sufficient. They are content with a superficial knowledge of God's Word.

If the followers of Christ would earnestly seek wisdom, God would lead them into rich fields of truth that they don't yet know exist. God's divine hand will guide those who give themselves fully to Him. As they treasure the lessons of divine wisdom, God will enable them to make their lives an honor to Him and a blessing to the world.

The Holy Spirit Produces Fruit in the Believer

Christ calls our attention to the growth of the vegetable world as an illustration of how His Spirit sustains spiritual life. The sap of the grapevine, going up from the root, goes out to the branches and produces fruit. So the Holy Spirit, sent from the Savior, fills the heart, renews the motives, and brings even the thoughts into obedience to God's will, enabling the person to bear precious fruit.

The exact method God uses to give spiritual life is beyond human minds to explain. Yet the workings of the Spirit are always in harmony with the written Word. As the natural life is not sustained by a direct miracle, but through the use of blessings God places within our reach, so the spiritual life is sustained by using resources that Providence has supplied. The follower of Christ must eat the bread of life and drink the water of salvation, following the instructions of God in His Word in all things.

There is another lesson in the experience of those Jewish converts. When they received baptism from John, they did not fully understand Jesus' mission as the Sin Bearer. But with clearer light, they gladly accepted Christ as their Redeemer, and as they received a purer faith, their lives changed in harmony with their new beliefs. To represent this change and to acknowledge their faith in Christ, they were rebaptized in the name of Jesus.

Paul continued his work at Ephesus for three months. In the synagogue he "spoke boldly . . . , reasoning and persuading concerning the things of the kingdom of God." As in other places, he was soon violently opposed. "Some stubbornly refused to believe and spoke evil of the Way before the congregation" (NRSV). As they persisted in rejecting the gospel, the apostle stopped preaching in the synagogue.

Paul presented enough evidence to win over all who honestly wanted the truth. But many refused to accept the most convincing evidence. Fearing that the believers would be in danger if they continued to associate with these opposers of the truth, Paul gathered the disciples into a group of their own, continuing his public instructions in the school of Tyrannus.

The Battle Between Christ and Satan at Ephesus

Paul saw that "a great and effective door" was opening before him, although there were "many adversaries" (1 Corinthians 16:9). Ephesus was not only the most magnificent city in Asia, but it was also the most corrupt. Superstition and sensual pleasure were in control. Under the shadow of her temples, criminals of every kind found shelter, and degrading sins multiplied.

Diana of the Ephesians had a magnificent temple there, whose fame extended worldwide. Its splendor made it the pride of the nation. People claimed that the idol within the temple had fallen from the sky. Books had been written to explain the meaning of symbols inscribed in it. Among those who studied these books diligently were many magicians, who exerted a powerful influence over the superstitious worshipers of the temple's image.

The power of God accompanied Paul's efforts at Ephesus, and many were healed of physical illnesses. These demonstrations of supernatural power were far stronger than any that had ever been seen in Ephesus, and no juggler's skill or sorcerer's spell could duplicate them. As Paul did these miracles in the name of Jesus, the people had opportunity to see that the God of heaven was more powerful than the magicians of the goddess Diana. And so the Lord exalted His servant far above the most powerful of the magicians.

But God, to whom all the spirits of evil are subject, was about to bring still greater defeat on those who despised and profaned His holy name. The Mosaic law had prohibited sorcery, yet apostate Jews had secretly practiced it. In Ephesus there were "some of the itinerant Jewish exorcists" who, seeing the wonders Paul performed, "took it upon themselves to call the name of the Lord Jesus over those who had evil spirits." "Also there were seven sons of Sceva, a Jewish high priest, who did so." Finding a man possessed with a demon, they said to him, "We exorcise you by the Jesus whom Paul preaches." But "the evil spirit answered and said, 'Jesus I know, and Paul I know; but who are you?'

"Then the man in whom the evil spirit was leaped on them, overpowered them, and prevailed against them, so that they fled out of that house naked and wounded."

This experience gave unmistakable proof of the sacredness of Christ's name and the danger of trying to use it without faith in the Savior's divinity. "Fear fell on them all; and the name of the Lord Jesus was magnified."

Facts hidden until then now came to light. To some extent some of the believers still continued to practice magic. Now, convinced of their error, many believers "came confessing and telling their deeds. Also, many of those who had practiced magic brought their books together and burned them in the sight of all. And they counted up the value of them, and it totaled fifty thousand pieces of silver. So the word of the Lord grew mightily and prevailed."

By burning their books on magic, the Ephesian converts showed that the things they had once delighted in, they now hated. Through magic they had especially offended God and put their spiritual life in danger, and now it was against magic that they showed such indignation. In this way they gave evidence of true conversion.

Why They Burned the Satanic Books

These books on sorcery were the regulations of Satan's worship—directions for requesting his help and obtaining information from him. By keeping these books the disciples would have exposed themselves to temptation. By selling them they would have placed temptation in the way of others. To destroy the power of the kingdom of darkness, they did not hesitate at any sacrifice. Truth triumphed over their love of money. The gospel won a great victory right in the stronghold of superstition. The influence of what took place there was more widespread than even Paul realized.

Sorcery is practiced today as surely as in the days of the old-time magicians. Through modern spiritualism Satan presents himself as though he were our departed friends. The Scriptures declare that "the dead know nothing" (Ecclesiastes 9:5). They do not communicate with the living. But Satan uses this ploy in order to gain control of minds. Through spiritualism many of the sick, the grieving, and the curious are communicating with evil spirits. All who do this are on dangerous ground.

The magicians of heathen times have their counterpart in the spiritualistic mediums and fortunetellers of today. The mystic voices at Endor and Ephesus are still misleading men and women by their lying words. Evil angels are using all their skills to deceive and destroy. Wherever an influence causes people to forget God, Satan is exercising his bewitching power there. When anyone yields to his influence, the mind is bewildered and the heart polluted. "Have no fellowship with the unfruitful works of darkness, but rather expose them" (Ephesians 5:11).

The Silversmiths Riot at Ephesus *

For more than three years Ephesus was the center of Paul's work. He raised up a flourishing church, and the gospel spread from this city throughout Asia among both Jews and Gentiles.

The apostle now "purposed in the Spirit, when he had passed through Macedonia and Achaia, to go to Jerusalem, saying, 'After I have been there, I must also see Rome.'" In harmony with this plan he "sent two of his helpers, Timothy and Erastus, to Macedonia" (NRSV), but feeling that Ephesus still needed his presence, he decided to stay there until after Pentecost. An event soon occurred, however, that made him leave sooner than planned.

Once a year, special ceremonies were held at Ephesus to honor the goddess Diana. These attracted great numbers of people. This gala season was a difficult time for those who had newly come to the faith. The believers who met in the school of Tyrannus were clearly out of harmony with the festive occasion, and people freely heaped ridicule and insult on them.

Paul's efforts had given the heathen worship a serious setback, and there was a noticeable drop in attendance at the national festival and in the enthusiasm of the worshipers. The influence of Paul's teachings extended far beyond the actual converts. Many who had not accepted the new doctrines had still gained enough light that they lost all confidence in their heathen gods.

There was also another cause of dissatisfaction. A profitable business had developed in selling small shrines and images, modeled after the temple and image of Diana. Those in this industry found their profits shrinking, and they all blamed the unwelcome change on Paul's ministry.

Demetrius, a manufacturer of silver shrines, called together the workmen of his craft and said: "Men, you know that we have our prosperity from this trade. Moreover you see and hear that not only at Ephesus, but throughout almost all Asia, this Paul has persuaded and turned away many people, saying that they are not gods which are made with hands. So not only is this trade of ours in danger of falling into disrepute, but also the temple of the great goddess Diana may be despised and her magnificence destroyed." The excitable people "were

---

* This chapter is based on Acts 19:21-41; 20:1.

full of wrath and cried out, saying, 'Great is Diana of the Ephesians!'"

A report of this speech quickly circulated, and "the whole city was filled with confusion." People searched for Paul, but the apostle was not to be found. His fellow believers had quickly removed him from the place. God sent angels to guard the apostle. His time to die as a martyr had not yet come.

When they failed to find the object of their anger, the mob seized "Gaius and Aristarchus, Macedonians, Paul's travel companions," and they "rushed into the theater" with them.

The Apostle Eager to Defend Truth

Paul was not far away, and he soon learned about the danger his friends were in. Forgetting his own safety, he wanted to go to the theater immediately to speak to the rioters. But "the disciples would not allow him." They didn't expect any serious harm to come to Gaius and Aristarchus, but if the apostle made an appearance, it would stir up the worst passions of the mob, and it would be humanly impossible to save his life.

Paul was finally persuaded not to go by a message from the theater. His friends "sent to him pleading that he would not venture into the theater."

The uproar there was continually growing stronger. "The assembly was confused, and most of them did not know why they had come together." The Jews, anxious to show that they did not sympathize with Paul and his work, brought forward one of their own people to speak to the mob. The speaker they chose was the craftsman Alexander, a coppersmith, who Paul later said had done him much harm. (See 2 Timothy 4:14.) Alexander applied all his energies to focusing the people's anger exclusively on Paul and his companions. But the crowd, seeing that he was a Jew, pushed him aside, and "all with one voice cried out for about two hours, 'Great is Diana of the Ephesians!'"

Finally, there was a moment of silence. Then the clerk of the city, because he was an important government officer, got the crowd's attention. He showed that there was no cause for the present uproar and appealed to their reason. "'What man is there who does not know that the city of the Ephesians is temple guardian of the great goddess Diana, and of the image which fell down from Zeus? . . . You ought to be quiet and do nothing rashly. . . . These men here . . . are neither robbers of temples nor blasphemers of your goddess. Therefore, if Demetrius and his fellow craftsmen have a case against anyone, the courts are open and there are proconsuls. Let them bring charges against one another. . . . We are in danger of being called in question for today's uproar, there being no reason which we may give to account for this disorderly gathering.' And when he had said these things, he dismissed the assembly."

In his speech Demetrius revealed the real cause of the commotion and also much of the persecution that followed the apostles: "This trade of ours [is] in danger of falling into disrepute." The spread of the gospel endangered the business of making idols. The income of pagan priests and craftsmen was at stake.

The decision of the clerk and of others in the city had upheld Paul before the people as innocent of any unlawful act. God had raised up a great city official to vindicate His apostle and keep the mob under control. Paul's heart was filled with gratitude to God for preserving his life and that Christianity had not been discredited by the near riot at Ephesus.

"After the uproar had ceased, Paul called the disciples to himself, embraced them, and departed to go to Macedonia."

Oppressed by Enemies
and Deserted by Friends

Paul's ministry in Ephesus involved constant labor, many hardships, and deep anguish. He had taught the people in public and from house to house, instructing and warning them. The Jews had opposed him at every turn. And while he was battling against opposition, he was carrying a heavy burden on his heart for all the churches. News of apostasy in some of the churches caused him deep sorrow. He spent many sleepless nights in earnest prayer as he learned of how people were trying to undo his work.

As he had opportunity, he wrote to the churches, giving correction, counsel, warnings, and encouragement. In these letters he sometimes gave glimpses of his sufferings in the service of Christ. Beatings and imprisonment, cold and hunger and thirst, dangers by land and by sea, in the city and in the wilderness, from his own countrymen, from the heathen, and from false believers—all this he endured for the gospel. He was "defamed," "reviled," made "the offscouring of all things," "perplexed," "persecuted," "hard pressed on every side," "in jeopardy every hour," "always delivered to death for Jesus' sake."

The brave apostle almost lost heart. But he looked to Calvary and with new spirit went forward to spread the knowledge of Jesus the Crucified. He was walking the blood-stained path Christ had traveled before him. He wanted no release from the warfare until it would be time for him to lay his armor down at the feet of his Redeemer.

Paul Challenges Lawsuits and Sexual Looseness*

For a year and a half Paul had worked among the believers in Corinth, pointing them to a crucified and risen Savior and urging them to rely completely on the transforming power of His grace. Before accepting them into church fellowship he had carefully taught them about the duties of the Christian believers, and he had tried to help them be faithful to their baptismal vows.

Paul had a clear sense of the conflict every Christian has to wage with the agencies of evil, and he had worked untiringly to strengthen those who were young in the faith. He had pleaded with them to make an entire surrender to God, for he knew that when the heart fails to make an entire surrender, sin is not forsaken, and temptations confuse the conscience. Every weak, doubting, struggling person who yields fully to the Lord comes into direct touch with heavenly powers that enable him to overcome. Angels help such Christians in every time of need.

The members of the church at Corinth were surrounded by idolatry and impurity. While Paul was with them, these influences had little power over them. Paul's prayers, earnest words of instruction, and godly life helped them to deny self, for Christ's sake, rather than to enjoy the pleasures of sin.

After Paul left, however, little by little many became careless and allowed natural tastes and desires to control them. Many who had put away evil habits when they were converted returned to the degrading sins of heathenism. Paul had written briefly, urging them "not to keep company" with members who persisted in immorality, but many argued over his words and excused themselves for ignoring his instruction.

The church sent a letter to Paul, asking for counsel on various matters, but saying nothing of the terrible sins existing among them. The Holy Spirit, however, impressed the apostle that church had hidden its true condition.

About this time members of the household of Chloe, a Christian family in Corinth, came to Ephesus. They told Paul that the strife that had arisen at the time of Apollos's visit had greatly increased. False teachers were leading the members to reject Paul's instructions. Pride, idolatry, and sexual sins were steadily increasing.

---

* This chapter is based on 1 Corinthians.

Paul saw that his worst fears had more than come true. But he did not allow himself to think that his work had been a failure. With "anguish of heart" and with "many tears" (2 Corinthians 2:4) he went to God for counsel. He would gladly have visited Corinth immediately, but he knew that in their present condition the believers would not be helped by his efforts, so he sent Titus to prepare the way for him to visit later on. Then the apostle wrote to the church at Corinth one of the richest, most instructive, most powerful of all his letters.

With remarkable clearness he answered questions and laid down general principles which, if they followed them, would lead the believers to a higher spiritual level. Faithfully he warned them of their dangers and rebuked them for their sins. He reminded them of the gifts of the Holy Spirit that they had received and showed them that it was their privilege to advance in the Christian life until they reached the purity and holiness of Christ. (See 1 Corinthians 1:4–8.)

Paul spoke plainly of the strife in the Corinthian church. "I appeal to you, brothers and sisters," he wrote, "that all of you be in agreement and that there be no divisions among you, but that you be united in the same mind and the same purpose. For it has been reported to me by Chloe's people that there are quarrels among you" (NRSV).

The Nature of a Prophet's Inspiration

Paul was an inspired apostle. The truth he taught he had received "by revelation," yet the Lord did not al-

ways directly reveal to him the condition of His people. In this case, those who were interested in the church had told the apostle about the situation, and from divine revelations he had received before, he was prepared to judge these developments. Even though the Lord did not give him a new revelation for that special time, those who wanted light from God accepted his message as expressing the mind of Christ. As evils developed, the apostle recognized their significance. God had commissioned him to defend the church. Wasn't it right for him to notice the reports of the divisions among them? Surely it was, and the reproof he sent was as certainly written under the inspiration of the Spirit of God as were any of his other letters.

The apostle did not mention the false teachers who were trying to destroy the fruit of his labor. He wisely decided not to irritate them by such references. He called attention to his own work as "a wise master builder" who had laid the foundation that others had built upon. "We are God's fellow workers." He acknowledged that divine power alone had made him able to present the truth in a way that was pleasing to God. Paul had communicated lessons that were to apply at all times, in all places, and under all conditions.

One former convert had backslidden so far that his sexual sins violated even the Gentile world's low standard of morality. The apostle pleaded with the church to put this evil person away from them. "Purge out the old leaven, that you may be a new lump, since you truly are unleavened."

Another serious evil was that church members were filing lawsuits against one another. Christ Himself had given instruction about how to resolve such matters: "If your brother sins against you, go and tell him his fault between you and him alone. If he hears you, you have gained your brother. But if he will not hear, take with you one or two more, that 'by the mouth of two or three witnesses every word may be established.' And if he refuses to hear them, tell it to the church" (Matthew 18:15–17).

How to Handle Lawsuits Among Church Members

"Dare any of you," Paul asked, "having a matter against another, go to law before the unrighteous, and not before the saints? Do you not know that the saints will judge the world? And if the world will be judged by you, are you unworthy to judge the smallest matters? Do you not know that we shall judge angels? How much more, things that pertain to this life? . . . I say this to your shame. Is it so, that there is not a wise man among you, not even one, who will be able to judge between his brethren? But brother goes to law against brother, and that before unbelievers!

"Now therefore, it is already an utter failure for you that you go to law against one another. Why do you not rather accept wrong?"

Satan is constantly looking to introduce distrust, resentment, and spite among God's people. We will often be tempted to feel that our rights are invaded, even when we have no real cause for such feelings. Those who will place their own interests first will go to almost any length to defend them. Pride and self-esteem keep many from going privately to those whom they think are in the wrong, to talk with them in the spirit of Christ and pray together. Instead of following the Savior's rule, some will even go to the law when they think their fellow church members have injured them.

Christians should not appeal to civil courts to settle differences among the members of the church. Even though someone may have done an injustice, the followers of the meek and lowly Jesus will allow themselves to "be cheated" rather than to present the sins of their fellow church members before the world.

Christians who go to court against one another expose the church to ridicule from her enemies. They are wounding Christ again and putting Him to open shame. By ignoring the authority of the church, they show contempt for God, who gave the church its authority.

In this letter Paul tried to show the Corinthians Christ's power to keep them from evil. To help them break from their slavery to sin, Paul reminded them of the claim of Him to whom they had dedicated their lives: "Do you not know that . . . you are not your own? For you were bought at a price; therefore glorify God in your body."

How to Live Pure Lives in an Ocean of Impurity

Paul begged them to control the lower passions and appetites. He stirred up their better nature and inspired them to make every effort for a higher life. He knew that Satan would oppose the Corinthian believers at every step in the Christian pathway and that they would have to face conflicts daily. They would have to force back old habits and natural desires, always mindful to pray. But Paul also knew that in Christ crucified they would find enough power to enable them to resist all temptations to evil.

The Corinthian believers had seen only the first rays of the early dawn of God's glory. Paul's desire for them was that they would follow on to know Him whose "going forth is established as the morning" (Hosea 6:3), and learn of Him until they would come into the full daylight of a perfect gospel faith.

Paul Strengthens the Church for All Time*

Of all the games established among the Greeks and the Romans, the ancient foot races near Corinth were considered the greatest. Kings, nobles, and statesmen were among the spectators. Young men of wealth and high social standing took part, and did not refuse any effort or discipline necessary to win the prize.

Strict regulations governed the contests, and there was no appeal from them. Those who wanted to enter had to endure severe training to prepare. They denied themselves any harmful food or drink, or anything that would lower their mental or physical vigor. The muscles must be strong and the nerves well under control. The physical powers must reach the highest level.

As the contestants made their appearance before the waiting crowds, their names were called, and they heard the rules of the race distinctly stated. Then they all started together, with the focused attention of the spectators inspiring them with determination to win. The judges sat near the goal to watch the race from beginning to end and give the prize to the true winner.

These games involved great risks. Some contestants never recovered from the terrible physical strain. It was not unusual for runners to fall on the course, bleeding at the mouth and nose, and sometimes a contestant would drop dead when about to grasp the prize.

As the winner reached the goal, applause filled the air. The judge presented him with the emblems of victory—a laurel crown and a palm branch to carry in his hand. People throughout the land sang his praises, his parents received their share of honor, and even the city in which he lived was held in high regard for having produced such a great athlete.

Paul referred to these races as an illustration of the Christian warfare. "Athletes," he wrote, "exercise self-control in all things" (NRSV). The runners put aside every indulgence that would tend to weaken their physical powers. How much more important that Christians bring appetite and passion under the control of reason and the will of God! We must never allow our attention to be turned to amusements, luxuries, or ease. Reason, enlightened by God's Word and guided by His Spirit, must sit at the controls.

---

* This chapter is based on 1 Corinthians.

In the Corinthian games the contestants made the last few strides of the race with agonizing effort to keep up their full speed. So Christians, as they near the goal, will push onward with even more determination than when they began.

Paul contrasts the fading laurel wreath received in the foot races with the crown of immortal glory that will be given to those who triumph in the Christian race. "They do it," he declares, "to obtain a perishable crown, but we for an imperishable crown." The Grecian runners did not hold back any effort or discipline. How much more willing should be our sacrifice and self-denial!

"Let us lay aside every weight, and the sin which so easily ensnares us, and let us run with endurance the race that is set before us, looking unto Jesus, the author and finisher of our faith" (Hebrews 12:1, 2). Envy, hatred, evil-thinking, evil-speaking, covetousness—these are weights that the Christian must lay aside. We must put away every practice that brings dishonor on Christ, no matter the sacrifice. One sin cherished is enough to degrade our own character and to mislead others.

In the ancient games, after the competitors had submitted to self-denial and rigid discipline, they still were not sure of victory. "Do you not know that those who run in a race all run, but one receives the prize?" One hand only could grasp the coveted laurel wreath. As some reached out to take hold of the prize, another, an instant before them, might grasp the coveted treasure.

The Race Where Everyone Can Win

In the Christian warfare, no one who complies with the conditions will be disappointed at the end of the race. The weakest believer, as well as the strongest, may wear the crown of immortal glory. Too often people look on the principles laid down in God's Word as unimportant—too trivial to demand attention. But nothing is small that will help or hinder. And the reward given to those who win will be proportional to the energy and earnestness they have put into the effort.

The apostle compared himself to a man running in a race, straining every nerve to win. "Therefore I run thus: not with uncertainty," he says. "Thus I fight: not as one who beats the air. But I discipline my body and bring it into subjection, lest, when I have preached to others, I myself should become disqualified." The words, "I discipline my body," literally mean to beat back the desires, impulses, and passions by severe discipline.

Paul realized that his conversation, his influence, his refusal to yield to self-gratification, must show that his religion was not just empty talk but a daily, living connection with God. One goal he always tried earnestly to reach was "the righteousness which is from God by faith" (Philippians 3:9).

Paul realized his need of putting a strict guard on himself, so that earthly desires might not overcome his spiritual zeal. He continued to battle against his natural inclinations. His words, his practices, his passions—he brought them all under the control of the Spirit of God.

Paul knew that the Corinthian believers had a life struggle ahead of them, from which they would have no release. He pleaded with them to put aside every weight and press onward to the goal of perfection in Christ.

He reminded them of the miraculous way in which God led the Hebrews from Egypt—He brought them through the Red Sea, while the Egyptians, trying to cross in the same way, were all drowned. Israel "all ate the same spiritual food, and all drank the same spiritual drink. For they drank of that spiritual Rock that followed them, and that Rock was Christ." The Hebrews had Christ as leader. The rock that Moses struck represented Him, wounded for our transgressions so that the stream of salvation could flow to everyone.

Yet, because of the Hebrews' craving for the luxuries left behind in Egypt, and because of their rebellion, God's judgments came on them. "Now these things occurred as examples for us," the apostle wrote, "so that we might not desire evil as they did" (NRSV). Their love of ease and pleasure had prepared the way for sins that brought the vengeance of God on them. When the Israelites sat down to eat and drink and rose up to play, they threw off the fear of God. They made a golden calf and worshiped it. And it was after a luxurious feast connected with the worship of Baal-peor that many Hebrews gave in to sexual sins. The anger of God was stirred, and 23,000 died by the plague in one day.

If the Corinthians became boastful and self-confident, they would fall into terrible sin. Yet Paul gave them the assurance: "God is faithful, who will not allow you to be tempted beyond what you are able, but with the temptation will also make the way of escape, that you may be able to bear it."

Paul urged the believers to do nothing, no matter how innocent, that would seem to approve of idolatry or offend those who might be weak in the faith. "Whether you eat or drink, or whatever you do, do all to the glory of God. Give no offense to the Jews or to the Greeks or to the church of God."

The apostle's words apply especially to our day. By idolatry he meant not only the worship of idols, but self-serving, love of ease, the gratifying of appetite and passion. A religion that treats self-indulgence lightly is not the religion of Christ.

By comparing the church with the human body, the apostle illustrated the close relationship that should exist among all members of the church. "The body does not consist of one member but of many. If the foot would say, 'Because I am not a hand, I do not belong to the body,' that would not make it any less a part of the body. And if the ear would say, 'Because I am not an eye, I do not belong to the body,' that would not make it any less a part of the body. . . . But as it is, God arranged the members in the body, each one of them, as he chose. . . . God has so arranged the body, giving the greater honor to the inferior member, that there may be no dissension within the body, but the members may have the same care for one another. If one member suffers, all suffer together with it; if one member is honored, all rejoice together with it.

"Now you are the body of Christ and individually members of it" (NRSV).

Importance of Love

And then Paul wrote about the importance of love: "Though I speak with the tongues of men and of angels, but have not love, I have become sounding brass or a clanging cymbal. And though I have the gift of prophecy, and understand all mysteries and all knowledge, and though I have all faith, so that I could remove mountains, but have not love, I am nothing. And though I bestow all my goods to feed the poor, and though I give my body to be burned, but have not love, it profits me nothing."

No matter how high the profession, those whose hearts are not filled with love for God and other people are not true disciples of Christ. In their zeal they might even die a martyr's death, but if love did not prompt them, they would be no more than deluded fanatics or ambitious hypocrites.

"Love is patient; love is kind; love is not envious or boastful" (NRSV). The noblest characters are built on the foundation of patience, love, and submission to God's will.

Love is not "arrogant or rude. It does not insist on its own way; it is not irritable or resentful" (NRSV). Christlike love places the best interpretation on the motives and acts of others. It does not listen eagerly to negative reports, but tries to bring to mind the good qualities of others.

This love "never ends" (NRSV). Those who have it will carry it through the gates of the city of God.

The Resurrection Clarifies All Scripture Truth

Among the Corinthian believers, some had gone so far as to deny the doctrine of the resurrection. Paul countered this heresy with a very plain testimony about the unmistakable evidence of Christ's resurrection. He "rose again the third day," and then "He was seen by Cephas, then by the twelve. After that He was seen by over five hundred brethren at once, of whom the greater part remain to the present, but some have fallen asleep. After that He was seen by James, then by all the apostles. Then last of all He was seen by me also, as by one born out of due time."

"If there is no resurrection of the dead," Paul argued, "then Christ is not risen. And if Christ is not risen, then our preaching is empty and your faith is also empty. . . . For if the dead do not rise, then Christ is not risen. And if Christ is not risen, your faith is futile; you are still in your sins! Then also those who have fallen asleep in Christ have perished. If in this life only we have hope in Christ, we are of all men the most pitiable."

"I tell you a mystery," he wrote. "We shall not all sleep, but we shall all be changed—in a moment, in the twinkling of an eye, at the last trumpet. For the trumpet will sound, and the dead will be raised incorruptible, and we shall be changed. For this corruptible must put on incorruption, and this mortal must put on immortality."

The apostle tried to draw the attention of the Corinthian believers to things that would lift them up from the selfish and the sensual and would glorify life with the hope of immortality.

"My beloved brethren, be steadfast, immovable, always abounding in the work of the Lord, knowing that your labor is not in vain in the Lord."

In this way the apostle spoke plainly, yet in love. Light was shining from the throne of God to reveal the hidden sins that were defiling their lives. How would they receive it?

Paul dreaded any further division and sometimes wished he could call his words back. Those who have felt responsible for churches or institutions can appreciate how he felt—depressed and self-accusing. Servants of God who bear the burden of His work for this time know something of the same experience of labor, conflict, and anxious care. Troubled by divisions in the church, realizing the danger of churches that tolerated dreadful sins, compelled to speak plain, hard truths in reproof of sin, Paul was at the same time weighed down with fear that he might have dealt too harshly with them. Anxiously he waited for some news about how they had received his message.

Corinth Accepts Paul's Counsel[*]

A "deep concern for all the churches," and particularly for the church at Corinth, rested heavily on Paul's heart. He had hoped to meet Titus at Troas and learn from him how the Corinthian believers had accepted his counsel and reproof, but he was disappointed. "My mind could not rest," he wrote, "because I did not find my brother Titus there" (NRSV). So he left Troas and crossed over to Macedonia, where he met Timothy at Philippi.

At times feelings of deep sadness swept over Paul's heart. He was afraid that the church at Corinth might misunderstand his counsel and warnings to them. Later he wrote, "We were troubled on every side. Outside were conflicts, inside were fears. Nevertheless God, who comforts the downcast, comforted us by the coming of Titus."

This faithful messenger brought the cheering news that a wonderful change had taken place among the Corinthian believers. Many had accepted the instruction in Paul's letter and had repented. Their lives were no longer a stain on Christianity.

Filled with joy, Paul sent another letter, expressing his gladness of heart: "Even if I made you sorry with my let-ter, I do not regret it; though I did regret it." He had sometimes regretted that he had written so severely. "I rejoice," he continued, "not that you were made sorry, but that your sorrow led to repentance. . . . For godly sorrow produces repentance leading to salvation, not to be regretted." The repentance that divine grace produces will lead people to confess and forsake their sin.

Paul had been carrying a heavy burden on his heart for the churches. False teachers had been urging their own doctrines in place of gospel truth. The discouragements that surrounded Paul are revealed in the words, "We were burdened beyond measure, above strength, so that we despaired even of life."

But now one cause of anxiety was gone. Paul broke into rejoicing: "Blessed be the God and Father of our Lord Jesus Christ, the Father of mercies and God of all comfort, who comforts us in all our tribulation, that we may be able to comfort those who are in any trouble, with the comfort with which we ourselves are comforted by God. . . . Our hope for you is steadfast, because we know that as you are

---

[*] *This chapter is based on 2 Corinthians.*

partakers of the sufferings, so also you will partake of the consolation."

Paul's Joy at Their Reconversion

Paul gave God all the praise for their reconversion and transformation of heart and life: "Thanks be to God," he exclaimed, "who always leads us in triumph in Christ, and through us diffuses the fragrance of His knowledge in every place. For we are to God the fragrance of Christ among those who are being saved and among those who are perishing." In those days a victorious general might return from war with a parade of captives. He would appoint incense bearers, and as the army marched triumphantly home, the fragrant odor was an aroma of death to the captives condemned to die, showing that they were nearing the time of their execution. But to the prisoners whose lives were to be spared, it was an aroma of life—it showed that their freedom was near.

Paul now felt that Satan was not going to triumph in Corinth. He and his fellow workers would celebrate their victory by going out with new zeal to spread the fragrance of the gospel like incense throughout the world. To those who would accept Christ, the message would be an aroma of life, but to those who would persist in unbelief, an aroma of death.

Realizing the overwhelming size of the work, Paul exclaimed, "Who is sufficient for these things?" Who is able to preach Christ in such a way that His enemies will have no valid reason to despise the messenger or the message? Only faithfulness in preaching the Word, united with a pure, consistent life, can make the efforts of ministers acceptable to God.

There were those who had accused Paul of promoting himself in his earlier letter. "Do we begin again to commend ourselves?" he asked. "Or do we need, as some others, epistles of commendation to you or letters of commendation from you?" Believers moving to a new place often carried letters of recommendation from the church, but the founders of these churches did not need any such recommendation. The Corinthian believers, whom he had led from idol worship to the gospel, were themselves all the recommendation Paul needed. Their reformed lives bore eloquent testimony to his work and authority as a minister of Christ.

"You are our epistle written in our hearts, known and read by all men; clearly you are an epistle of Christ, ministered by us, written not with ink but by the Spirit of the living God, not on tablets of stone but on tablets of flesh, that is, of the heart."

The Most Wonderful Career Possible

The conversion of sinners and their godly living through the truth is the strongest proof a minister can have that God has called him. The evidence of his apostleship is written on the hearts of those converted, and their renewed lives testify to it. A minister is greatly strengthened by these evidences of his ministry.

Though today there are many preachers, there is a great lack of capable, holy ministers who are filled with the love found in Christ's heart. The fruits many Christians bear are pride, self-confidence, love of the world, and faultfinding. Their lives offer sad testimony to the character of the ministerial labor that "converted" them.

A Christian can have no greater honor than to be accepted by God as a minister of the gospel. But those whom the Lord blesses with power and success recognize their complete dependence on Him. They have no power of their own. With Paul they say, "Not that we are sufficient of ourselves to think of anything as being from ourselves, but our sufficiency is from God, who also made us sufficient as ministers of the new covenant." True ministers realize that they have a relationship to the church and to the world similar to what Christ had. They work untiringly to lead sinners to a nobler, higher life. They lift up Jesus as the sinner's only hope. Their hearers know that they have drawn close to God in fervent, effective prayer. The Holy Spirit has rested on them. Their hearts have felt the vital, heavenly fire. When they present the love of God, people's hearts are broken, and many are led to ask, "What must I do to be saved?"

"For we do not preach ourselves, but Christ Jesus the Lord, and ourselves your bondservants for Jesus' sake. For it is the God who commanded light to shine out of darkness, who has shone in our hearts to give the light of the knowledge of the glory of God in the face of Jesus Christ."

In this way Paul praised the grace and mercy of God. He and his fellow workers had been kept through affliction and danger. They had not held back truth in order to make their teaching attractive. And they had brought their own conduct into harmony with their teaching, so that truth might recommend itself to everyone's conscience.

"We have this treasure in earthen vessels," the apostle continued, "that the excellence of the power may be of God and not of us." God did not intend to proclaim His truth through sinless angels. He has placed priceless treasure in earthen vessels, human beings. Through them His glory is to shine out. They are to meet the sinful and the needy and lead them to the cross.

Paul showed that no selfish motives had prompted him to choose the service of Christ. "We are hard pressed on every side," he wrote, "yet not crushed; we are perplexed, but not in despair; persecuted, but not forsaken; struck down, but not destroyed—always carrying about in the body the dying of the Lord Jesus, that the life of Jesus also may be manifested in our body."

As Christ's messengers he and his fellow workers were constantly in danger. "We who live," he wrote, "are always delivered to death for Jesus' sake, that the life of Jesus also may be manifested in our mortal flesh." Through poverty and toil, these ministers were accepting a death like Christ's, but what was leading to death in them was bringing life to the Corinthians. In view of this, Jesus' followers were not to increase the burdens and difficulties of the workers.

Nothing could tempt Paul to conceal the conviction of his soul. He would not buy wealth or pleasure by conforming to the world's opinions.

Though he was in constant danger of being killed for his faith, he was not intimidated. He knew that Jesus who had died and risen again would raise him from the grave and present him to the Father.

The Cross Accomplishes True Conversion

The apostles did not preach the gospel to exalt themselves. The hope of saving lost people kept them from stopping their efforts because of danger or suffering.

"Therefore we do not lose heart," Paul wrote. "Even though our outward man is perishing, yet the inward man is being renewed day by day." Though his physical strength was declining, yet he declared the gospel without flinching. This hero of the cross pushed forward in the conflict. "We do not look at the things which are seen, but at the things which are not seen. For the things which are seen are temporary, but the things which are not seen are eternal."

The apostle appealed to his fellow believers in Corinth to consider again the matchless love of their Redeemer: "For you know the grace of our Lord Jesus Christ, that though He was rich, yet for your sakes He became poor, that you through His poverty might become rich." You know the height from which He stooped, the depth of humiliation to which He descended. There was no rest for Him between the throne and the cross. Paul lingered over point after point, so that those who read his letter could comprehend how much Savior had sacrificed for us.

The apostle recounted Christ's path to reach the depths of humiliation. Paul was convinced that if his readers could comprehend the amazing sacrifice made by the Majesty of heaven, they would banish all selfishness from their lives. The Son of God had humbled Himself as a servant, becoming obedient unto death, "even the death of the cross" (Philippians 2:8), so that He could lift fallen humanity from its degraded condition.

When we study the divine character in the light of the cross, we see mercy and forgiveness blended with fairness and justice. We see at the throne One who bears in His hands and feet and side the marks of the suffering He endured to reconcile us to God. We see a Father receiving us to Himself through the merits of His Son. In the light reflected from the cross, the cloud of vengeance that threatened misery and despair reveals the writing of God: Repentant, believing heart, live! I have paid a ransom.

In contemplating Christ, we linger on the shore of a love that is beyond measuring. We tell of it, but language fails us. "In this is love, not that we loved God but that he loved us and sent his Son to be the atoning sacrifice for our sins" (1 John 4:10, NRSV).

It was on earth that the love of God was revealed through Christ. It is on earth that His children are to reflect this love through blameless lives.

The Joy of Liberal Giving

In his first letter to the Corinthian believers, Paul gave instruction about supporting God's work. He asked:

"Who ever goes to war at his own expense? Who plants a vineyard and does not eat of its fruit? Or who tends a flock and does not drink of the milk of the flock? . . .

"For it is written in the law of Moses, 'You shall not muzzle an ox while it treads out the grain.' Is it oxen God is concerned about? Or does He say it altogether for our sakes? For our sakes, no doubt, this is written, that he who plows should plow in hope, and he who threshes in hope should be partaker of his hope."

The apostle further asked, "Do you not know that those who minister the holy things eat of the things of the temple, and those who serve at the altar partake in the offerings of the altar? Even so the Lord has commanded that those who preach the gospel should live from the gospel." (1 Corinthians 9:7–10, 13, 14.)

The priests who ministered in the temple were supported by the people to whom they ministered spiritual blessings. "Those who are of the sons of Levi, who receive the priesthood, have a commandment to receive tithes from the people according to the law"

(Hebrews 7:5). The tribe of Levi was chosen by the Lord for the priesthood. (See Deuteronomy 18:5.) The Lord claimed one tenth of all the increase as His own, and He regarded withholding of the tithe as robbery.

Paul referred to this plan for supporting the ministry when he said, "Even so the Lord has commanded that those who preach the gospel should live from the gospel." "The laborer is worthy of his wages" (1 Timothy 5:18).

Payment of the tithe was just one part of God's plan for the support of His service. The people were taught to cultivate a spirit of liberality. The law of Moses specified many gifts and offerings. At the harvest and the vintage, the people dedicated the first fruits of the field to the Lord. Produce that the reapers missed and what grew in the corners of the field were reserved for the poor. The first fruits of the wool when the sheep were shorn, and of the grain when the wheat was threshed, were set apart for God. So were the firstborn of all animals, and families paid a redemption price for the firstborn son.

In this way the people were reminded that God was the owner of their fields, flocks, and herds. It was

He who sent the sunshine and the rain that ripened the harvest. They were only managers of His goods.

Should Followers of Christ Give Less?

The liberality that God required of the Hebrews was mainly to benefit their own nation. Today Christ has given His followers the responsibility of taking the good news of salvation to the world. Our obligations are much greater than ancient Israel's were. As God's work spreads, calls for help will come more frequently. Christians should obey the command, "Bring all the tithes into the storehouse, that there may be food in My house" (Malachi 3:10). If professing Christians would faithfully bring their tithes and offerings to God, there would be no need to resort to fairs, lotteries, or parties of pleasure to raise funds.

Many church members do not hesitate to spend extravagantly to gratify their appetite, adorn themselves, or embellish their homes. But when they are asked to give to the Lord's treasury, they object and dole out an amount much less than they often spend for things they don't need. They show no real love for Christ's service, no deep interest in the salvation of others. The Christian life of such people is no more than a dwarfed, sickly existence!

Anyone whose heart glows with the love of Christ will find it a pleasure to help in advancing the highest, holiest work committed to mankind—presenting to the world the riches of truth. The spirit of liberality is the spirit of heaven. This spirit finds its highest expression in Christ's sacrifice on the cross. The Father gave His only Son, and Christ gave Himself, so that we could be saved. The cross of Calvary should appeal to the generosity of every follower of the Savior. The principle illustrated there is to give, give.

The spirit of selfishness is the spirit of Satan. The principle illustrated in the lives of people without Christ is to get, get. But the fruit they harvest is misery and death.

Blessings in Gratitude Offerings

Not only should God's children return to the Lord the portion that belongs to Him, they should also bring a gratitude offering, the first fruits of their rich blessings—their most excellent possessions, their best and holiest service. In this way they will gain rich blessings. God will make their hearts like a watered garden. And the harvest that they are enabled to bring to the Master will be the reward of their unselfish use of the talents He has lent them.

God's chosen messengers should never have to serve at their own expense, without the help of hearty support from their fellow Christians. It is the responsibility of church members to deal liberally with those who leave secular employment to give themselves to the ministry. When God's ministers are encouraged, His cause is greatly strengthened.

God is displeased with those who allow consecrated workers to suffer without the necessities of life. These selfish ones will have to give an account for their misuse of money and for the depression brought on His faithful servants. Those who heed the call of duty and give up everything to engage in God's service should receive wages that are enough to support themselves and their families.

In secular labor, workers can earn good wages. Isn't the work of leading people to Christ more important than any ordinary business? Aren't those who faithfully engage in this work entitled to decent pay?

A solemn responsibility rests on ministers to keep their churches aware of the needs of God's cause and to educate them to give liberally. When the churches fail to give, not only does the work of the Lord suffer, but God withholds the blessing that should come to believers.

Why the Gifts of the Poor Are Valuable

Even the very poor should bring their offerings to God. They are to share in the grace of Christ by helping those whose need is more urgent than their own. The poor person's gift, the fruit of self-denial, comes up before God as fragrant incense. And every act of self-sacrifice allies the giver more closely to the One who was rich, yet for our sakes became poor.

Christ called the disciples' attention to the widow who dropped two tiny coins—"her whole livelihood" (Mark 12:44)—into the treasury. He judged her gift to be more valuable than the large offerings of those whose donations did not call for self-denial. The widow had deprived herself of even the necessities of life, trusting God to meet her needs. "This poor widow has put in more than all those who have given to the treasury" (verse 43). God measures the value of the gift not by the amount, but by the proportion that is given, and the motive that prompts the giver.

The apostle Paul said, "Remember the words of the Lord Jesus, that He said, 'It is more blessed to give than to receive.' " "He who sows sparingly will also reap sparingly, and he who sows bountifully will also reap bountifully. So let each one give as he purposes in his heart, not grudgingly or of necessity; for God loves a cheerful giver." (Acts 20:35; 2 Corinthians 9:6, 7.)

Nearly all the Macedonian believers were poor in this world's goods, but they gladly gave to support the gospel. Paul held up the liberality of the converts in Macedonia as an example to other churches: "In a great trial of affliction the abundance of their joy and their deep poverty abounded in the riches of their liberality" (2 Corinthians 8:2).

Moved by the Spirit of God, they "first gave themselves to the Lord" (2 Corinthians 8:5). Then they were willing to give freely of their money to support the gospel work. It was not necessary to urge them. Instead, they were happy for the privilege of denying themselves even necessary things in order to meet the needs of others.

When Paul sent Titus to Corinth to strengthen the believers there, in a personal letter he added his own appeal: "Now as you excel in everything—in faith, in speech, in knowledge, in utmost earnestness, and in our love for you—so we want you to excel also in this generous undertaking." "And God is able to provide you with every blessing in abundance, so that by always having enough of everything, you may share abundantly in every good work. . . . You will be enriched in every way for great generosity, which will produce thanksgiving to God through us." (2 Corinthians 8:7; 9:8–11, NRSV.)

Unselfish liberality brought great joy to the early church. The believers knew that their efforts were helping to send the gospel to those in darkness. Their generosity showed that they had not received the grace of God in vain. In the eyes of believers and unbelievers this kind of liberality was a miracle of grace.

Spiritual prosperity goes hand-in-hand with Christian generosity. As the followers of Christ give to the Lord, they have the assurance that their treasure is going ahead of them to the heavenly courts. Would you like to make your property secure? Place it in the hands that bear the marks of the Crucifixion. Do you want to enjoy your wealth? Use it to bless the needy. Do you want to increase your possessions?

"Honor the Lord with your
    possessions,
And with the firstfruits of all your
    increase;
So your barns will be filled with
    plenty,
And your vats will overflow with new
    wine."

Proverbs 3:9, 10

Try to keep your possessions for selfish purposes, and you will experience eternal loss. But treasure we give to God is securely marked with His name.

"Some give freely, yet grow all the richer; others withhold what is due, and only suffer want" (Proverbs 11:24, NRSV). The sower multiplies his seed by throwing it away. So those who are faithful in sharing God's gifts increase their blessings. (See Luke 6:38.)

Working Under Great Difficulties

The Jews considered it a sin to allow youth to grow up ignorant of physical labor. Every young man, whether his parents were rich or poor, was taught some trade. Early in his life, Paul had learned the trade of tentmaking.

Before he became a disciple of Christ, he held a high position and was not dependent on working with his hands for support. But afterward, when he had used all his wealth in advancing the cause of Christ, at times he resorted to his trade to earn a living.

At Thessalonica Paul worked with his hands in self-supporting labor while preaching the Word. Writing to the believers there, he reminded them: "You remember, brethren, our labor and toil; for laboring night and day, that we might not be a burden to any of you, we preached to you the gospel of God" (1 Thessalonians 2:9). And again, he wrote, "nor did we eat anyone's bread free of charge, but worked with labor and toil night and day, that we might not be a burden to any of you, not because we do not have authority, but to make ourselves an example of how you should follow us" (2 Thessalonians 3:8, 9).

At Thessalonica Paul had opposed those who refused to work with their hands. "We hear that there are some who walk among you in a disorderly manner, not working at all, but are busybodies. Now those who are such we command and exhort through our Lord Jesus Christ that they work in quietness and eat their own bread." "Even when we were with you," he wrote, "we commanded you this: If anyone will not work, neither shall he eat." (Verses 11, 12, 10.)

In every age Satan has tried to introduce fanaticism into the church. It was that way in Paul's day, and later, during the Reformation. Wycliffe, Luther, and many others met up with overzealous, unbalanced, and unsanctified minds. Misguided people have taught that it is a sin to work, that Christians should devote their lives entirely to spiritual things. Paul's teaching and example rebuke such extreme views.

Paul was not completely dependent on the work of his hands at Thessalonica. He wrote to the Philippian believers to acknowledge the gifts he had received from them, saying, "Even in Thessalonica you sent aid once and again for my necessities" (Philippians 4:16). Despite the fact that he received this help, he set an example of diligence, giving a practical rebuke to those who held fanatical views about manual labor.

The Greeks were skilled traders, trained in sharp business practices. They had come to believe that making money was commendable, whether by fair means or not. Paul would give them no reason to say that he preached the gospel to enrich himself. He was willing to do without support from his Corinthian hearers rather than allow his usefulness as a minister to be injured by unjust suspicion that he was preaching for profit.

Priscilla and Aquila Encourage Paul

At Corinth Paul found "a certain Jew named Aquila, born in Pontus, who had recently come from Italy with his wife Priscilla." These were "of the same trade" that he was. Aquila and Priscilla had established a business manufacturing tents. Learning that they feared God and were trying to avoid the contaminating influences around them, "he stayed with them and worked. . . . And he reasoned in the synagogue every Sabbath, and persuaded both Jews and Greeks" (Acts 18:2–4).

In his second letter to the believers in Corinth, Paul reviewed his manner of life among them. "And when I was present with you, and in need, I was a burden to no one, for what I lacked the brethren who came from Macedonia supplied. And in everything I kept myself from being burdensome to you, and so I will keep myself" (2 Corinthians 11:9).

While he had worked at tentmaking, Paul had also faithfully proclaimed the gospel. He wrote this about his

work: "For what is it in which you were inferior to other churches, except that I myself was not burdensome to you? Forgive me this wrong!

"Now for the third time I am ready to come to you. And I will not be burdensome to you; for I do not seek yours, but you. . . . I will very gladly spend and be spent for your souls" (2 Corinthians 12:13–15).

During his ministry in Ephesus Paul worked at his trade again. As in Corinth, the apostle was happy to associate with Aquila and Priscilla, who had accompanied him to Asia at the close of his second missionary journey.

Some objected to Paul's working with his hands, claiming that it was inconsistent with the work of a gospel minister. Why should Paul connect mechanical work with the preaching of the Word? Why should he spend time in making tents that he could be put to better use?

But Paul did not regard the time he spent this way as lost. His mind was always reaching out for spiritual knowledge. He gave his fellow workers instruction in spiritual things, and he also set an example by being industrious. He was a quick, skillful worker, diligent in business, "fervent in spirit; serving the Lord" (Romans 12:11). Working at his trade, the apostle had access to people he could not have reached in other ways. He showed that skill in common trades is a gift from God, who provides both the gift and the wisdom to use it correctly. Paul's work-hardened hands took nothing away from the force of his appeals as a Christian minister.

Paul sometimes worked night and

day, not only for his own support, but in order to help his fellow laborers. He even suffered hunger at times so that he could provide for the needs of others. He lived an unselfish life. When he gave his farewell talk to the elders at Ephesus, he could lift up his work-worn hands and say, "I have coveted no one's silver or gold or apparel. Yes, you yourselves know that these hands have provided for my necessities, and for those who were with me. I have shown you in every way, by laboring like this, that you must support the weak. And remember the words of the Lord Jesus, that He said, 'It is more blessed to give than to receive'" (Acts 20:33–35).

A Suggestion for Modern Gospel Ministers

If ministers feel they are suffering hardship, let them in imagination visit Paul's workshop. Let them bear in mind that while this man of God is cutting and stitching the canvas, he is working for food that he has already earned by his labors as an apostle.

Work is a blessing, not a curse. Idleness grieves the Spirit of God. A stagnant pool of water is offensive, but a pure, flowing stream spreads health and gladness over the land. Paul wanted to teach young ministers that by exercising their muscles, they would become strong to endure the work and hardships ahead of them. His own teachings would lack vitality and force if he did not exercise.

Thousands of human beings exist only to consume the benefits that God bestows on them. They forget they are to be producers as well as consumers.

Young men whom God chooses for the ministry will give proof of their high calling. They will work at gaining an experience that will fit them to plan, organize, and execute. By self-discipline they will become more and more like their Master, revealing His goodness, love, and truth.

Not all who feel called to preach should immediately throw themselves and their families on the church for financial support. Money dedicated to the work of God should not be consumed by those who desire to preach only so that they can receive support.

Although he was an eloquent speaker and God had chosen him to do a special work, Paul was never above labor, nor did he ever tire of sacrificing for the cause he loved. "To the present hour," he wrote to the Corinthians, "we both hunger and thirst, and we are poorly clothed, and beaten, and homeless. And we labor, working with our own hands" (1 Corinthians 4:11, 12). He worked at this trade, but he always stood ready to lay aside his secular work in order to oppose the enemies of the gospel or to win people to Jesus. His zeal and industry are a rebuke to idleness and desire for ease.

Paul illustrated what consecrated laymen could do in many places. Many can advance the cause of God while at the same time supporting themselves in daily labor. God used Aquila and Priscilla to show Apollos the way of truth more perfectly. While God chooses some with special talents to devote all their energies to the work of the gospel, He calls many others to an important part in bringing people to Jesus.

There are many opportunities for self-supporting gospel workers. Many may gain valuable experiences in ministry while working part time at manual labor. By this method, people may develop into strong workers for important service in needy fields.

The Heart Burden Carried by Servants of Christ

The self-sacrificing servants of God do not measure their work by hours. Their wages do not influence them in their efforts. They have received their commission from heaven, and to heaven they look for their reward.

Such workers should be freed from unnecessary cares. While they should be careful to exercise to keep the mind and body vigorous, yet they should not have to spend a large part of their time at secular employment. These faithful workers are not immune to temptation. When burdened with worry because the church has failed to give them proper financial support, some are fiercely attacked by the tempter. They become depressed. Their families must have food and clothing. If they could feel released from their divine commission, they would be willing to labor with their hands. But they realize that their time belongs to God, and they continue to advance the cause that is dearer than life itself to them. However, for a while they may be forced to engage in manual labor while doing ministerial work.

Sometimes because of lack of funds it seems impossible to do the work that needs to be done. Some people fear that they cannot do everything that they feel is their duty. But if they move forward in faith, success will follow their efforts. Jesus, who has asked His followers to go into all the world, will sustain every worker who tries to proclaim His message.

In the building up of His work, the Lord sometimes tests the confidence of His people by bringing about circumstances that compel them to move forward in faith. Often He tells them to advance when their feet seem to be touching the waters of Jordan. (See Joshua 3:14–17.) At such times, when their prayers go up to Him in earnest faith, God opens the way before them and blesses their efforts beyond their expectations. Angels will prepare the way before them, and the funds necessssary for the work will be provided. Those whom God has enlightened will give freely to support the work. The Spirit of God will move on their hearts to maintain the Lord's cause, not only in home fields, but in the regions beyond. And so the work of the Lord will advance in His own appointed way.

The Joy of Working With Christ

God does not live for Himself. "He makes His sun rise on the evil and on the good, and sends rain on the just and on the unjust" (Matthew 5:45). By His example Jesus taught what it means to minister. He served all, ministered to all.

Again and again He tried to establish this principle among His disciples. "Whoever desires to become great among you, let him be your servant. And whoever desires to be first among you, let him be your slave—just as the Son of man did not come to be served, but to serve, and to give His life a ransom for many" (Matthew 20:26–28).

Since his ascension Christ has carried forward His work by chosen ambassadors, through whom He speaks to people and ministers to their needs. In Christ's place they are to plead with men and women to be reconciled to God.

Their work has been compared to that of watchmen. In ancient times sentinels were stationed on the walls of cities, where they could keep watch over important posts to be guarded and warn of approaching enemies. At prearranged times they called to one another, to make sure that all were awake and that no harm had come to any. Each one repeated the call of good cheer or of warning until it echoed through the city.

The words of the prophet Ezekiel declare the solemn responsibility of those who are appointed as guardians of the church: "So you, son of man, I have made a watchman for the house of Israel; therefore you shall hear a word from My mouth and warn them for Me. When I say to the wicked, 'O wicked man, you shall surely die!' and you do not speak to warn the wicked from his way, that wicked man shall die in his iniquity; but his blood I will require at your hand. Nevertheless if you warn the wicked to turn from his way, . . . you have delivered your soul" (Ezekiel 33:7–9).

People are in danger of falling under temptation, and they will die eternally unless God's ministers are faithful. If the ministers' spiritual senses become so benumbed that they are unable to recognize danger, God will hold them responsible for the blood of those who are lost.

Christ's Love a Greater Motivation Than Money

Watchmen on the walls of Zion may live so near to God and be so receptive to the impressions of His Spirit that He can work through them to tell men and women of their danger and point them to safety. They should not relax their vigilance at any time, and never are they to give one wavering, uncertain note of warning. They are not to work only for wages, but because they realize that there is a judgment on them if they fail to preach the gospel. God has chosen them, and they are to rescue men and women from destruction.

Co-workers with Christ do not put their own ease or convenience first. They are forgetful of self. In their search for the lost sheep they do not realize that they are themselves weary, cold, and hungry. They have only one goal in view—saving the lost.

The soldiers of the cross stand without flinching in the forefront of the battle. As the enemy attacks them severely, they turn to God for help and find strength for the duties of the hour. The victories they gain do not lead to self-exaltation, but cause them to lean more and more heavily on the Mighty One. Relying on that Power, they are enabled to present the message of salvation so forcibly that it vibrates in other minds.

Those who teach the Word must live in constant contact with God through prayer and study of His Word. This will give their efforts a power greater than the influence of their preaching. They must not allow themselves to be deprived of this power. They must plead with God to strengthen them and touch their lips with living fire. By the power and light that God gives they can understand more and accomplish more than their finite judgment had thought possible.

Satan's deceptions are more successful against those who are depressed. When discouragement threatens, let the minister present his needs before God. When the heavens were as brass (see Deuteronomy 28:23) over Paul, he trusted most fully in God. He was afflicted, but listen to his triumphant cry: "This slight momentary affliction is preparing us for an eternal weight of glory beyond all measure, because we look not at what can be seen but at what cannot be seen" (2 Corinthians 4:17, 18, NRSV). By seeing Him who is invisible, we gain strength and vigor of heart.

Come Close to the People

When a minister has preached a sermon, his work has only begun. He should visit the people in their homes and point them to the higher way. Let ministers teach the truth in families, drawing close to those they are working to save. Christ will give them words that will sink deep into the hearts of the listeners. Paul said, "I kept back nothing that was helpful, but proclaimed it to you, and taught you publicly and from house to house, . . . repentance toward God and faith toward our Lord Jesus Christ" (Acts 20:20, 21).

The Savior went from house to house, healing the sick and speaking peace to the discouraged. He took little children in His arms and spoke words of hope and comfort to the weary mothers. He was the servant of all. And as men and women listened to the truths that fell from His lips, hope sprang up in their hearts. He spoke with an earnestness that sent

His words straight to the heart with convicting power.

God's ministers are to learn Christ's method of working. This is the only way they can fulfill their trust. The same Spirit that lived in Christ is to be the source of their knowledge and the secret of their power.

Some ministers have failed to succeed because they have not given their full attention to the Lord's work. Ministers should have no absorbing interests apart from the great work of leading people to the Savior. The fishermen whom Christ called left their nets and followed Him. Ministers cannot work for God and carry the burden of large personal business ventures at the same time. The minister needs all his energies for his high calling. His best powers belong to God.

The Danger of Side Businesses

"No one engaged in warfare entangles himself with the affairs of this life, that he may please him who enlisted him as a soldier" (2 Timothy 2:4). With these words the apostle emphasized that ministers need to be completely dedicated to the Master's service. They are not working hard to gain earthly riches. Their one desire is to bring the indifferent and the disloyal to appreciate the realities of eternity. They may be asked to take other opportunities that promise large worldly gain, but they answer, "What will it profit a man if he gains the whole world, and loses his own soul?" (Mark 8:36).

Satan presented this enticement to Christ, knowing that if He accepted it, the world would never be ransomed. And in different ways he presents the same temptation to God's ministers today, knowing that those who are deceived by it will be untrue to their trust.

"The love of money is a root of all kinds of evil, for which some have strayed from the faith in their greediness, and pierced themselves through with many sorrows.

"But you, O man of God, flee these things." By example as well as by word, the ambassador for Christ is to "command those who are rich . . . not to be haughty, nor to trust in uncertain riches but in the living God, who gives us richly all things to enjoy. Let them do good, that they be rich in good works, ready to give, willing to share." (1 Timothy 6:10, 11, 17, 18.)

Paul's heart burned with love for sinners, and he put all his energies into the work of winning people to Christ. The blessings he received he used in blessing others. He went from place to place, establishing churches. Wherever he could he worked to counteract wrong and to turn men and women to righteousness.

The apostle made it part of his work to educate young men for the ministry. He took them on his missionary journeys, and they gained experience from this that enabled them to fill positions of responsibility. When he was apart from them, he still kept in touch with their work.

Paul never forgot that if people were lost because he had been unfaithful, God would hold him accountable. Christ "we proclaim, warning everyone and teaching everyone in all wisdom, so that we may present everyone mature in Christ. For this I toil and struggle with all the energy which he powerfully inspires within me" (Colossians 1:28, 29, NRSV).

All who put themselves under the control of the great Teacher can reach this high goal. The minister who dedicates himself fully to the Lord may be assured that he will receive what he needs to bring the word of life to his hearers. Paul has left us a picture of his own work in his letter to the Corinthian believers: "As servants of God we have commended ourselves in every way: through great endurance, in afflictions, hardships, calamities, beatings, imprisonments, riots, labors, sleepless nights, hunger; . . . in honor and dishonor, in ill repute and good repute. We are treated as impostors, and yet are true; as unknown, and yet are well known; as dying, and see— we are alive; as punished, and yet not killed; as sorrowful, yet always rejoicing; as poor, yet making many rich" (2 Corinthians 6:4–10, NRSV).

There is nothing more precious in the sight of God than His ministers, who go out into the unpromising places of the earth to sow the seeds of truth. God gives His Spirit to them to turn people from sin to righteousness. God is calling for workers who are willing to leave their farms, their businesses, if need be their families, to become missionaries for Him. And many will answer the call. In the past men have left home and friends, even wife and children, to go among idol worshipers and savages, to proclaim the message of mercy. Many have lost their lives in the attempt, but others have sprung up to carry on the work. So the seed sown in sorrow has yielded an abundant harvest. The knowledge of God has been extended widely.

If Christ left the ninety and nine so that He could seek and save one lost sheep, can we do less? If we neglect to work as Christ worked, to sacrifice as He sacrificed, isn't this a betrayal of sacred trusts?

The heart of the true minister is filled with an intense longing to save others. They must hear the truths that brought to his own soul such peace and joy. With eyes fixed on the cross of Calvary, believing that the Savior will be with him until the end, he seeks to win people to Jesus, and Heaven regards him among those who are "called, chosen, and faithful" (Revelation 17:14).

God's Special Plan for the Jews*

After many delays, Paul reached Corinth, where he had invested so much effort in the past. Many of the early believers still felt warmly toward the one who had first brought the gospel to them. As he saw the evidences of their faithfulness, he rejoiced that his work in Corinth had not been in vain. The Corinthian believers had developed strength of Christian character and were now a strong force for good in that center of heathenism and superstition. In the fellowship of these faithful converts, the apostle's worn and troubled spirit found rest.

At Corinth the possibility of going to Rome especially filled Paul's thoughts. To see the Christian faith firmly established at the great center of the known world was one of his dearest hopes. The apostle wanted the church already established in Rome to cooperate in the work to be done in Italy and other countries. To prepare the way he sent these fellow Christians a letter announcing his intention to visit Rome and his hope of planting the banner of the cross in Spain.

In his letter, clearly and powerfully Paul presented the doctrine of justification by faith in Christ. He hoped that the instruction might also help other churches, but how dimly could he foresee the far-reaching influence of his words! Through all the ages, the great truth of justification by faith has stood as a mighty lighthouse to guide sinners into the way of life. This light scattered the darkness that clouded Luther's mind and revealed to him the power of Christ's blood to cleanse from sin. The same light has guided thousands to the true Source of pardon and peace.

Ever since his conversion, Paul had longed to help his Jewish brethren gain a clear understanding of the gospel. "My heart's desire and prayer to God for Israel is," he wrote, "that they may be saved." The Israelites had failed to recognize Jesus of Nazareth as the promised Messiah. Paul assured the believers at Rome, "I could wish that I myself were accursed from Christ for my brethren, my countrymen according to the flesh." Through the Jews God had intended to bless the entire human race. Many prophets among them had foretold the coming of a Redeemer who would be rejected and killed by those who should have

---

* This chapter is based on Paul's letter to the Romans.

recognized Him as the Promised One.

But even though Israel rejected His Son, God did not reject them. Paul continued: "I say then, has God cast away His people? Certainly not! For I also am an Israelite, of the seed of Abraham, of the tribe of Benjamin. God has not cast away His people whom He foreknew. . . . At this present time also there is a remnant according to the election of grace."

Those Who Fall Can Rise Again

Israel had stumbled and fallen, but this did not make it impossible for them to rise again. In answer to the question, "Have they stumbled that they should fall?" the apostle replied: "Certainly not! But through their fall, to provoke them to jealousy, salvation has come to the Gentiles. . . .

"For if their being cast away is the reconciling of the world, what will their acceptance be but life from the dead?"

It was God's decision to reveal His grace among the Gentiles as well as among the Israelites. "Does not the potter have power over the clay, from the same lump to make one vessel for honor and another for dishonor?" he inquired. "What if God, wanting to show His wrath and to make His power known, endured with much longsuffering the vessels of wrath prepared for destruction, and that He might make known the riches of His glory on the vessels of mercy, which He had prepared beforehand for glory, even us whom He called, not of the Jews only, but also of the Gentiles?"

Despite Israel's failure as a nation, there were faithful men and women who had gladly received the message of John the Baptist and so had been led to study again the prophecies about the Messiah. The early Christian church was composed of these faithful Jews. Paul referred to this "remnant": "If the part of the dough offered as first fruits is holy, then the whole batch is holy; and if the root is holy, then the branches also are holy" (NRSV).

Paul compared the Gentiles to branches from a wild olive tree, grafted into the parent stock. "If some of the branches were broken off," he wrote, "and you, being a wild olive tree, were grafted in among them, and with them became a partaker of the root and fatness of the olive tree, do not boast against the branches. . . .

"Because of unbelief they were broken off, and you stand by faith. Do not be haughty, but fear. For if God did not spare the natural branches, He may not spare you either."

All Who Believe Are the True Israel

By rejecting Heaven's plan for her, Israel as a nation had lost her connection with God. But God was able to take the branches that had been separated from the parent stock and reunite them with the true stock of Israel. "If you were cut out of the olive tree which is wild by nature, and were grafted contrary to nature into a cultivated olive tree, how much more will these, who are natural branches, be grafted into their own olive tree? . . .

"Blindness in part has happened to Israel until the fullness of the Gentiles has come in. And so all Israel will be saved. . . .

"For the gifts and the calling of God are irrevocable. For as you were once disobedient to God, yet have now obtained mercy through their disobedience, even so these also have now been disobedient, that through the mercy shown you they also may obtain mercy. . . .

"Oh, the depth of the riches both of the wisdom and knowledge of God! How unsearchable are His judgments and His ways past finding out!"

God is abundantly able to transform the hearts of Jew and Gentile alike. "For He will finish the work and cut it short in righteousness, because the Lord will make a short work upon the earth."

When Jerusalem was destroyed and the temple laid in ruins, many Jews were sold as slaves in heathen lands, scattered among the nations like wrecks on a deserted shore. Maligned, persecuted, from century to century they have had a heritage of suffering.

Even though God pronounced doom on the nation, through the years there have been many noble, God-fearing Jewish men and women. God has comforted their hearts in their affliction and has looked with pity on their terrible situation. Some who have turned to Him for a right understanding of His Word have learned to see the lowly Nazarene as the true Messiah. As their minds have grasped the significance of prophecies long obscured by tradition and misinterpretation, their hearts have overflowed with gratitude to God for the unspeakable gift of Christ as a personal Savior.

What Is Needed in Order to Awaken the Sincere Jews

Isaiah said in his prophecy, "The remnant will be saved." From Paul's day to the present time, the Holy Spirit has been calling the Jew as well as the Gentile. "God shows personal favoritism to no man" (Galatians 2:6), Paul declared. "The gospel . . . is the power of God to salvation for everyone who believes, for the Jew first and also for the Greek. For in it the righteousness of God is revealed from faith to faith; as it is written, 'The just shall live by faith.' " This gospel is equally effective for Jew and Gentile.

When this gospel will be presented in its fullness to the Jews, many will accept Christ. Only a few Christian ministers feel called to labor for the Jewish people; but the message of Christ is to come to those who have often been passed by.

In the gospel's closing proclamation, God expects His messengers to take particular interest in the Jewish people. Many of the Jews will see the Christ of the gospel in the pages of the Old Testament and will grasp how the New Testament explains the Old. They will recognize Christ as the Savior of the world. To them God will fulfill the words, "As many as received Him, to them He gave the right to become children of God, to those who believe in His name" (John 1:12).

Some Jews, like Saul of Tarsus, are mighty in the Scriptures, and they

Paul's Timeless Letter to the Galatians*

Through the influence of false teachers, heresy and immorality were gaining ground among the believers in Galatia. These false teachers were mixing Jewish traditions with the truths of the gospel. The evils they introduced threatened to destroy the Galatian churches.

Paul was heartbroken. He immediately wrote to the deceived believers, exposing the false ideas that they had accepted.

"I marvel that you are turning away so soon from Him who called you in the grace of Christ, to a different gospel, which is not another; but there are some who trouble you and want to pervert the gospel of Christ. But even if we, or an angel from heaven, preach any other gospel to you than what we have preached to you, let him be accursed." The Holy Spirit had confirmed his work, and he warned his fellow believers not to listen to anything that contradicted the truths he had taught.

"O foolish Galatians!" he exclaimed, "Who has bewitched you that you should not obey the truth, before whose eyes Jesus Christ was clearly portrayed among you as crucified?" Refusing to

recognize the doctrines of the false teachers, the apostle tried to lead the converts to see that they had been terribly deceived, but that by returning to their earlier faith in the gospel, they could still defeat Satan's plans. His complete confidence in the message he gave helped many, whose faith had failed, to return to the Savior.

How different this was from Paul's way of writing to the Corinthian church! He rebuked the Corinthians with tenderness, but the Galatians with words of the plainest reproof. It would take caution and patience to teach the Corinthians to tell the difference between the false and the true. But in the Galatian churches, open, unmasked error was replacing the gospel. The Galatians had essentially rejected Christ for the ceremonies of Judaism. The apostle saw that if the believers were to be saved from the dangerous influences that threatened them, he must take decisive action.

Why Paul Was So Abrupt

In his letter Paul briefly reviewed events connected with his own conversion and early Christian experi-

---

* This chapter is based on Paul's letter to the Galatians.

ence. By doing this, he was trying to show that it was through a special display of divine power that he had come to see the great truths of the gospel. God Himself led Paul to write to the Galatians in such strong language. With unshakeable conviction and absolute knowledge, he clearly outlined the difference between human teaching and instruction that had come directly from Christ.

The people who had tried to lead the Galatians from the gospel were hypocrites, with unholy hearts and corrupt lives. They expected to win favor with God through performing a round a ceremonies. They had no desire for a gospel that called for obeying the word, "Unless one is born again, he cannot see the kingdom of God" (John 3:3). A religion based on a doctrine like this required too great a sacrifice, and they clung to their errors.

It is still pleasing to the unconverted person to substitute external forms for holiness of heart and life. Satan deliberately tries to divert minds from the hope of salvation through faith in Christ and obedience to the law of God. The archenemy adapts his temptations to the preferences of the ones he is trying to deceive. In the apostles' times he led the Jews to value the ceremonial law and reject Christ. Today he leads professing Christians to scorn the moral law and to teach that we may break it with no consequences. Every servant of God must firmly withstand these perverters of the faith and expose their errors.

Success Followed the Letter

Paul ably defended his position as an apostle, "not from men nor through man, but through Jesus Christ and God the Father who raised Him from the dead." He received his commission from the highest Authority in heaven, and a general council at Jerusalem acknowledged his position. Those who tried to throw contempt on his calling and work were fighting against Christ, who demonstrated His grace and power through Paul. The opposition of his enemies forced the apostle to take a firm stand in maintaining his authority, not to exalt himself, but to magnify the grace of God.

Paul pleaded with those who had once experienced the power of God to return to their first love of gospel truth. He showed them what a privilege to become free in Christ, whose atoning grace enables all who make a full surrender to be clothed with the robe of His righteousness. Everyone who wants to be saved must have a genuine, personal experience in the things of God.

The apostle's earnest words bore fruit. Many who had wandered into strange paths returned to their former faith. Ever afterward, they were faithful in the liberty in which Christ had made them free. God was glorified, and many joined the ranks of the believers throughout that region.

Paul's Farewell Journey to Jerusalem*

Paul always held on to the hope that he might help to remove the prejudice of his unbelieving countrymen so that they would accept the gospel. He also wanted to meet the church at Jerusalem and give them the gifts the Gentile churches had sent. And he hoped to bring about a closer tie between Jewish and Gentile converts to the faith.

He was about to step aboard the ship to sail for a port in Palestine when he learaned that the Jews were plotting to take his life. In the past, these opposers had failed in their efforts to end the apostle's work.

Paul's success in preaching the gospel stirred up the Jews' anger again. This teaching released Jews from the ceremonial law and made Gentiles equal with Jews as children of Abraham! Paul's enemies called it blasphemy when he said emphatically, "There is neither Greek nor Jew, circumcised nor uncircumcised" (Colossians 3:11), and they determined to silence his voice.

Paul received warning of the plot and decided to go by way of Macedonia. He had to give up his plan to reach Jerusalem in time for the Passover, but he hoped to be there at Pentecost. He had a large amount of money with him from the Gentile churches, and because of this he made arrangements for representatives to go with him from the various churches that had contributed.

At Philippi he stopped to keep the Passover. Only Luke remained with him, while the others went ahead to Troas to wait for him there. The Philippians were the apostle's most loving and truehearted converts, and he enjoyed happy fellowship with them.

Sailing from Philippi, Paul and Luke reached Troas five days later and remained for seven days with the believers there.

The Saturday Evening Farewell Meeting

On the last evening the Christians "came together to break bread." The fact that their beloved teacher was about to leave had called together a larger group than usual. They met in an "upper room" on the third story. There, in the intensity of his care for them, the apostle preached until midnight.

In one of the open windows sat a young man named Eutychus, who

---

* This chapter is based on Acts 20:4 to 21:16.

went to sleep and fell to the courtyard below. He died from the fall, and many gathered around him crying and mourning. But Paul prayed earnestly that God would restore the dead to life. Above the sound of weeping, the apostle's voice was heard, "Do not trouble yourselves, for his life is in him." With joy the believers again gathered in the upper room. They celebrated the Communion service, and then Paul "talked a long while, even till daybreak."

The ship was about to sail, and Paul's companions hurried on board. The apostle, however, chose to take the shorter route by land and meet his traveling companions at Assos. His mind was troubled over the difficulties connected with his visit to Jerusalem, the attitude of the church there toward him, and the needs of the gospel work in other fields, so he took advantage of this special opportunity to seek God for strength and guidance.

As the travelers sailed south from Assos, they passed Ephesus. Paul had wanted to visit the church there, but he decided to hurry on, because he wanted "to be at Jerusalem, if possible, on the Day of Pentecost." At Miletus, however, about thirty miles from Ephesus, he learned that it might be possible to communicate with the church before the ship set sail. So he sent a message to the elders, urging them to hurry to Miletus, so that he could see them.

They came, and he spoke touching words of counsel and farewell to them. "You know," he said, "from the first day that I came to Asia, in what manner I always lived among you, . . .

how I kept back nothing that was helpful, but proclaimed it to you, and taught you publicly and from house to house, testifying to Jews, and also to Greeks, repentance toward God and faith toward our Lord Jesus Christ."

Paul had always exalted God's law. He had shown that sinners must repent, humble themselves before God, and exercise faith in the blood of Christ. The Son of God had died as their sacrifice and had gone up to heaven as their representative. By repentance and faith they could be free from condemnation, and through the grace of Christ be enabled to obey to the law of God.

"And see," Paul continued, "now I go bound in the spirit to Jerusalem, not knowing the things that will happen to me there, except that the Holy Spirit testifies in every city, saying that chains and tribulations await me. . . .

"I know that you all, among whom I have gone preaching the kingdom of God, will see my face no more."

The Holy Spirit Moves Paul to Say Goodbye

While he was speaking, the Spirit of inspiration came on him, confirming his fears that this would be his last meeting with the Ephesian believers.

"I have not shunned to declare to you the whole counsel of God." No fear of offending someone could lead Paul to keep back the words that God had given him to warn or correct them. If the ministers of Christ today see that any of their flock are cherishing sin, as faithful shepherds they must open God's Word and give them the instruction that applies to their case.

Pastors must give their people faithful instruction, showing them what they must be and do in order to stand perfect in the day of God. At the close of their work, faithful teachers of the truth will be able to say with Paul, "I am innocent of the blood of all men."

"Therefore take heed to yourselves and to all the flock, among which the Holy Spirit has made you overseers, to shepherd the church of God which He purchased with His own blood." Ministers are dealing with people whom Christ's blood has purchased. As representatives of Christ, they are to keep intact the honor of His name. By purity of life they are to prove themselves worthy of their high calling.

Dangers would threaten the church at Ephesus: "I know this, that after my departing savage wolves will come in among you, not sparing the flock. And from among yourselves men will rise up, speaking perverse things, to draw away the disciples after themselves." Looking into the future, Paul saw the attacks the believers would experience from enemies both outside and inside the church. "Therefore watch, and remember that for three years I did not cease to warn everyone night and day with tears.

"So now, brethren," he continued, "I commend you to God and to the word of His grace, which is able to build you up and give you an inheritance among all those who are sanctified. I have coveted no one's silver or gold or apparel." Paul had never tried to get anything for himself from the Ephesian Christians who were wealthy. "These hands," he stated, "have provided for my necessities, and for those

who were with me. I have shown you . . . by laboring like this, that you must support the weak. And remember the words of the Lord Jesus, that He said, 'It is more blessed to give than to receive.'

"And when he had said these things, he knelt down and prayed with them all. Then they all wept freely, and fell on Paul's neck and kissed him, sorrowing most of all for the words which he spoke, that they would see his face no more. And they accompanied him to the ship."

From Miletus the travelers sailed to Patara, where, "finding a ship sailing over to Phoenicia," they "went aboard and set sail." At Tyre, where the ship was unloaded, the Holy Spirit warned a few disciples about the dangers waiting for Paul at Jerusalem. They urged him not to go on. But the apostle would not allow any fear to turn him from his purpose.

At Caesarea Paul spent a few peaceful, happy days—the last of perfect freedom he would enjoy for a long time. While he was there "a certain prophet named Agabus came down from Judea. When he had come to us," Luke says, "he took Paul's belt, bound his own hands and feet, and said, 'Thus says the Holy Spirit, "So shall the Jews at Jerusalem bind the man who owns this belt, and deliver him into the hands of the Gentiles." ' "

Paul Would Not Turn Aside From Duty

But Paul would not turn aside from the path of duty. He would follow Christ to prison and to death if needed. "What do you mean by weeping and breaking my heart?" he exclaimed. "For I am ready not only to be bound, but also to die at Jerusalem for the name of the Lord Jesus."

The time soon came for his brief stay at Caesarea to end, and Paul and his companions set out for Jerusalem, their hearts shadowed by the premonition of coming evil.

The apostle knew he would find few friends and many enemies at Jerusalem. Remembering his own bitter prejudice against the followers of Christ, he felt the deepest pity for his mistaken countrymen. And yet how little hope he had that he would be able to help them! The same blind hatred that had once burned in his own heart was now inflaming the hearts of a whole nation against him.

And he could not count on the sympathy of even his own brothers in the faith. Even among the apostles and elders, some had believed the most unfavorable reports about Paul as true, making no attempt to contradict what they had heard and showing no desire to support him.

Yet the apostle did not despair. He trusted that the Voice that had spoken to his own heart would still speak to the hearts of his countrymen, and that the Master whom his fellow disciples served would still unite their hearts with his in the work of the gospel.

Paul Receives Bad Advice*

Paul gave the leaders at Jerusalem the contributions the Gentile churches had sent for the support of the poor among the Jewish believers. The amount far exceeded what the elders at Jerusalem had expected. It represented severe sacrifice and self-denial on the part of the Gentile believers.

These freewill offerings showed the Gentile converts' loyalty to the organized work of God throughout the world. Yet some were clearly unable to appreciate the spirit of brotherly love that had prompted the gifts.

In earlier years, some of the leaders at Jerusalem had not cooperated cheerfully with Paul. In their concern to preserve a few meaningless forms and ceremonies, they had lost sight of the blessing that would come through trying to unite all parts of the Lord's work into one. They had failed to keep up with God's leading forward and tried to put many unnecessary restrictions on the workers. Men who did not know the particular needs in distant fields insisted that they had the authority to direct the workers there to follow certain specific ways of working.

Several years had gone by since the Jerusalem leadership had carefully considered the methods used by those working among the Gentiles and had made recommendations about certain rites and ceremonies. At this general council the leaders had also united in recommending Barnabas and Paul as missionaries worthy of every believer's full confidence. At this meeting some had severely criticized the apostles who were carrying the gospel to the Gentile world, but during the council their views of God's plans had broadened, and they united in making decisions that made it possible to unite the entire body of believers.

Some Leaders Continue to Hurt Paul's Ministry

Afterward, when converts among the Gentiles were increasing rapidly, a few leaders at Jerusalem began to revive their former prejudices against Paul's methods. Some of the leaders determined that from then on the work must be conducted according to their own ideas. If Paul would conform to their policies, they would recognize and support his work. Otherwise, they could no longer support it.

These men had lost sight of the fact that God is the teacher of His

---

* This chapter is based on Acts 21:17 to 23:35.

people. Every worker in His cause is to follow the divine Leader, not looking to others for direct guidance. God's workers are to be molded in the divine likeness.

Paul had taught the people "not with persuasive words of human wisdom, but in demonstration of the Spirit and of power" (1 Corinthians 2:4). He had looked to God for direct guidance, yet he had been careful to work in harmony with the decisions of the general council at Jerusalem. As a result, the churches were "strengthened in the faith, and increased in number daily" (Acts 16:5). Despite the lack of sympathy that some showed him, he had encouraged a spirit of loyalty, generosity, and brotherly love in his converts, as the liberal contributions he placed before the Jewish elders showed.

Paul "told in detail those things which God had done among the Gentiles through his ministry." This brought the conviction, even to those who had been doubting, that God had blessed his work. "When they heard it, they glorified the Lord." The methods the apostle followed bore the approval of Heaven. The leaders who had urged arbitrary control saw Paul's ministry in a new light and were convinced that they had been wrong. Jewish customs and traditions had held them in bondage, and they had obstructed the work of the gospel by not recognizing that the death of Christ had broken down the dividing wall between Jew and Gentile.

This was the golden opportunity for all the leadership to freely admit that God had worked through Paul and that sometimes they had been wrong to allow his enemies to stir up their jealousy and prejudice. But instead of doing what was right to the one who had been injured, they showed that they still wanted to hold Paul largely responsible for the existing prejudice. They did not stand nobly in his defense but tried to strike a compromise.

Advice to Compromise Leads to Disaster

"You see, brother," they said in response to his testimony, "how many thousands of believers there are among the Jews, and they are all zealous for the law. They have been told about you that you teach all the Jews living among the Gentiles to forsake Moses, and that you tell them not to circumcise their children or observe the customs. . . . So do what we tell you. We have four men who are under a vow. Join these men, go through the rite of purification with them, and pay for the shaving of their heads. Thus all will know that there is nothing in what they have been told about you, but that you yourself observe and guard the law. But as for the Gentiles who have become believers, we have sent a letter with our judgment that they should abstain from what has been sacrificed to idols and from blood and from what is strangled and from fornication" (NRSV).

These men assured Paul that the former council's decision about Gentile converts and the ceremonial law was still good. But the advice they now gave was not consistent with that decision. The Spirit of God did not prompt this instruction. It was the fruit of cowardice.

Many of the Jews who had accepted the gospel still cherished the ceremonial law. They were only too willing to make unwise concessions in the hope of removing prejudice and winning their countrymen to faith in Christ as the world's Redeemer. Paul realized that as long as many leading members of the church at Jerusalem continued to hold prejudice against him, they would constantly work against his influence. He felt that if he could win them to the truth by a reasonable concession, he would remove a great obstacle to the success of the gospel in other places. But God did not authorize him to go as far as they asked.

When we think of Paul's great desire to be in harmony with other believers, his tenderness toward those who were weak in faith, and his deep respect for the apostles who had been with Christ, it is less surprising that he felt it necessary to depart from the firm course he had followed up to then. But his efforts to satisfy others' concerns only brought on his predicted sufferings more quickly, separated him from the other believers, and deprived the church of one of its strongest pillars.

The next day Paul began to follow the counsel of the elders. He took the four men under the Nazirite vow (see Numbers 6) into the temple. Those who advised Paul to do this had not considered how it would put him in great danger. He had visited many of the world's largest cities and was well known to thousands who had come to Jerusalem to attend the feast. Among these were men who hated Paul bitterly. He would risk his life to enter the temple on a public occasion. For several days he was apparently unnoticed, but as he was talking with a priest about the sacrifices to be offered, some Jews from Asia recognized him.

With the fury of demons they rushed at him. "Men of Israel, help! This is the man who teaches all men everywhere against the people, the law, and this place." And as the people responded to the call for help, another accusation was added—"furthermore he also brought Greeks into the temple and has defiled this holy place."

By Jewish law, for an uncircumcised person to enter the inner courts of the sacred temple was a crime punishable by death. Paul had been seen in the city with Trophimus, an Ephesian, and people concluded that he had brought him into the temple. He had not done so, and since he was a Jew himself, his own act of entering the temple was no violation of the law.

The Hatred Shown to Christ Repeated Against Paul

But although the charge was completely false, it served to stir up popular prejudice. Wild excitement spread through Jerusalem. "All the city was disturbed, and the people ran together, seized Paul, and dragged him out of the temple; and immediately the doors were shut. Now as they were seeking to kill him, news came to the commander of the garrison that all Jerusalem was in an uproar." Claudius Lysias "immediately took soldiers and centurions, and ran down to them. And when they saw the commander and the soldiers, they stopped beating

Paul." Seeing that the crowd's rage was directed at Paul, the Roman captain "took him, and commanded him to be bound with two chains; and he asked who he was and what he had done." Immediately many voices rose in loud and angry accusation. "So when he could not ascertain the truth because of the tumult, he commanded him to be taken into the barracks. . . . For the multitude of the people followed after, crying out, 'Away with him!' "

Paul was calm and self-possessed. He knew that angels of heaven were around him. As he was about to be led into the barracks, he said to the chief captain, "May I speak to you?" Lysias responded, "Are you not the Egyptian who . . . stirred up a rebellion and led the four thousand assassins out into the wilderness?".

In reply Paul said, "I am a Jew from Tarsus, in Cilicia, a citizen of no mean city; and I implore you, permit me to speak to the people."

The Unreasoning Hatred of Paul's Enemies

Lysias agreed, and "Paul stood on the stairs and motioned with his hand to the people." His bearing invited respect. "And when there was a great silence, he spoke to them in the Hebrew language, saying, 'Brethren and fathers, hear my defense before you now.' " In the universal hush he continued:

"I am indeed a Jew, born in Tarsus of Cilicia, but brought up in this city at the feet of Gamaliel, taught according to the strictness our fathers' law, and was zealous toward God as you all are today." The facts he referred to were well known. He then spoke of his pre-

vious zeal in persecuting the disciples of Christ, and he told the story of his conversion, how his proud heart had come to bow to the crucified Nazarene. His account of his experience seemed to soften and subdue the hearts of his opponents.

He then showed that he had wanted to work for his own nation, but in that very temple the voice of God had spoken to him, directing him to go "far from here to the Gentiles."

The Rage of Exclusivism

The people were listening with close attention, but when Paul reached the point where he was appointed ambassador to the Gentiles, their fury broke out again. They were unwilling to let the despised Gentiles share the privileges they had thought of as exclusively their own. They shouted, " 'Away with such a fellow from the earth, for he is not fit to live!' Then, as they cried out, . . . the commander ordered him to be brought into the barracks, and said that he should be examined under scourging, that he might know why they shouted so against him. And as they bound him with thongs, Paul said to the centurion who stood by, 'Is it lawful for you to scourge a man who is a Roman, and uncondemned?'

"When the centurion heard that, he went and told the commander, saying, 'Take care what you do, for this man is a Roman.'

"Then the commander came and said to him, 'Tell me, are you a Roman?'

"He said, 'Yes.'

"The commander answered, 'With

a large sum I obtained this citizenship.'

"And Paul said, 'But I was born a citizen.'

"Then immediately those who were about to examine him withdrew from him; and the commander was also afraid after he found out that he was a Roman, and because he had bound him.

"The next day, because he wanted to know for certain why he was accused by the Jews, he released him from his bonds, and commanded the chief priests and all their council to appear, and brought Paul down and set him before them."

Paul Before the Court of Law

As he stood before the Jewish rulers, Paul's face revealed the peace of Christ. "'Men and brethren, I have lived in all good conscience before God until this day.' And the high priest Ananias commanded those who stood by him to strike him on the mouth." At this inhuman command, Paul exclaimed, "'God will strike you, you whitewashed wall! For you sit to judge me according to the law, and do you command me to be struck contrary to the law?'

"And those who stood by said, 'Do you revile God's high priest?'"

With his usual courtesy Paul answered, "'I did not know, brethren, that he was the high priest; for it is written, "You shall not speak evil of a ruler of your people."'

"But when Paul perceived that one part were Sadducees and the other Pharisees, he cried out in the council, 'Men and brethren, I am a Pharisee,

the son of a Pharisee; concerning the hope and resurrection of the dead I am being judged!'"

The two parties began to argue between themselves, and this broke the strength of their opposition to Paul. "The scribes of the Pharisees' party arose and protested, saying, 'We find no evil in this man; but if a spirit or an angel has spoken to him, let us not fight against God.'"

The Sadducees were eagerly trying to take custody of the apostle so that they could kill him, and the Pharisees were as eager to protect him. "The commander, fearing lest Paul might be pulled to pieces by them, commanded the soldiers to go down and take him by force from among them, and bring him into the barracks."

Later, Paul began to fear that his actions might not have been pleasing to God. Had he made a mistake in visiting Jerusalem? Had his great desire to be in union with His fellow believers led to this terrible result?

How would those heathen officers think of the Jews as God's professed people—taking a sacred office, yet giving themselves up to blind anger, trying to destroy even their fellow countrymen who dared to differ with them in religious faith, and turning their solemn council into a scene of wild confusion? The name of God had suffered disgrace in the eyes of the heathen.

And now he knew that his enemies would stop at nothing to kill him. Could it be that his work for the churches was over and that vicious wolves were to enter in now? He thought of the dangers facing the scattered churches, exposed to the persecutions of people like he had encountered in the Sanhedrin council. In distress he wept and prayed.

In this dark hour the Lord revealed Himself to His faithful witness in response to his earnest prayers for guidance. "The following night the Lord stood by him and said, 'Be of good cheer, Paul; for as you have testified for Me in Jerusalem, so you must also bear witness at Rome.' "

While the Lord encouraged His servant, Paul's enemies were plotting to destroy him. Conspirators "came to the chief priests and elders, and said, 'We have bound ourselves under a great oath that we will eat nothing until we have killed Paul. Now you, therefore, together with the council, suggest to the commander that he be brought down to you tomorrow, as though you were going to make further inquiries concerning him; but we are ready to kill him before he comes near.' "

The priests and rulers eagerly agreed. Paul had spoken the truth when he compared Ananias to a "whitewashed wall."

Paul's Nephew Foils the Plot

But God stepped in to save His servant. Paul's sister's son heard about the assassins' ambush, and he "entered the barracks and told Paul. Then Paul called one of the centurions to him and said, 'Take this young man to the commander, for he has something to tell him.' So he took him and brought him to the commander and said, 'Paul the prisoner called me to him and asked me to bring this young man to you. He has something to say to you.' "

Claudius Lysias received the youth kindly. "What is it that you have to tell me?" The youth replied: " 'The Jews have agreed to ask that you bring Paul down to the council tomorrow, as though they were going to inquire more fully about him. But do not yield to them, for more than forty of them lie in wait for him, men who have bound themselves by an oath that they will neither eat nor drink till they have killed him; and now they are ready, waiting for the promise from you.'

"So the commander let the young man depart, and commanded him, 'Tell no one that you have revealed these things to me.' "

Lysias "called for two centurions, saying, 'Prepare two hundred soldiers, seventy horsemen, and two hundred spearmen to go to Caesarea at the third hour of the night; and provide mounts to set Paul on, and bring him safely to Felix the governor.' "

They were to lose no time. "So the soldiers, according to their instructions, took Paul and brought him during the night to Antipatris" (NRSV). The horsemen went on with the prisoner to Caesarea. The officer in charge delivered his prisoner to Felix, also presenting a letter:

"Claudius Lysias, to the most excellent governor Felix: Greetings. This man was seized by the Jews and was about to be killed by them. Coming with the troops I rescued him, having learned that he was a Roman. . . . And when it was told me that the Jews lay in wait for the man, I sent him immediately to you, and also commanded his accusers to state before you the charges against him."

Adding Crime to Crime

In their rage against Paul, the Jews had added another crime to the dark record that marked their history and had made their doom more certain. In the synagogue at Nazareth, Christ reminded His hearers that in the past God had turned away from His chosen people because of their unbelief and rebellion and had revealed Himself to people in heathen lands who had not rejected the light of heaven. The faithful messenger of God would find no safety with backsliding Israel. The Jewish leaders were taking the people further and further from obedience to God—where He could not defend them in the day of trouble.

The Savior's words of rebuke to the people of Nazareth applied in Paul's case of Paul to his own brethren in the Christian faith. If the leaders in the church had fully surrendered their bitterness toward the apostle and accepted him as one God had specially called to carry the gospel to the Gentiles, the Lord would have preserved him for them. God had not decreed that Paul's work should end so soon.

The same spirit is still depriving the church of many blessings. How often would the Lord have prolonged the work of some faithful minister if the church had appreciated his efforts. But if church members misrepresent and misinterpret the words and acts of Christ's servant, allowing themselves to stand in his way, the Lord sometimes removes the blessing He had given them.

Those God has chosen to accomplish a great and good work may be ready to sacrifice even life itself for the cause of Christ, yet the great deceiver will suggest doubts about them to their fellow believers to undermine confidence in their integrity and cripple their usefulness. Too often, through their own fellow Christians, Satan succeeds in bringing upon them such sorrow of heart that God graciously intervenes to give His persecuted servants rest. After the voice of warning and encouragement goes silent, then these hardened opposers may see and value the blessings they have thrown away. The death of God's servants may accomplish what their life failed to do.

Paul's Trial at Caesarea*

Five days after Paul arrived at Caesarea, his accusers came from Jerusalem, bringing their lawyer, Tertullus. Paul was brought before the assembly, and Tertullus "began his accusation." The sly orator began his speech by flattering Felix: "Seeing that through you we enjoy great peace, and prosperity is being brought to this nation by your foresight, we accept it always and in all places, most noble Felix, with all thankfulness."

In saying this, Tertullus stooped to bold-faced lying, for Felix's character was shameful. Those who heard Tertullus knew his words were untrue.

Tertullus accused Paul of high treason against the government: "We have found this man a plague, a creator of dissension among all the Jews throughout the world, and a ringleader of the sect of the Nazarenes. He even tried to profane the temple." The Jews who were there noisily supported all the charges, making no effort to hide their hatred of the prisoner.

Felix was perceptive enough to know the motives of Paul's accusers in flattering him. He also saw that they had failed to prove their charges. Turning to Paul, he motioned to him to answer for himself.

Paul wasted no words in compliments. Referring to the charges brought against him, he plainly showed that not one of them was true. He had caused no disturbance in any part of Jerusalem, nor had he defiled the sanctuary. While acknowledging that he worshiped God "according to the Way," he stated that He had always believed "all things which are written in the Law and in the Prophets," and he believed in the resurrection of the dead. The guiding principle of his life was to "always strive to have a conscience without offense toward God and men."

Simply and clearly he told the purpose of his visit to Jerusalem and the circumstances of his arrest and trial: "I came to bring alms and offerings to my nation, in the midst of which some Jews from Asia found me purified in the temple, neither with a mob nor with tumult."

The apostle's words rang true. Claudius Lysias, in his letter to Felix, had given a similar report about Paul's conduct. Paul's plain statement of the facts enabled Felix to understand the

---

* This chapter is based on Acts 24.

motives of the Jews in trying to convict the apostle of stirring up rebellion and of treason. The governor would not satisfy them by unjustly condemning a Roman citizen or giving him up to them. Yet Felix knew no higher motivation than self-interest. He was afraid to offend the Jews, and this held him back from doing full justice to a man he knew was innocent. So he decided to suspend the trial until Lysias was present.

The apostle remained a prisoner, but Felix commanded that he should "have liberty," and "not to forbid any of his friends to provide for or visit him."

Felix and Drusilla Hear the Wonderful Good News

Not long after this, Felix and his wife Drusilla sent for Paul, to hear him "concerning the faith in Christ." They were eager to listen to these new truths—truths that, if rejected, would witness against them in the day of God.

Paul knew that he stood in the presence of a ruler who had power to put him to death or to set him free, yet he did not speak to Felix and Drusilla with flattery. Forgetting all selfish considerations, he tried to awaken them to a sense of their danger. The apostle realized that one day they would stand either among the holy around the great white throne, or with those to whom Christ would say, "Depart from Me, you who practice lawlessness" (Matthew 7:23).

Few had ever before dared even to hint to Felix that his character and conduct were not faultless. But Paul had no fear of any human being. So God led him to speak about those virtues that are essential to Christian character, which the haughty pair before him so greatly lacked.

He held up before Felix and Drusilla God's righteousness, justice, and the nature of His law. He showed that it is our duty to live a sober, temperate life in obedience to God's law, preserving the physical and mental powers in a healthy condition. There would surely come a day of judgment when it would be clear that wealth, position, or titles cannot deliver anyone from the results of sin. This life is our time of preparation for the future life. If we neglect present opportunities, we will experience eternal loss. We will receive no second chance then.

Paul especially showed how God's law extends to the deep secrets of our moral nature. The law searches our thoughts, motives, and purposes. Dark passions hidden from human view—jealousy, hatred, lust, and ambition, evil deeds we may think about yet never do for lack of opportunity—all these God's law condemns.

Paul pointed to the one great Sacrifice for sin, Christ, as the only source of life and hope for fallen humanity. As holy men centuries earlier saw the dying agonies of the sacrificial animals, they looked across the gap of ages to the Lamb of God that was to take away the sin of the world.

God justly claims the love and obedience of His creatures. But many forget their Maker and give Him back hatred instead of love. God cannot lower the requirements of His law. Neither can we meet the demands of the law in our own power. Only by faith in Christ can the sinner find cleansing from guilt and power to be obedient to the law of his Maker.

In this way Paul the prisoner urged the claims of the divine law and presented Jesus as the Son of God, the world's Redeemer.

Felix and His Wife Reject Their Golden Opportunity

The Jewish princess understood the law she had so shamelessly broken, but her prejudice against the Man of Calvary hardened her heart against the word of life. But Felix was deeply troubled, and he felt that Paul's words were true. With terrible clarity the secrets of his life came up before him. He saw himself lustful, cruel, greedy. Never before had truth come home to his heart like this. The thought that his career of crime was open to the eye of God and that he must be judged for his deeds made him tremble.

But instead of letting his convictions lead him to repentance, he tried to dismiss these unwelcome thoughts. "Go away for now; when I have a convenient time I will call for you."

How wide the contrast between Felix's actions and those of the jailer at Philippi! The servants of the Lord were brought to the jailer in chains, as Paul was to Felix. The evidence they gave that a divine power sustained them, combined with their spirit of forgiveness, sent conviction to the jailer's heart. With trembling he confessed his sins and found pardon. Felix also trembled, but he did not repent. The jailer welcomed the Spirit of God; Felix told the divine Messenger to leave. One chose to become an heir of heaven; the other chose to unite with evildoers. For two years Paul remained a prisoner. Felix visited him several times and hinted that by paying a large sum of money Paul could secure his release. The apostle, however, was too noble to free himself by a bribe. He would not stoop to commit a wrong in order to gain freedom. He felt that he was in the hands of God, and he would not interfere with God's plan for him.

Felix was finally summoned to Rome because of terrible wrongs he committed against the Jews. Before leaving Caesarea he thought he would "do the Jews a favor" by allowing Paul to remain in prison. But Felix did not succeed in regaining the confidence of the Jews. He was removed from office in disgrace, and Porcius Festus was appointed to follow him.

A ray of light from heaven had come to Felix when Paul reasoned with him "about righteousness, self-control, and the judgment to come." But he said to the messenger of God, "Go away for now; when I have a convenient time I will call for you."

He never received another call from God.

Paul Appeals to Caesar[*]

Now when Festus had come to the province, after three days he went up from Caesarea to Jerusalem. And the high priest and the chief men of the Jews informed him against Paul; and they petitioned him, asking a favor against him, that he would summon him to Jerusalem." In making this request they intended to ambush Paul along the road and murder him.

But Festus had a high sense of responsibility, and he courteously declined. He declared that it is "not the custom of the Romans to deliver any man to destruction before the accused meets the accusers face to face, and has opportunity to answer for himself."

The Jews had not forgotten their earlier defeat at Caesarea. Again they urged Festus to send Paul to Jerusalem for trial, but Festus held firmly to his plan to give Paul a fair trial at Caesarea. God controlled the decision of Festus, to lengthen the life of the apostle.

The Jewish leaders immediately prepared to testify against Paul at the court of the procurator. Festus, "sitting on the judgment seat, . . . commanded Paul to be brought. . . . The Jews who had come down from Jerusalem stood about and laid many serious complaints against Paul, which they could not prove." As the trial went along, Paul clearly showed, calmly and openly, that his accusers' statements were not true.

Festus recognized that nothing in the charges against Paul would make him subject to death or even imprisonment. Yet he saw clearly the storm of rage that would follow if he did not condemn Paul or turn him over to his accusers. And so, "wanting to do the Jews a favor," Festus asked Paul if he was willing to go to Jerusalem under his protection, to be tried by the Sanhedrin.

The apostle knew that he would be safer among the heathen than with those who had rejected light from heaven and hardened their hearts against the gospel. So he decided to exercise his right, as a Roman citizen, to appeal to Caesar: "I stand at Caesar's judgment seat, where I ought to be judged. To the Jews I have done no wrong, as you very well know. For if I am an offender, or have committed anything deserving of death, I do not object to dying; but if there is nothing in these things of which these men ac-

---

*This chapter is based on Acts 25:1–16.

cuse me, no one can deliver me to them. I appeal to Caesar."

Festus knew nothing about the conspiracies of the Jews to murder Paul and was surprised by this appeal to Caesar. However, the words of the apostle put a stop to the court's proceedings. "Festus . . . answered, 'You have appealed to Caesar? To Caesar you shall go!' "

Those Who Serve God Need Firm Courage

Once more, because of hatred, a servant of God was driven to the heathen for protection. This same hatred forced Elijah to escape to the widow of Sarepta, and it forced the gospel messengers to turn from the Jews to the Gentiles. The people of God living in this age will one day have to meet this hatred as well. People claiming to be Christ's representatives will act much like the priests and rulers did in their treatment of Christ and the apostles. Faithful servants of God will face the same hardness of heart, the same cruel determination, the same unyielding hatred.

Those who are true to God will be persecuted, their motives misrepresented, their best efforts misinterpreted, and their names condemned as evil. Satan will work with all his deceptive power to make evil appear good and good evil. He will work fiercely to stir up rage against God's people from those who claim to be righteous while they trample on God's law. It will require the firmest trust, the most heroic determination, to hold tightly to the faith that God gave His followers long ago.

Prepared or unprepared, God's people must all meet the soon-coming crisis. Only those who have brought their lives into harmony with the divine standard will stand firm. When secular rulers unite with ministers of religion to dictate in matters of conscience, then it will be clear who really fears and serves God. And while the enemies of truth watch the Lord's servants for evil, God will watch over them for good. To them He will be like the shadow of a great rock in a weary land.

The King Who Refused the Cross*

Festus could do nothing else than send Paul to Rome. But some time passed before a suitable ship could be found. This gave Paul opportunity to present the reasons of his faith before the leaders of Caesarea and also before King Agrippa II.

"After some days King Agrippa and Bernice came to Caesarea to greet Festus." Festus outlined the circumstances that led to the prisoner's appeal to Caesar, telling of Paul's recent trial before him and saying that the Jews had brought "some questions against him about their own religion and about a certain Jesus, who had died, but whom Paul affirmed to be alive."

Agrippa became interested and said, "I also would like to hear the man myself." A meeting was arranged for the following day, and "at Festus' command Paul was brought in."

Festus had tried to make this an occasion of impressive display. The rich robes of the procurator and his guests, the swords of the soldiers, and the gleaming armor of their commanders gave brilliance to the scene.

And now Paul, in chains, stood before the company. What a contrast! Agrippa and Bernice possessed power and position, but they were completely lacking the character that God values. They were transgressors of His law, corrupt in heart and life.

The aged prisoner, chained to his guard, had nothing in his appearance that would lead the world to honor him. Yet in this man, apparently without friends, wealth, or position, all heaven was interested. Angels were by his side. If the glory of only one of those shining messengers had flashed out, the king and court attendants would have been struck to the earth like the Roman guards at the tomb of Christ.

Festus presented Paul to the assembly with the words: "King Agrippa and all the men who are here present with us, you see this man about whom the whole assembly of the Jews petitioned me, both at Jerusalem and here, crying out that he was not fit to live any longer. But when I found that he had committed nothing deserving of death, and that he himself had appealed to Augustus, I decided to send him. I have nothing certain to write to my lord concerning him. . . . It seems to me unreasonable to send a prisoner and not to specify the charges against him."

---

* This chapter is based on Acts 25:13–27; 26.

will powerfully proclaim the unchangeable nature of God's law. The God of Israel will fulfill this in our day. As His servants work in faith for those who have long been neglected, God will reveal His salvation.

Paul Not Intimidated by Earthly Pomp

Agrippa now gave Paul permission to speak. The apostle was not unsettled by the brilliant display or the high rank of his audience. Earthly pomp could not drain his courage or rob him of his self-control.

"I consider myself fortunate that it is before you, King Agrippa, I am to make my defense today against all the accusations of the Jews, because you are especially familiar with all the customs and controversies of the Jews" (NRSV). Paul told the story of his conversion. He described the heavenly vision—a revelation of divine glory, in the midst of which sat enthroned the One whom he had despised and hated, whose followers he was seeking to destroy. From that hour Paul had been a strong believer in Jesus.

With power Paul outlined before Agrippa the leading events in the life of Christ. He testified that the Messiah had already appeared—as Jesus of Nazareth. The Old Testament Scriptures had declared that the Messiah was to appear as a man among men. In Jesus every specification outlined by Moses and the prophets had been fulfilled. The Son of God had endured the cross and had ascended to heaven triumphant over death.

Once it had seemed incredible to Paul that Christ could rise from the dead, but how could he disbelieve what he himself had seen and heard? At the gate of Damascus he had looked on the crucified and risen Christ. He had seen and talked with Him. The Voice had told him to proclaim the gospel of a risen Savior, and how could he disobey? Throughout Judea and in regions far away he had given his witness concerning Jesus the Crucified, showing all classes "that they should repent, turn to God, and do works befitting repentance.

"For these reasons the Jews seized me in the temple and tried to kill me. Therefore, having obtained help from God, to this day I stand, witnessing both to small and great, saying no other things than those which the prophets and Moses said would come."

Worldly "Great" People Reject the Cross

The whole assembly listened spellbound. But Festus interrupted the apostle by calling out, "Paul, you are beside yourself! Much learning is driving you mad!"

The apostle replied, "I am not mad, most noble Festus, but speak the words of truth and reason. For the king, before whom I also speak freely, knows these things." Then, turning to Agrippa, he spoke to him directly: "King Agrippa, do you believe the prophets? I know that you do believe."

For the moment Agrippa forgot his surroundings and dignity. Seeing only the humble prisoner standing before him as God's ambassador, he answered involuntarily, "You almost persuade me to become a Christian."

The apostle answered, "I would to God that not only you, but also all who hear me today, might become . . . such as I am," adding, as he raised his bound hands, "except for these chains."

Festus, Agrippa, and Bernice, all guilty of terrible crimes, heard that day the offer of salvation through the name of Christ. One of them, at least, had almost been persuaded to accept. But Agrippa refused the cross of a crucified Redeemer.

The king's curiosity was satisfied, and he indicated that the interview was over. Though Agrippa was a Jew, he did not share the blind prejudice of the Pharisees. "This man," he said to Festus, "might have been set free if he had not appealed to Caesar."

But the case was now beyond the jurisdiction of either Festus or Agrippa.

Paul Experiences Shipwreck in a Storm*

Paul was finally on his way to Rome. "They delivered Paul and some other prisoners to one named Julius, a centurion of the Augustan Regiment. So," Luke writes, "entering a ship of Adramyttium, we put to sea."

In the first century, traveling by sea was dangerous. Sailors navigated mostly by the sun and stars. When a storm seemed to be coming, the ship owners were afraid of the open sea. During part of the year, safe navigation was almost impossible.

The apostle would now suffer the trying experiences of a prisoner in chains during the long voyage to Italy. Aristarchus shared Paul's captivity by choice, so that he could care for him in his hardships (see Colossians 4:10).

The voyage began well. The following day they dropped anchor in the harbor of Sidon. Here Julius "treated Paul kindly" and "gave him liberty to go to his [Christian] friends and receive care." The apostle, who was in frail health, appreciated this.

Leaving Sidon, the ship faced contrary winds. At Myra the centurion found a large Alexandrian ship bound for Italy, and he transferred his prisoners to it. But the winds were still contrary. Luke writes: "When we had sailed slowly many days, . . . passing . . . with difficulty, we came to a place called Fair Havens."

They remained there for some time, waiting for better winds. Winter was coming quickly, and "sailing was now dangerous." The question now was whether to stay in Fair Havens or try to reach a better place to stay for the winter.

Paul's Inspired Advice Rejected

The centurion finally asked Paul, who had won the respect of sailors and soldiers, for his opinion. Without hesitation the apostle advised remaining where they were. "I perceive that this voyage will end with disaster and much loss, not only of the cargo and ship, but also of our lives." But "the owner of the ship" and the majority of passengers and crew were unwilling to accept this counsel. They "advised to set sail from there also, if by any means they could reach Phoenix . . . and winter there."

The centurion decided to follow the judgment of the majority. "When the south wind blew softly, . . . putting out to sea, they sailed close by Crete.

But not long after, a tempestuous head wind arose. . . . The ship was caught, and could not head into the wind."

Driven by the storm, the ship neared the small island of Clauda, and the sailors prepared for the worst. The lifeboat, their only means of escape, was in tow and in danger of being smashed in pieces at any moment. Their first work was to hoist this boat on board. They took every possible precaution to prepare the ship to ride out the storm. The slight protection that the little island provided did not last long, and soon they were exposed to the full violence of the storm again.

All night the storm raged, and the ship leaked. Night came again, but the wind did not die down. The storm-beaten ship, with shattered mast and torn sails, was tossed this way and that. It seemed that the groaning timbers must surely break as the ship quivered under the shock of the storm. The leak increased rapidly, and passengers and crew worked continually at the pumps. Writes Luke, "When neither sun nor stars appeared for many days, and no small tempest beat on us, all hope that we would be saved was finally given up."

For fourteen days they drifted. Though the apostle was suffering physically, he had words of hope for the darkest hour and a helping hand in every emergency. By faith he grasped the arm of Infinite Power. He knew that God would preserve him to witness at Rome for the truth of Christ, but his heart longed for the poor souls around him, sinful and unprepared to die. He pleaded earnestly with God to spare their lives, and God granted his request.

Disaster to the Ship

Taking advantage of a lull in the storm, Paul stood on deck and said: "Now I urge you to take heart; for there will be no loss of life among you, but only of the ship. For there stood by me this night an angel of the God to whom I belong and whom I serve, saying, 'Do not be afraid, Paul; you must be brought before Caesar; and indeed God has granted you all those who sail with you.' Therefore take heart, men, for I believe God that it will be just as it was told me. However, we must run aground on a certain island."

When they heard these words, the passengers and crew began to revive from their hopelessness. They must put forth every effort within their power to avoid destruction.

On the fourteenth night of tossing on the huge waves, about midnight the sailors heard the sound of breakers. "Then," Luke writes, "fearing lest we should run aground on the rocks, they dropped four anchors from the stern, and prayed for day to come."

At daybreak the outlines of the stormy coast were dimly visible, but the outlook was so gloomy that the heathen sailors lost all courage and "were seeking to escape from the ship." "Under pretense of putting out anchors from the prow," they had let down the lifeboat, when Paul saw what they were planning to do. He said to the centurion and the soldiers, "Unless these men stay in the ship, you cannot be saved." The soldiers immediately "cut away the ropes of the skiff and let it fall off" into the sea.

The most critical time was still ahead of them. The apostle again spoke words of encouragement and urged both sailors and passengers to eat something. " 'Today is the fourteenth day you have waited and continued without food, and eaten nothing. Therefore I urge you to take nourishment, for this is for your survival, since not a hair will fall from the head of any of you.' "

"When he had said these things, he took bread and gave thanks to God in the presence of them all; and when he had broken it he began to eat." Then that weary and discouraged company of 275 people, who would have become desperate were it not for Paul, joined the apostle in eating some food. "So when they had eaten enough, they lightened the ship and threw out the wheat into the sea."

Daylight had now come. "They observed a bay with a beach, onto which they planned to run the ship if possible. And they let go the anchors and left them in the sea, meanwhile loosening the rudder ropes; and they hoisted the mainsail to the wind and made for shore. But striking a place where two seas met, they ran the ship aground; and the prow stuck fast and remained immovable, but the stern was being broken up by the violence of the waves."

The Prisoners About to Be Killed

The prisoners now faced a threat more terrible than shipwreck. The soldiers saw that to reach land they would have all they could do to save themselves. Yet if any prisoners were missing, the Roman authorities would execute those who were responsible for them. For this reason the soldiers wanted to put all the prisoners to death. Roman law allowed this cruel policy. But Julius knew that Paul had helped to save the lives of all on board, and, convinced that the Lord was with him, he was afraid to do him harm. So he "commanded that those who could swim should jump overboard first and get to land, and the rest, some on boards and some on parts of the ship. And so it was that they all escaped safely to land." When they checked the prisoner list, not one was missing.

The heathen people of Malta "kindled a fire," Luke writes, "and made us all welcome, because of the rain that was falling and because of the cold." Having gathered "a bundle of sticks," Paul "laid them on the fire," and a poisonous snake came out "because of the heat, and fastened on his hand." Seeing by his chain that Paul was a prisoner, the bystanders said, " 'No doubt this man is a murderer, whom, though he has escaped the sea, yet justice does not allow to live.' . . . But after they had looked for a long time and saw no harm come to him, they changed their minds and said that he was a god."

During the three months that they stayed on Malta, Paul found many opportunities to preach the gospel. The Lord worked through him. For his sake the entire shipwrecked group was treated with kindness. And when they left Malta they were provided with everything they needed for their voyage. Luke says:

"Publius . . . entertained us courteously for three days. And it happened that the father of Publius lay sick of a fever and dysentery. Paul went in to him and prayed, and he laid his hands on him and healed him. So when this was done, the rest of those on the island who had diseases also came and were healed. They also honored us in many ways; and when we departed, they provided such things as were necessary."

Paul in Rome: Big-City Evangelist in Chains[*]

When sailing was safe again, the centurion and his prisoners set out on their journey to Rome. An Alexandrian ship had wintered at Malta on her way westward, and the travelers were able to get passage on it. When it safely completed the voyage, the ship dropped anchor in the beautiful harbor of Puteoli in Italy, where a few Christians urged the apostle to stay with them for seven days, a privilege that the centurion kindly granted.

Since receiving Paul's letter to the Romans, the Christians of Italy had eagerly looked forward to a visit from the apostle. His sufferings as a prisoner only made him more precious to them. The seaport was only 140 miles from Rome, so some of the Christians started out to meet and welcome him.

On the eighth day after landing, the centurion and his prisoners set out for Rome. Julius willingly granted the apostle every favor he was able to give, but he could do nothing about the fact that Paul was a prisoner. With a heavy heart Paul went forward to the world's metropolis. How was he to proclaim the gospel while chained like a criminal?

At last the travelers reached Appii Forum, 40 miles from Rome. The gray-haired old man, chained with a group of hardened-looking criminals, received many a scornful glance and was made the subject of rude jokes.

Suddenly there was a cry of joy, and a man leaped out from the passing crowd and embraced the prisoner with tears and rejoicing, like a son would welcome a long-absent father. This scene happened again and again. Many recognized the chained captive as the one who at Corinth, Philippi, or Ephesus had spoken to them the words of life.

As the warmhearted disciples eagerly flocked around their father in the gospel, the whole group was brought to a standstill. The soldiers, impatient with the delay, did not have the heart to interrupt this happy meeting, for they too had learned to appreciate their prisoner. The disciples saw the image of Christ reflected in that pain-stricken face. They assured Paul that they had not stopped loving him. In the depth of their love they would carry him on their shoulders the whole way to the city, if they could only have the privilege.

When Paul saw his fellow Christians, "he thanked God and took courage."

---

[*] *This chapter is based on Acts 28:11–31 and the letter to Philemon.*

The weeping, sympathizing believers were not ashamed of his shackles. The cloud of sadness that had rested on his spirit was swept away. Chains and afflictions were waiting for him, but he knew that it had been his privilege to deliver others from a bondage infinitely more terrible, and he rejoiced in his sufferings for Christ's sake.

Paul, in Chains, Appeals to the Jews

At Rome Julius delivered his prisoners to the captain of the emperor's guard. The good account that he gave of Paul, with the letter from Festus, caused the chief captain to look with favor on the apostle, and instead of Paul's being thrown into prison, he was permitted to live in his own rented house. Although still chained to a soldier, he was able freely to receive his friends and to work for the cause of Christ.

Many of the Jews previously banished from Rome had been allowed to return. Paul determined to present the facts concerning himself and his work to these people first of all, before his enemies had opportunity to prejudice them against him. Three days after his arrival he called their leading men together and said:

"Though I have done nothing against our people or the customs of our fathers, yet I was delivered as a prisoner from Jerusalem into the hands of the Romans, who, when they had examined me, wanted to let me go, because there was no cause for putting me to death. But when the Jews spoke against it, I was compelled to appeal to Caesar. . . . For the hope of Israel I am bound with this chain."

He said nothing of the repeated plots to assassinate him. He was not trying to win sympathy but to defend the truth and maintain the honor of the gospel.

His hearers said that none of the Jews who had come to Rome had accused him of any crime. They also expressed a strong desire to hear for themselves the reasons for his faith in Christ. Paul asked them to set a day, and when the time arrived, many came to hear him. "He explained and solemnly testified of the kingdom of God, persuading them concerning Jesus from both the Law of Moses and the Prophets." He told of his own experience and presented arguments from the Old Testament Scriptures.

Religion Is Practical and Experiential

The apostle showed that religion is a practical, personal experience of God's renewing power in the life. Moses had pointed Israel to Christ as that Prophet whom they were to hear. All the prophets had testified of Him as the guiltless One who was to bear the sins of the guilty. Paul showed that while the Jews performed the ritual service with great exactness, they were rejecting Him who was the fulfillment of all that system.

Paul told them that he had rejected Jesus of Nazareth as an impostor because He did not fulfill his cherished idea of the Messiah to come. But now his views of Christ were more spiritual, for he had been converted. To get a glimpse of Christ by faith, to have a spiritual knowledge of Him, was more important than a personal acquaintance with Him in His human form on the earth as only an earthly and human companion.

As Paul spoke, those who were honestly searching for truth were convinced. His words made an impression on some minds that they would never forget. But other people stubbornly refused to accept the testimony of the Scriptures. They could not refute Paul's arguments, but they refused to accept his conclusions.

As a Prisoner, Paul Has Stronger Influence

Many months passed before the Jews of Jerusalem appeared to present their accusations against the prisoner. Now that Paul was to be tried before the highest court of the Roman Empire, they had no desire to risk another defeat. Delay would give them time to try to influence the emperor secretly in their favor, so they waited a while before making their charges against the apostle.

This delay helped the spread of the gospel. Paul was permitted to live in a spacious house, where he could present the truth every day to those who came to hear. So for two years he continued his work, "preaching the kingdom of God and teaching the things which concern the Lord Jesus Christ with all confidence, no one forbidding him."

During this time Paul did not forget the churches he had established in many lands. The apostle addressed their needs in letters of practical instruction, and from Rome he sent consecrated workers to labor in fields that he had not visited himself. The apostle kept in constant communication with them, and he was able to exercise wise supervision over them all.

In this way Paul exerted a wider and more lasting influence than if he had been free to travel among the churches as he had in earlier years. As a "prisoner of Christ Jesus," he had a firmer hold on the affections of the believers, and his words commanded greater attention and respect than when he was personally with them. Up to then the believers had usually excused themselves from carrying responsibilities and burdens because they did not have his wisdom, tact, and boundless energy. But now they valued his warnings and instructions more than they had appreciated his personal work. And as they learned of his courage and faith during his long imprisonment, they determined to be even more faithful in the cause of Christ.

At Rome, Luke, "the beloved physician," who had been Paul's companion on the journey to Jerusalem, through the two years' imprisonment at Caesarea, and on his dangerous voyage to Rome, was still with him. Timothy also did what he could to make him comfortable. Tychicus stood nobly by the apostle. Demas and Mark were with him. Aristarchus and Epaphras were his "fellow prisoners." (See Colossians 4:7–14.)

Mark's Christian experience had deepened as he had studied the life and death of Christ more closely. Now, sharing the living conditions of Paul the prisoner, he understood better than ever before that it is infinite gain to win Christ, infinite loss to win the world and lose the soul. In the face of severe difficulties, Mark remained faithful, a wise and beloved helper of the apostle.

Paul wrote, "Demas has forsaken me, having loved this present world" (2 Timothy 4:10). For worldly gain, Demas traded away every high and noble consideration. But Mark, choosing to suffer for Christ's sake, had eternal riches.

The Beautiful Story of Onesimus the Slave

Among those who gave their hearts to God in Rome was Onesimus, a pagan slave who had wronged his master, Philemon, a Christian believer in Colosse, and had escaped to Rome. In the kindness of his heart, Paul tried to relieve the needs of the poor fugitive and then worked to bring the light of truth into his darkened mind. Onesimus listened, confessed his sins, and was converted to Christ.

He endeared himself to Paul by tenderly caring for the apostle's comfort and by his zeal in promoting the gospel. Paul saw that he could be a useful helper in missionary work and counseled him to return immediately to Philemon, beg his forgiveness, and plan for the future. Paul was about to send Tychicus with letters to various churches in Asia Minor, so he sent Onesimus with him to the master he had wronged. It was a severe test, but this servant had been truly converted, and he did not turn aside from duty.

Paul gave Onesimus a letter to take to Philemon in which the apostle pleaded for the repentant slave. He reminded Philemon that everything he possessed was due to the grace of

Christ. This alone made him different from the wicked and the sinful. The same grace could make the corrupt criminal a child of God and a useful laborer in the gospel.

The apostle asked Philemon to receive the repentant slave as his own child, "no longer as a slave but more than a slave—a beloved brother." He expressed his desire to keep Onesimus with him as one who could minister to him in his imprisonment as Philemon himself would have done, but he did not want his services unless Philemon himself was willing to set the slave free.

The apostle knew how severely masters could treat their slaves. He knew also that Philemon was angry over what his servant had done. He tried to write in a way that would appeal to Philemon's tenderest feelings as a Christian. Paul would regard any punishment inflicted on this new convert as inflicted on himself.

Paul volunteered to pay the debt of Onesimus in order to spare the guilty one the disgrace of punishment. "If then you count me as a partner," he wrote to Philemon, "receive him as you would me. But if he has wronged you or owes anything, put that on my account. I, Paul, am writing with my own hand. I will repay."

How fitting an illustration of the love of Christ! The sinner who has robbed God of years of service has no way to cancel the debt. Jesus says, I will pay the debt. I will suffer in his place.

Paul reminded Philemon how much he himself owed the apostle. God had made Paul the instrument of his conversion. As Philemon had refreshed the believers by his generosity, so he would refresh the spirit of the apostle by giving him this reason to rejoice. "Having confidence in your obedience," he added, "I write to you, knowing that you will do even more than I say."

Paul's letter to Philemon shows the influence of the gospel on the relationship between master and servant. Slaveholding was an established institution throughout the Roman Empire, and masters and slaves were found in most churches where Paul worked. In the cities where slaves often greatly outnumbered the free population, laws of terrible cruelty were thought necessary to keep slaves under control. A wealthy Roman often owned hundreds of slaves. With full control over the souls and bodies of these helpless beings, he could inflict on them any suffering he chose. If in retaliation or self-defense a slave dared to raise a hand against his owner, the whole family of the offender might be inhumanely sacrificed.

Some masters were more humane than others, but the vast majority, living for lust, passion, and appetite, made their slaves the miserable victims of tyranny. The whole system was hopelessly degrading.

It was not the apostle's work suddenly to overturn the established order of society. Trying to do this would prevent the success of the gospel. But he taught principles that struck at the foundation of slavery and would surely undermine the whole system. "Where the Spirit of the Lord is, there is liberty" (2 Corinthians 3:17). When converted, the slave became a member of the body of Christ, to be loved and treated as a brother, a fellow heir with his master to the blessings of God. On the other hand, servants were to perform their duties "not with eyeservice, as menpleasers, but as bondservants of Christ, doing the will of God from the heart" (Ephesians 6:6).

Master and slave, king and subject, have been washed in the same blood and made alive by the same Spirit. They are one in Christ.

Paul Wins Converts in the Emperor's Palace

The gospel has always had its greatest success among the humbler classes. "Not many wise according to the flesh, not many mighty, not many noble, are called" (1 Corinthians 1:26). No one could expect Paul, a poor, friendless prisoner, to be able to gain the attention of the wealthy classes of Roman citizens. Sin held them as willing captives. But many among the weary, deprived victims of their oppression, even poor slaves, gladly listened to Paul, and in Christ they found hope and peace. The apostle's work began with the poor, but its influence spread until it reached the emperor's palace.

Rome was the metropolis of the world. The haughty Caesars were giving laws to nearly every nation on earth. King and officials were either ignorant of the humble Nazarene or hated and scorned Him. And yet in less than two years the gospel found its way into the emperor's halls. "The word of God is not chained," said Paul (2 Timothy 2:9).

Earlier, the apostle had publicly proclaimed the faith of Christ with appealing power before the wise men of Greece, before kings and governors. Haughty rulers trembled as if they were already seeing the terrors of the day of God.

Now the apostle, confined to his house, was able to proclaim the truth only to those who looked for him there. Yet at this very time, when its chief spokesman was cut off from public work, the gospel experienced a great victory. Members were added to the church from the household of the king.

In the Roman court, Nero seemed to have obliterated from his soul the last trace of the divine, and even of the human. His attending officials, in general, were of the same character—fierce, debased, and corrupt. Yet even in Nero's household, trophies of the cross were won. From the evil attendants of the more evil king came converts who became children of God—Christians not ashamed of their faith.

Paul's Afflictions Do Not Restrict the Gospel

How did Christianity gain a footing where it seemed impossible? Paul believed his imprisonment helped give him success in winning converts from Nero's household. He assured the Philippians, "I want you to know, brethren, that the things which happened to me have actually turned out for the furtherance of the gospel" (Philippians 1:12).

When the Christian churches first

learned that Paul would visit Rome, they looked forward to the gospel's triumph in that city. Wouldn't this champion of the faith succeed in winning souls even in the metropolis of the world? But Paul had gone to Rome as a prisoner. How great was their disappointment! Human expectations had failed, but not the plans of God. As a captive, Paul broke the chains that held many people in the slavery of sin. His cheerfulness during his long, unjust imprisonment, his courage and faith, were a continual sermon. His example spurred Christians on to greater energy as spokesmen for the cause, and when his usefulness seemed cut off, then it was that he gathered a harvest for Christ in fields from which he seemed completely excluded.

Before the close of two years' imprisonment, Paul was able to say, "It has become evident to the whole palace guard, and to all the rest, that my chains are in Christ" (Philippians 1:13). Among those who sent greetings to the Philippians he mentions "those who are of Caesar's household" (Philippians 4:22).

Christians who show patience in grief and suffering, who meet even death with the calmness of an unshaken faith, may accomplish more for the gospel than they could have by a long life of faithful work. Often the mysterious circumstances that our shortsighted vision would mourn turn out to be something God designed to accomplish a work that otherwise would never be done.

God never sets aside Christ's true witnesses. In health and sickness, in life and death, He still uses them.

When the servants of Christ have been persecuted because Satan hates them, when they have been thrown into prison or dragged to the executioner's scaffold, it was so that truth could gain a greater victory. People who had been in doubt were convinced of the faith of Christ and took their stand for Him. From the ashes of martyrs, a harvest for God has sprung up.

The apostle might have argued that it would be useless to call the servants of Nero to repentance and faith in Christ when they faced such huge obstacles. Even if they became convinced of the truth, how could they obey it? But in faith Paul presented the gospel to these people, and some decided to obey at any cost. They would accept the light and trust God to help them let it shine out to others.

After their conversion they still stayed in Caesar's household. They did not feel free to leave their post of duty because their surroundings were no longer friendly. The truth had found them there, and that is where they remained, testifying of their new faith's transforming power.

No Excuse for Unfaithfulness

Consider the disciples in Caesar's household—the depravity of the emperor, the immorality of the court. Yet they remained true to God. Because of obstacles that seem too great to overcome, some Christians may try to excuse themselves from obeying the truth as it is in Jesus. But no excuse will hold up under investigation. If we could find legitimate excuses, we would prove that God is unjust—that He had made conditions of salvation for His children that they could not fulfill.

Difficulties will be powerless to stop those who seek first the kingdom of God and His righteousness. In the strength that comes from prayer and study of the Word, they will choose virtue and forsake vice. He whose word is truth has promised enough help and grace to meet every circumstance. We may rest safely in His care, saying, "I will trust in You" (Psalm 56:3).

By His own example the Savior has shown that the Christian may remain spotless in any surroundings. We develop Christian character not in freedom from difficulties, but in the midst of them. Snubs and opposition lead the follower of Christ to pray more earnestly to the mighty Helper. Severe trial develops patience, strength, and a deep trust in God. The Christian faith enables its follower to suffer and be strong; to submit, and by doing so to conquer; to be "killed all day long," and yet to live; to bear the cross, and in this way to win the crown of glory.

The Letters Paul Wrote From Rome*

Paul acknowledged that he had received many "visions and revelations of the Lord." His understanding of the gospel was equal to that of "the most eminent apostles." (2 Corinthians 12:1, 11.) He had clearly understood "the width and length and depth and height" of "the love of Christ which passes knowledge" (Ephesians 3:18, 19).

Paul could not tell everything that he had seen in vision. Some hearers would have misused his words. But what had been revealed to him molded the messages that in later years he sent to the churches. He gave a message that has brought strength to the church of God ever since. To believers today this message speaks plainly of dangers that will threaten the church.

The apostle wanted those to whom he addressed his letters to "no longer be children, tossed to and fro and carried about with every wind of doctrine," but to come into "the unity of the faith and of the knowledge of the Son of God, to a perfect man, to the measure of the stature of the fullness of Christ" (Ephesians 4:14, 13). Christ, who "loved the church and gave Himself for her," would "present her to Himself . . .

not having spot or wrinkle or any such thing"—a church "holy and without blemish" (Ephesians 5:25, 27).

In these messages, written not with human power but with God's power, we find principles that every church should follow, and the way that leads to eternal life is made plain.

In his letter to "the saints" at Colosse, written while he was a prisoner in Rome, Paul mentions his joy over their faithfulness: "We also, since the day we heard it, do not cease to pray for you, and to ask that you may be filled with the knowledge of His will in all wisdom and spiritual understanding; that you may walk worthy of the Lord, fully pleasing Him, being fruitful in every good work and increasing in the knowledge of God."

There is no limit to the blessings that the children of God may receive. They may grow stronger and stronger until they are made "qualified . . . to be partakers of the inheritance of the saints in the light."

Christ, the Creator

The apostle exalted Christ as the One by whom God created all things. The hand that sustains the world in

---

* This chapter is based on the letters to the Colossians and the Philippians.

space is the hand that was nailed to the cross: "For by Him all things were created that are in heaven and that are on earth, visible and invisible. . . . All things were created through Him and for Him. And He is before all things, and in Him all things consist."

The Son of God came to this earth to be "wounded for our transgressions" and "bruised for our iniquities" (Isaiah 53:5). In all things He was made like us. He became flesh, even as we are. He knew what it meant to be hungry, thirsty, and weary. He was sustained by food and refreshed by sleep. He was tempted and tried as men and women of today are tempted and tried, yet He lived a life free from sin.

Surrounded by the influences of heathenism, the Colossian believers were in danger of being drawn away from the gospel's simplicity. Paul pointed them to Christ as the only safe guide: "This I say lest anyone should deceive you with persuasive words. . . .

"As you therefore have received Christ Jesus the Lord, so walk in Him, rooted and built up in Him and established in the faith, as you have been taught. . . .

"Beware lest anyone cheat you through philosophy and empty deceit, according to the tradition of men, according to the basic principles of the world, and not according to Christ."

Christ had warned that deceivers would come and that through their influence "lawlessness will abound" and "the love of many will grow cold" (Matthew 24:12). The church would be in more danger from this evil than from persecution by her enemies. By letting false teachers in, they would open the door to errors that the enemy would use to shake the confidence of those who had just come to the faith. They were to reject everything that was not in harmony with Christ's teachings.

As people tried to use philosophy to destroy faith in the Scriptures in the apostles' day, so today, by higher criticism, evolution, spiritualism, mysticism, and pantheism the enemy of righteousness is working to lead people into forbidden paths. To many the Bible is like a lamp without oil, because they have turned their minds to speculations and suppositions that bring confusion. The work of higher criticism in taking the Bible apart, guessing about other meanings, and reconstructing it along different lines is destroying faith, robbing God's Word of its power to control and inspire human lives. Spiritualism teaches that desire is the highest law, that license is liberty, and that human beings are accountable only to themselves.

The followers of Christ will confront spiritualistic interpretations of the Scriptures, but we are not to accept them. We must discard all ideas that are not in harmony with Christ's teaching. We must accept the Bible as the voice of God speaking directly to us. The knowledge of God as revealed in Christ is the knowledge that everyone who is saved must have. This knowledge transforms the character. Apart from this knowledge, everything else is vanity and nothingness.

In every generation and in every country, the true foundation for character building has been the same—the principles contained in the Word of God. With the Word the apostles overcame the false theories of their day, saying, "No other foundation can anyone lay than that which is laid" (1 Corinthians 3:11).

In his letter, Paul urged the Colossian believers not to forget that they must make a constant effort: "If then you were raised with Christ, seek those things which are above, where Christ is, sitting at the right hand of God. Set your mind on things above, not on things on the earth. For you died, and your life is hidden with Christ in God."

How to Break the Chains of Habit

Through the power of Christ, men and women have broken the chains of sinful habits. They have turned away from selfishness. The irreligious have become reverent, the drunken sober, the immoral pure. This change is the miracle of miracles—"Christ in you, the hope of glory."

When the Spirit of God controls mind and heart, the converted person begins to sing a new song. The promise of God has been fulfilled, and the sinner's transgression has been forgiven. The changed person has repented to God for disobeying the divine law and has exercised faith in Christ, who died to justify us.

But Christians are not to fold their hands, content with what Christ has accomplished for them. They will find that all the powers and passions of their natural hearts rise up against them. Each day they must renew their commitment. Old habits, inherited tendencies to wrong, will try to take control, and the Christian

is to fight against these in Christ's strength.

"As God's chosen ones, holy and beloved, clothe yourselves with compassion, kindness, humility, meekness, and patience. Bear with one another and, if anyone has a complaint against another, forgive each other; just as the Lord has forgiven you, so you also must forgive" (NRSV).

The power of a higher, purer life is our great need. The world has too much of our thought and the kingdom of heaven too little. To reach God's ideal, the Christian must never give up. Moral and spiritual perfection through Christ's grace is promised to all. Jesus is the source of power. He brings us to His Word. He puts a prayer into our mouth to bring us into close contact with Himself. To help us, He sets in operation the all-powerful agencies of heaven. At every step we touch His living power.

To the Philippians: How to Reach Perfection

The church at Philippi had sent gifts to Paul by Epaphroditus, whom Paul calls "my brother, fellow worker, and fellow soldier." While in Rome, Epaphroditus was sick, "almost unto death; but God had mercy on him, and not only on him but on me also, lest I should have sorrow upon sorrow." The believers at Philippi were deeply concerned about Epaphroditus, and he decided to return to them. "He was longing for you all," Paul wrote, "and was distressed because you had heard that he was sick. . . . For the work of Christ he came close to death, not regarding his life, to supply what was lacking in your service toward me."

Paul sent a letter with Epahroditus for the Philippian believers. Of all the churches, Philippi had been the most generous in supplying Paul's needs. "Not that I seek the gift; but I seek the profit that accumulates to your account. I have been paid in full and have more than enough; I am fully satisfied, now that I have received from Epaphroditus the gifts you sent" (NRSV).

"I thank my God upon every remembrance of you, always in every prayer of mine making request for you all with joy, for your fellowship in the gospel from the first day until now, being confident of this very thing, that He who has begun a good work in you will complete it until the day of Jesus Christ. . . .

"And this I pray, that your love may abound still more and more in knowledge and all discernment, . . . that you may be sincere and without offense till the day of Christ."

Paul's imprisonment had resulted in progress for the gospel. "The things which happened to me have actually turned out for the furtherance of the gospel, so that it has become evident to the whole palace guard, and to all the rest."

There is a lesson for us in this experience. The Lord can bring victory out of what may seem like defeat to us. When misfortune or disaster comes, we are ready to accuse God of neglect or cruelty. If He sees fit to bring an end to our usefulness in some area, we mourn, not stopping to think that He may be working for our good. Painful experiences are a part of His great plan. While suffering, the Christian may sometimes do more for the Master than when giving active service.

Paul pointed the Philippians to Christ, who,

"though he was in the form of God,
  did not regard equality with God
  as something to be exploited,
but emptied himself, taking the form
  of a slave, being born in human
  likeness.
And being found in human form, he
  humbled himself and became
  obedient to the point of death—
  even death on a cross" (NRSV).

"Therefore, my beloved," Paul continued, "it is God who works in you both to will and to do for His good pleasure.

"Do all things without complaining and disputing, that you may become blameless and harmless, children of God without fault in the midst of a crooked and perverse generation."

Paul holds up the standard of perfection and shows how to reach it: "Work out your own salvation . . . for it is God who works in you." The work of gaining salvation is a joint operation between God and the repentant sinner. We are to make earnest efforts to overcome, but we are completely dependent on God for success. Without the aid of divine power, human effort is useless. God works and we work. Resistance to temptation must come from us, and we must draw our power from God.

God wants us to overcome self, but He cannot help us without our consent and cooperation. The divine Spirit works through the powers and abilities given to us. By ourselves we cannot bring our desires and our leanings into harmony with the will of God. But if we are "willing to be made willing," the Savior will accomplish this for us, "casting down arguments . . . , bringing every thought into captivity to the obedience of Christ" (2 Corinthians 10:5).

Those who want to be well-balanced Christians must give all and do all for Christ. Every day they must learn what it means to surrender self. They must study the Word of God, obeying its instructions. Day by day God works with them, perfecting the character that will stand in the final test. And day by day the believers work out a wonderful experiment for others and even angels to see, showing what the gospel can do for fallen human beings.

The True Motive That Leads to Perfection

"I do not consider that I have made it my own," Paul wrote, "but this one thing I do: forgetting what lies behind and straining forward to what lies ahead, I press on toward the goal for the prize of the heavenly call of God in Christ Jesus" (NRSV).

In all the busy activities of his life, Paul never lost sight of one great purpose—to press toward the goal for the prize of his high calling. To exalt the cross—this was his all-absorbing motive that inspired his words and acts.

Though he was a prisoner, Paul was not discouraged. A note of triumph rings through the letters that he wrote from Rome. "Rejoice!" he wrote. "In everything by prayer and supplication, with thanksgiving, let your requests be made known to God; and the peace of God, which surpasses all understanding, will guard your hearts and minds through Christ Jesus."

"My God shall supply all your need according to His riches in glory by Christ Jesus."

Paul Is Free Once More

Clouds were gathering that threatened not only Paul's own safety, but also the prosperity of the church. In Rome he had been placed in the charge of the captain of the imperial guards, who was a man of integrity. The captain left him comparatively free to carry on the gospel work. But this man was replaced by an official who was unlikely to offer the apostle any special favor.

In their efforts against Paul the Jews found an able helper in the immoral Jewish convert whom Nero had made his second wife. Paul had little hope of justice from Nero, who had low morals and was capable of terrible cruelty. The first year of his reign had seen the poisoning of his young stepbrother, the rightful heir to the throne. Nero had then murdered his own mother and his wife. In every noble mind he inspired only horror and contempt.

His shameless wickedness created disgust, even in many who were forced to share his crimes. They were in constant fear over what he would suggest next. Yet Nero was acknowledged as the absolute ruler of the civilized world. More than this, he was worshiped as a god.

It seemed certain that such a judge would condemn Paul. But the apostle felt that as long as he was loyal to God, he had nothing to fear. His Protector could shield him from the hatred of the Jews and the power of Caesar.

And God did shield His servant. At Paul's trial the charges against him were dismissed. With a respect for justice completely opposite his character, Nero declared the prisoner guiltless. Paul was again a free man.

If he had been held in Rome until the following year, he would surely have died in the persecution that took place then. During Paul's imprisonment, there had been so many converts that the authorities had become alarmed. The emperor became especially angry over the conversion of members of his own household, and he soon found an excuse to bring his merciless cruelty on the Christians.

A terrible fire occurred in Rome, burning nearly half the city. According to rumors, Nero himself had caused it, but he made a show of great generosity by assisting the homeless and destitute. He was, however, accused of the crime. The people were enraged, and in order to clear himself, Nero turned the accusation on the Christians. Thousands of men, women, and children were cruelly put to death.

Paul's Last Period of Freedom

Soon after his release Paul left Rome. Working among the churches, he tried to establish a stronger tie between the Greek and the Eastern churches and to fortify the believers against the false doctrines that were creeping in to corrupt the faith.

The trials that Paul had endured had taken a toll on his physical powers. He felt he was now doing his last work, and as time grew shorter, he intensified his efforts. There seemed to be no limit to his zeal. Strong in faith, he traveled from church to church in many lands to strengthen the believers, so that in the difficult times they were starting to face, they could win souls and remain true to the gospel, bearing faithful witness for Christ.

Paul's Final Arrest and Imprisonment

Paul's work among the churches could not escape his enemies' attention. Under Nero the Christians had been outlawed everywhere. After a time, the unbelieving Jews devised the idea of blaming Paul for the crime of provoking the burning of Rome. Not one of them thought he was guilty, but they knew that an accusation like this would seal his doom. Paul was again arrested and hurried away to Rome to his final imprisonment.

Several companions went with him, but he refused to permit them to be imprisoned with him and put their lives in danger. Thousands of Christians in Rome had been martyred for their faith. Many had left, and those who remained were greatly discouraged.

In Rome, Paul was placed in a gloomy dungeon. Accused of stirring up one of the most terrible crimes against the city and nation, he was the object of universal hatred.

His few friends now began to leave, some deserting him, others going on missions to various churches. Demas, frightened by the thickening clouds of danger, abandoned the persecuted apostle. Writing to Timothy, Paul said, "Only Luke is with me" (2 Timothy 4:11). The apostle had never needed his fellow Christians as much as now, weakened as he was by age, toil, and illnesses, and confined in the damp, dark vaults of a Roman prison. Luke, the beloved disciple and faithful friend, was a great comfort and enabled Paul to communicate with his fellow church members.

In this difficult time Paul's heart was cheered by frequent visits from Onesiphorus. This warmhearted Ephesian spared no effort to make Paul's situation more bearable. In his last letter the apostle wrote: "The Lord grant mercy to the household of Onesiphorus, for he often refreshed me, and was not ashamed of my chain; but when he arrived in Rome, he sought me out very zealously and found me. The Lord grant to him that he may find mercy from the Lord in that Day" (2 Timothy 1:16–18).

Christ longed for the sympathy of His disciples in His hour of agony in Gethsemane. And Paul yearned for sympathy and companionship at a time of loneliness and desertion. Onesiphorus brought gladness and cheer to Paul, who had spent his life in service for others.

Paul Again Before Nero

When Paul was called before Nero for trial, he expected soon to meet certain death. Among the Greeks and Romans it was customary to allow an accused person a lawyer or other representative who, by force of argument, impassioned eloquence, or tears, often secured a decision in favor of the prisoner or succeeded in reducing the severity of the sentence. But no one dared to act as Paul's spokesman. No friend was at hand even to record the charge against him or the arguments he presented in his own defense. Among the Christians at Rome, not one came forward to stand by him in that difficult hour.

The only reliable record of the occasion comes from Paul himself: "At my first defense no one stood with me, but all forsook me. May it not be charged against them.

"But the Lord stood with me and strengthened me, so that the message might be preached fully through me, and that all the Gentiles might hear. Also I was delivered out of the mouth of the lion" (2 Timothy 4:16, 17).

Nero had reached the peak of earthly power, authority, and wealth, as well as the lowest depths of iniquity. No one dared question his authority. The decrees of senators and the decisions of judges were no more than the echo of his will. The name of Nero made the world tremble. To come under his displeasure was to lose property, liberty, life.

Without money, friends, or an attorney, the aged prisoner stood before Nero. The face of the emperor showed the shameful record of passions that raged within. The face of the accused told of a heart at peace with God. In spite of constant misrepresentation, blame, and abuse, Paul had fearlessly held high the standard of the cross. Like his Master, he had lived to bless humanity. How could Nero understand or appreciate the character and motives of this son of God?

The huge hall was filled with an eager crowd that pushed its way to the front. High and low, rich and poor, educated and ignorant, proud and humble, all alike were in desperate need of a true knowledge of the way of life and salvation.

The Jews brought against Paul the old charges of treason and heresy, and both Jews and Romans accused him of stirring people up to burn the city. The people and the judges looked at Paul in surprise. They had gazed at many a criminal, but they had never seen a man wear a look of such holy calmness. The keen eyes of the judges searched Paul's face for some evidence of guilt, without finding any. When he was permitted to speak in his own behalf, everyone listened with eager interest.

Once more Paul uplifted the banner of the cross before an amazed crowd, his heart stirred with an intense desire for their salvation. Losing sight of the terrible fate that seemed so near, he saw only Jesus, the Intercessor, pleading for sinful humanity. With eloquence and power, Paul pointed to the sacrifice Jesus made for the fallen race. Christ had paid an infinite price for our redemption. He had made provision for us to share the throne of God. Angel messengers connect earth with heaven, and all mankind's deeds are open to the eye of Infinite Justice. Paul's words were like a shout of victory above the roar of battle. Though he might die, the gospel would not perish.

Never had that assembly listened to words like these. They struck a chord that vibrated in the hearts of even the most hardened. Light blazed into the minds of many who later gladly followed its rays. The truths Paul spoke on that day were destined to shake nations and to live through all time, still influencing people when the lips that had spoken them would be silent in a martyr's grave.

Nero Hears God's Last Call

Never had Nero heard truth as he heard it on this occasion. He trembled with terror at the thought of a tribunal where he, the ruler of the world, would finally be arraigned. He feared the apostle's God, and he dared not pass sentence on Paul. A sense of awe restrained his bloodthirsty spirit.

For a moment, heaven was opened to the hardened Nero, and its peace and purity seemed desirable. But only for a moment did he welcome the thought of pardon. Then he issued the command to take Paul back to his dungeon. As the door closed on the messenger of God, the door of repentance closed forever against the emperor of Rome. No ray of light would ever again penetrate the darkness that surrounded him.

Not long after this, Nero sailed on his infamous expedition to Greece, where he disgraced himself and his kingdom by his degrading antics. Returning to Rome, he engaged in scenes of revolting immorality. In the midst of these low festivities, there was an alarming sound in the streets. Galba, at the head of an army, was marching rapidly on Rome, rebellion had broken out in the city, and the streets were filled with an enraged mob threatening death to the emperor and his supporters.

Afraid that the mob would torture him, the wretched tyrant thought to take his own life, but at the critical moment his courage failed. He fled from the city in cowardly disgrace and sought shelter at a country retreat a few miles away. But his hiding place was soon discovered, and as the pursuing horsemen drew near, he called a slave to his aid and killed himself. In this way the tyrant Nero died at the age of thirty-two.

Paul Pours Out His Heart in His Last Letter[*]

Paul returned to his cell from the judgment hall, realizing that his enemies would not rest until they had brought about his death. But for a time truth had triumphed. For Paul to have proclaimed a crucified and risen Savior to that huge crowd was a victory in itself. The work that had begun that day would grow, and neither Nero nor all other enemies of Christ would be able to destroy it.

Sitting in his gloomy cell day after day, knowing that at a word from Nero his life could be sacrificed, Paul thought of Timothy and decided to send for him. He had left Timothy at Ephesus when he made his last journey to Rome. Timothy had shared Paul's labors and sufferings, and their friendship had grown deeper and more sacred until to Paul, Timothy was everything that a son could be to an honored father. In his loneliness, Paul longed to see him.

Even under the best of circumstances, it would take several months for Timothy to reach Rome from Asia Minor. Paul knew that his life was uncertain, and while he urged Timothy to come without delay, he dictated the testimony that he might not live long enough to speak in person. His heart was filled with loving concern for his son in the gospel and for the church under his care.

The apostle urged Timothy: "Stir up the gift of God which is in you through the laying on of my hands. For God has not given us a spirit of fear, but of power and of love and of a sound mind.

"Therefore do not be ashamed of the testimony of our Lord, nor of me His prisoner, but share with me in the sufferings for the gospel according to the power of God." "For this reason I also suffer these things; nevertheless I am not ashamed, for I know whom I have believed and am persuaded that He is able to keep what I have committed to Him until that Day."

Through his long service Paul had never wavered in his allegiance to his Savior. Before scowling Pharisees or Roman authorities or the convicted sinners in the Macedonian dungeon, reasoning with panic-stricken sailors on the shipwrecked vessel, or standing alone before Nero—he had never been ashamed of the cause he represented. No opposition or persecution had been able to make him stop presenting Jesus.

---

* This chapter is based on 2 Timothy.

"You therefore, my son," Paul continued, "be strong in the grace that is in Christ Jesus. . . . Endure hardship as a good soldier of Jesus Christ."

Grace Enlarges the Minister's Capabilities

True ministers of God will not refuse hardship. From the Source that never fails, they draw strength to overcome temptation and to perform the duties God places on them. Their hearts go out in longing desire to do acceptable service. "The grace that is in Christ Jesus" enables them to be faithful witnesses of the things they have heard. They commit this knowledge to faithful Christians, who in their turn teach others.

In this letter Paul held up before the younger worker a high ideal: "Do your best to present yourself to God as one approved by him, a worker who has no need to be ashamed, rightly explaining the word of truth" (NRSV). "Flee also youthful lusts; but pursue righteousness, faith, love, peace with those who call on the Lord out of a pure heart. But avoid foolish and ignorant disputes, knowing that they generate strife." Be "able to teach, patient, in humility correcting those who are in opposition, if God perhaps will grant them repentance, so that they may know the truth."

The apostle warned Timothy against false teachers who would try to enter the church: "Know this, that in the last days perilous times will come: For men will be lovers of themselves, lovers of money, boasters, proud, blasphemers, disobedient to parents, unthankful, unholy, . . . having a form of godliness but denying its power. And from such people turn away!"

"But you must continue in the things which you have learned and been assured of, knowing from whom you have learned them, and that from childhood you have known the Holy Scriptures, which are able to make you wise for salvation. . . .

"All scripture is given by inspiration of God, and is profitable for doctrine, for reproof, for correction, for instruction in righteousness, that the man of God may be complete, thoroughly equipped for every good work." The Bible is the armory where we may get equipped for the struggle. The shield of faith must be in our hand, and with the sword of the Spirit—the Word of God—we are to cut our way through the obstructions and entanglements of sin.

Timothy's Call to Preach

Paul knew that faithful, earnest work would have to be done in the churches, and he wrote to Timothy: "Preach the word! Be ready in season and out of season. Convince, rebuke, exhort, with all longsuffering and teaching." Calling Timothy before the judgment bar of God, Paul urged him to be ready to witness for God before large congregations and private circles, along the road and at the fireside, to friends and to enemies, in safety or hardship and danger.

Fearing that Timothy's mild, yielding personality might lead him to avoid an essential part of his work, Paul called on him to be faithful in condemning sin. Yet he was to do this "with all longsuffering and teaching," explaining his rebukes by the Word.

It is difficult to hate sin and at the same time show tenderness for the sinner. We must guard against being too severe with the wrongdoer, but we must not lose sight of how terribly sinful sin is. There is danger of showing such great toleration for error that the person doing wrong will look on himself as not deserving any correction.

How Ministers Can Become Tools of Satan

Ministers of the gospel sometimes allow their patience with those in error to degenerate into toleration of sins, and even participation in them. They excuse what God condemns, and after a time they become so blinded that they commend the ones whom God commands them to rebuke. Those who have blunted their spiritual senses by being sinfully lenient toward those whom God condemns will soon commit a greater sin by being severe and harsh toward those whom God approves.

By their pride in human wisdom and by their distaste for the truths of God's Word, many who feel well able to teach others will turn away from the requirements of God. "The time will come when they will not endure sound doctrine, but according to their own desires, because they have itching ears, they will heap up for themselves teachers; and they will turn their ears away from the truth, and be turned aside to fables."

In these words the apostle refers to professing Christians who make their own desires their guide and in this way become slaves to self. Such people are willing to listen only to doctrines that do not rebuke sin or condemn their pleasure-loving lives. They choose teachers who flatter them. And among professing ministers there are those who preach human opinions instead of the Word of God.

God has decreed that until the close of time His holy law, unchanged in the smallest detail, is still to hold its claim on human beings. Christ came to show that it is based on the broad foundation of love to God and love to man, and that obedience to its instructions is the whole duty of mankind. His own life was an example of obedience to the law of God.

But the enemy of all righteousness has led men and women to disobey the law. As Paul foresaw, the majority has chosen teachers who present myths. Many, both ministers and people, are trampling the commandments of God under their feet. The Creator is insulted, and Satan laughs triumphantly over his success.

The True Remedy for Social Evils

Contempt for God's law results in an increasing distaste for religion, an increase of pride, love of pleasure, disobedience to parents, and self-indulgence. Thoughtful people everywhere are anxiously asking, What can be done to correct these evils? The answer is, "Preach the Word." The Bible is a transcript of the will of God, an expression of divine wisdom. It will guide all who obey its instruction, keeping them from wasting their lives in misguided effort.

After Infinite Wisdom has spoken, there can be no doubtful questions for us to settle. God simply requires obedience.

Paul was about to finish his life's course, and he wanted Timothy to take his place, guarding the church from fables and heresies. He urged him to resist all activities and entanglements that would prevent him from giving himself completely to his work for God; to endure cheerfully the opposition, accusations, and persecution; to show beyond a doubt that his ministry was genuine.

Paul clung to the cross as his only guarantee of success. The Savior's love was the motive that upheld him in his conflicts with self and in his struggles against the unfriendliness of the world and the opposition of his enemies.

In these days of danger the church needs an army of workers who have educated themselves to be useful and who have a deep experience in the things of God. It needs people who will not run from trial and responsibility, who are brave and true, and who will "preach the Word" with lips touched with holy fire. Because there are so few workers of this kind, fatal errors, like deadly poison, stain the morals and crush the hopes of a large part of the human race.

Will young men accept the holy trust? Will they obey the apostle's charge and hear the call to duty, in spite of all the temptations to selfishness and ambition?

Paul concluded his letter with the urgent request for Timothy to come soon, before winter if possible. He spoke of his loneliness and mentioned that he had sent Tychicus to Ephesus. After speaking about his trial before Nero, how the other Christians had deserted him, and about the sustaining grace of God, Paul closed by entrusting his beloved Timothy to the Chief Shepherd who, though the undershepherds might be struck down, would still care for His flock.

Paul Dies for the One Who Died for Him

At Paul's final trial, Nero had been so strongly impressed with the force of the apostle's words that he put off making a decision, neither acquitting nor condemning the servant of God. But the emperor's evil disposition soon returned. Exasperated by his inability to stop the spread of the Christian religion even in the imperial household, Nero condemned Paul to a martyr's death. Because a Roman citizen could not be subjected to torture, the apostle was sentenced to be beheaded.

Few spectators were allowed to come to the execution, for Paul's persecutors feared that converts might be won to Christianity by the scene of his death. But even the hardened soldiers listened to his words and were amazed to see him cheerful, even joyous, as he neared his death. More than one accepted the Savior, and soon they also fearlessly sealed their faith with their blood.

Even to his last hour the life of Paul testified to the truth of his words to the Corinthians: "For it is the God who commanded light to shine out of darkness, who has shone in our hearts to give the light of the knowledge of the glory of God in the face of Jesus Christ. . . .

"We are hard pressed on every side, yet not crushed; we are perplexed, but not in despair; persecuted, but not forsaken; struck down, but not destroyed" (2 Corinthians 4:6–9).

The heaven-born peace on Paul's face won many to the gospel. All who associated with him felt the influence of his union with Christ. His own life gave convincing power to his preaching. Here lies the power of truth: the spontaneous, unconscious influence of a holy life is the most convincing sermon we can give in favor of Christianity. Argument may only stir up opposition, but a godly example is impossible to resist completely.

The apostle forgot about his own approaching sufferings in his concern for those whom he was about to leave to cope with prejudice, hatred, and persecution. He assured the few Christians who accompanied him to the place of execution that of all the promises given for the Lord's tried and faithful children, none would fail. For a little while the Christians might not have earthly comforts, but they could encourage their hearts with the assurance of God's faithfulness. Soon the glad morning of peace and perfect day would dawn.

Why Paul Was Not Afraid

The apostle was looking into the great future with joyous hope and longing expectation. As he stood at the place of martyrdom, he did not see the executioner's sword or the earth that would so soon receive his blood. He looked up through the calm blue heaven of that summer day to the throne of the Eternal.

This man of faith saw the ladder of Jacob's vision—Christ connecting earth with heaven. He called to mind how patriarchs and prophets relied on the One who was his support, and from these holy men he heard the assurance that God is true. His fellow apostles who did not count their lives dear to themselves so that they could bear the light of the cross in the dark mazes of unfaithfulness—these he heard witnessing to Jesus as the Son of God, the Savior of the world. From the rack, the stake, the dungeon, from dens and caves of the earth, there fell on his ear the martyr's shout of triumph, declaring, "I know whom I have believed."

Ransomed by Christ's sacrifice and clothed in His righteousness, Paul had the assurance of the Spirit in himself that He who conquered death is able to keep that which is committed to His trust. His mind grasped the Savior's promise, "I will raise him up at the last day" (John 6:40). His hopes centered on the second coming of his Lord, and as the sword of the executioner came down, the martyr's thought sprang forward to meet the Life-Giver.

Nearly twenty centuries have passed since Paul poured out his blood for the Word of God and the testimony of Jesus. No faithful hand recorded the last scenes in the life of this holy man, but Inspiration has preserved his dying testimony. Like a trumpet fanfare his voice has rung out through all the ages since, giving courage to thousands of witnesses for Christ, and in sorrow-stricken hearts awakening the echo of his own triumphant joy: "I have fought the good fight, I have finished the race, I have kept the faith. Finally, there is laid up for me the crown of righteousness, which the Lord, the righteous Judge, will give me on that Day, and not to me only but also to all who have loved His appearing" (2 Timothy 4:7, 8).

The Apostle Peter, a Faithful Undershepherd*

During the busy years that followed the Day of Pentecost, the apostle Peter worked untiringly to reach the Jews who came to Jerusalem at the time of the annual festivals. The talents he possessed were invaluable to the early Christian church. He carried a double responsibility: he was an effective witness about the Messiah to unbelievers, and at the same time strengthened the believers' faith in Christ.

After Peter had been led to surrender self and rely entirely on divine power, he received his call as an undershepherd. Christ had said to Peter before his denial, "When you have returned to Me, strengthen your brethren" (Luke 22:32), and these words told of the work he was to do for those who would come to the faith. Peter's experience of sin and repentance had prepared him for this work. Not until he learned his weakness could he know the believer's need to depend on Christ. He had come to understand that we can walk safely only as we rely on the Savior, in complete distrust of self.

At the last meeting by the sea, Jesus tested Peter by repeating the question three times, "Do you love Me?" (John 21:15–17), and then He restored him to his place among the Twelve. Jesus gave him his work: he was not only to seek those outside the fold, but to be a shepherd to the sheep.

Christ mentioned only one condition of service—"Do you love Me?" Knowledge, a generous spirit, eloquence, zeal—all are essential, but without the love of Christ in the heart, the Christian minister is a failure. This love is a living principle revealed in the heart. If the character of the shepherd illustrates the truth he teaches, the Lord will set the seal of His approval on the work.

Christ's Patience With Peter Is a Lesson

Although Peter had denied his Lord, the love Jesus had for him never wavered. And, remembering his own weakness and failure, the apostle was to deal with the sheep and lambs as tenderly as Christ had dealt with him.

Human beings are prone to deal harshly with those who do wrong. They cannot read the heart; they do not know its struggle and pain. They need to learn about the rebuke that is love, the warning that speaks hope.

---

* This chapter is based on 1 Peter.

Throughout his ministry Peter faithfully watched over the flock and proved himself worthy of the responsibility the Lord had given him. He exalted Jesus as the Savior and brought his own life under the discipline of the Master Worker. He worked to educate the believers for active service and inspired many young men to give themselves to the work of the ministry. His influence as a teacher and leader increased. While he never lost his burden for the Jews, he gave his testimony in many countries.

In the later years of his ministry, his letters strengthened the faith of those who were experiencing trial and affliction and those who were in danger of losing their hold on God. These letters bear the marks of one whose entire being had been transformed by grace and whose hope of eternal life was solid and unchanging.

Even in severe trouble, the early Christians rejoiced in this hope of an inheritance in the new earth. "In this you greatly rejoice," Peter wrote, "though now for a little, if need be, you have been grieved by various trials, that the genuineness of your faith, being much more precious than gold that perishes, though it is tested by fire, may be found to praise, honor, and glory at the revelation of Jesus Christ."

The apostle's words have special significance for those who live when "the end of all things is at hand." His words of courage are needed by every Christian who would keep the faith "steadfast to the end" (Hebrews 3:14).

The apostle worked to teach the believers to keep the mind from wandering to forbidden themes or from using its energies on unimportant subjects. They must avoid reading, seeing, or hearing things that will suggest impure thoughts. The heart must be faithfully guarded, or evils from outside will awaken evils within, and the believer will wander in darkness. "Gird up . . . your mind," Peter wrote, "be sober, and rest your hope fully upon the grace that is to be brought to you at the revelation of Jesus Christ, . . . not conforming yourselves to the former lusts, as in your ignorance."

"You were not redeemed with corruptible things, like silver or gold, from your aimless conduct received by tradition from your fathers, but with the precious blood of Christ, as of a lamb without blemish and without spot."

If silver and gold were enough to purchase salvation, how easily it could have been accomplished by Him who says, "The silver is Mine, and the gold is Mine" (Haggai 2:8). But the transgressor could be redeemed only by the blood of the Son of God. And as the crowning blessing of salvation, "the gift of God is eternal life in Christ Jesus our Lord" (Romans 6:23).

The Fruit Produced by the Love of Truth

Peter continued, "Love one another fervently with a pure heart." The Word of God is the channel through which the Lord reveals His Spirit and power. Obedience to the Word produces fruit—"sincere love of the brethren." When truth becomes a living principle in the life, the person is "born anew, not of perishable but of imperishable seed, through the living and enduring word of God" (NRSV). This new birth is the result of receiving Christ as the Word. When the Holy Spirit impresses divine truths on the heart, He awakens new understandings and stirs up energies that had been dormant to help us cooperate with God.

The Great Teacher spoke many of His most precious lessons to those who did not understand them at the time. After His ascension, when the Holy Spirit brought His teachings to their remembrance, their slumbering senses awoke. The meaning of these truths flashed on their minds as a new revelation. Then the men He had appointed proclaimed the mighty truth, "The Word became flesh and dwelt among us, . . . full of grace and truth." "And of His fullness we have all received, and grace for grace" (John 1:14, 16).

The apostle urged the believers to study the Scriptures. Peter realized that every Christian who is finally victorious will experience perplexity and trial. But an understanding of the Scriptures will bring to mind promises that will comfort the heart and strengthen faith in the Mighty One.

Many to whom Peter addressed his letters were living among the heathen, and much depended on their remaining true to their calling. "You are a chosen generation, a royal priesthood, a holy nation, His own special people, that you may proclaim the praises of Him who called you out of darkness into His marvelous light. . . .

"Beloved, I beg you as sojourners and pilgrims, abstain from fleshly lusts which war against the soul."

Our Duty to the Government

The apostle outlined the attitude that believers should have toward civil authorities. "Submit yourselves to every ordinance of man for the Lord's sake, whether to the king as supreme, or to governors, as to those who are sent by him for the punishment of evildoers and for the praise of those who do good. For this is the will of God, that by doing good you may put to silence the ignorance of foolish men."

Those who were servants were to remain obedient to their masters, "for this is commendable," the apostle explained, "if because of conscience toward God one endures grief, suffering wrongfully. For what credit is it if, when you are beaten for your faults, you take it patiently? But when you do good and suffer, if you take it patiently, this is commendable before God. . . . Christ also suffered for us, leaving us an example, that you should follow in His steps:

'Who committed no sin,
Nor was deceit found in His mouth';

who, when He was reviled, did not revile in return; when He suffered, He did not threaten, but committed Himself to Him who judges righteously."

The apostle encouraged the women in the faith to be modest. "Do not let your adorning be merely outward—arranging the hair, wearing gold, or putting on fine apparel—rather let it be the hidden person of the heart, with the incorruptible beauty of a gentle and quiet spirit, which is very precious in the sight of God."

The lesson applies in every age. In

the life of the true Christian the outward adorning is always in harmony with the inward peace and holiness. Self-denial and sacrifice will mark the Christian's life. In the way we dress, people will see evidence that our choices are converted. It is right to love beauty and desire it, but God wants us to love first the highest beauty, the one that is imperishable—the "fine linen, white and clean" (Revelation 19:14), that all the holy ones of earth will wear. This robe of Christ's righteousness will make them beloved here and will be their badge of admission to the palace of the King.

Looking ahead to the dangerous times that the church was about to enter, the apostle wrote: "Do not be surprised at the fiery ordeal that is taking place among you to test you" (NRSV). Trial is to purify God's children from the impurities of earthliness. It is because God is leading His children that hard experiences come to them. Trials and obstacles are His chosen methods of discipline and the condition of success. Some people have qualifications that, rightly directed, they could use in His work. He brings these followers of His into various situations and circumstances where they can discover the defects they don't even know they have. He gives them opportunity to overcome these defects. Often He permits the fires of affliction to burn so that they may be purified.

God permits no affliction to come to His children except what is essential for their good now and eternally. Everything that He brings in test and trial comes so that they may gain deeper devotion and greater strength to carry forward the victories of the cross.

There had been a time when Peter was unwilling to see the cross in the work of Christ. When the Savior made known His approaching sufferings and death, Peter exclaimed, "Far be it from You, Lord; this shall not happen to You!" (Matthew 16:22). It was a bitter lesson, one that he learned slowly—that the path of Christ on earth went through agony and humiliation. Now, when his once-active body was stooped with the burden of years, he could write, "Beloved, . . . rejoice to the extent that you partake of Christ's sufferings, that when His glory is revealed, you may also be glad with exceeding joy."

Undershepherds Are to Be Watchful

Addressing the church elders about their responsibilities as undershepherds of Christ's flock, the apostle wrote: "Shepherd the flock of God which is among you, . . . not for dishonest gain but eagerly; not as being lords over those entrusted to you, but being examples to the flock; and when the Chief Shepherd appears, you will receive the crown of glory that does not fade away."

Ministry means earnest, personal labor. Pastors are needed—faithful shepherds—who will neither flatter God's people nor treat them harshly, but who will feed them the bread of life.

God calls the undershepherd to meet alienation, bitterness, and jealousy in the church, and he will need to labor in the spirit of Christ. People may misjudge and criticize the servant of God. When this happens, let him remember that "the wisdom that is from above is first pure, then peaceable, gentle, willing to yield. . . . Now the fruit of righteousness is sown in peace by those who make peace" (James 3:17, 18).

If the gospel minister chooses the least self-sacrificing part, leaving the work of personal ministry for someone else, his labors will not be acceptable to God. He has mistaken his calling if he is unwilling to do the personal work that the care of the flock demands.

The true shepherd loses sight of self. By personal ministry in the homes of the people, he learns their needs and comforts their distresses, relieves their spiritual hunger, and wins their hearts to God. The angels of heaven assist the minister in this work.

The apostle outlined some general principles that everyone in church fellowship is to follow. The younger members are to follow the example of their elders in showing Christlike humility:

" 'God resists the proud,
But gives grace to the humble.'

Therefore humble yourselves under the mighty hand of God, that He may exalt you in due time, casting all your care upon Him, for He cares for you."

Peter wrote this way at a time of special trial to the church. Soon the church was to undergo terrible persecution. Within a few years many leaders would lay down their lives for the gospel. Soon grievous "wolves" would enter in, not sparing the flock. But with words of encouragement and cheer Peter pointed the believers "to an inheritance incorruptible and undefiled and that does not fade away." "May the God of all grace," he prayed fervently, "after you have suffered a while, perfect, establish, strengthen, and settle you."

Peter Crucified at Rome[*]

In his second letter the apostle Peter explains the divine plan for developing Christian character. He writes that God has "given to us exceedingly great and precious promises, that through these you may be partakers of the divine nature, having escaped the corruption that is in the world through lust."

"Giving all diligence, add to your faith virtue, to virtue knowledge, to knowledge self-control, to self-control perseverance, to perseverance godliness, to godliness brotherly kindness, and to brotherly kindness love."

The apostle presents the ladder of Christian progress to the believers. Every step represents advancement in knowing God. We are saved by climbing rung after rung to the height of Christ's ideal for us. God wants to see men and women reaching the highest standard, and when they lay hold of Christ by faith, when they claim His promises as their own, when they seek for the Holy Spirit, God will make them complete in Him.

Having received the faith of the gospel, the believer is to add virtue to his character, and in this way prepare the mind for the knowledge of God. This knowledge is the foundation of all true service and the only real protection against temptation. This alone can make us like God in character. No good gift is kept back from anyone who sincerely desires the righteousness of God.

No one needs to fail to reach, in his or her sphere, perfection of Christian character. God places before us the example of Christ's character. In His humanity, perfected by a life of constant resistance of evil, the Savior showed that through cooperation with Divinity, human beings may reach perfection of character in this life. We may obtain complete victory.

Overcoming Every Fault by Grace

The Bible holds out to the believer the wonderful possibility of being obedient to all the principles of the law. But by ourselves we are unable to reach this condition. The holiness that we must have is the result of divine grace's working as we submit to the discipline and restraining influences of the Spirit of truth. The incense of Christ's righteousness fills every act of obedience with divine fragrance. Christians are never to give up in overcoming every fault. Constantly they are to ask the

---

[*] This chapter is based on 2 Peter.

Savior to heal the disorders of their sin-sick lives. The Lord grants strength to overcome to those who in repentance turn to Him for help.

The work of transformation from unholiness to holiness is a continuous one. Day by day God works for our sanctification, and we are to cooperate with Him. Our Savior is always ready to answer the prayer of the humble person. He gladly grants the blessings we need in our struggle against the evils that surround us.

Those who become weary and allow the enemy of souls to rob them of the Christian graces that have been developing in their hearts and lives are in a truly sad condition. "He who lacks these things," says the apostle, "is shortsighted, even to blindness, and has forgotten that he was cleansed from his old sins."

Peter's faith in God's power to save had become stronger over the years. He had proved that there is no possibility of failure for the Christian who climbs by faith to the top rung of the ladder. Knowing that soon he would die as a martyr for his faith, Peter once more urged his fellow believers to keep going steadily in Christ's path: "Therefore, brethren, be even more diligent to make your call and election sure, for if you do these things you will never stumble; for so an entrance will be supplied to you abundantly into the everlasting kingdom of our Lord and Savior Jesus Christ."

"I think it is right, as long as I am in this tent, to stir you up by reminding you, knowing that shortly I must put off my tent, just as our Lord Jesus Christ showed me. Moreover I will be careful to ensure that you always have a reminder of these things after my decease."

Why Peter Was Sure of Gospel Truth

"We did not follow cleverly devised myths" about Jesus, he reminded the believers, "but we had been eyewitnesses of his majesty. For he received honor and glory from God the Father when that voice was conveyed to him by the Majestic Glory, saying, 'This is my Son, my Beloved, with whom I am well pleased.' We ourselves heard this voice come from heaven, while we were with him on the holy mountain" (NRSV).

Yet there was another even more convincing witness. Peter declared, "We have the prophetic word confirmed, which you do well to heed as a light that shines in a dark place, until the day dawns and the morning star rises in your hearts . . . prophecy never came by the will of man, but holy men of God spoke as they were moved by the Holy Spirit."

While exalting true prophecy, the apostle solemnly warned the church against the torch of false prophecy, lifted up by "false teachers" who would bring in "destructive heresies, even denying the Lord." The apostle compared these false teachers, who many of the believers thought were true, to "wells without water, clouds carried by a tempest, for whom is reserved the blackness of darkness forever. . . .

"It would have been better for them not to have known the way of righteousness, than having known it, to turn from the holy commandment delivered to them."

Looking down the ages, Peter was inspired to outline conditions in the world just before the second coming of Christ. "Scoffers will come in the last days," he wrote, "walking according to their own lusts, and saying, 'Where is the promise of His coming?'" However, not everyone would be ensnared by the enemy's traps. There would be faithful ones able to recognize the signs of the times, a remnant who would endure to the end.

Peter's Faith in the Second Coming of Christ

Peter kept the hope of Christ's return alive in his heart, and he assured the church that the Savior's promise, "I will come again" (John 14:3), would certainly be fulfilled. His coming might seem to be delayed for a long time, but the apostle assured them, "The Lord is not slow about his promise, as some think of slowness, but is patient with you, not wanting any to perish, but all to come to repentance" (NRSV).

"Since all these things will be dissolved, what manner of persons ought you to be in holy conduct and godliness, looking for and hastening the coming of the day of God, because of which the heavens will be dissolved, being on fire, and the elements will melt with fervent heat? Nevertheless we, according to His promise, look for new heavens and a new earth in which righteousness dwells."

"Beloved, since you know this beforehand, beware lest you also fall from your own steadfastness, being led away with the error of the wicked; but grow in the grace and knowledge of our Lord and Savior Jesus Christ."

Peter closed his ministry in Rome, where the emperor Nero ordered his imprisonment about the time of Paul's final arrest. In this way the two apostles, for many years widely separated in their labors, were to bear their last witness for Christ in the world's greatest city, and on its soil to shed their blood as the seed of an immense harvest of believers.

Peter had faced danger bravely and had shown a noble courage in preaching a crucified, risen, and ascended Savior. As he lay in his cell, he called to mind Christ's words: "When you were younger, you girded yourself and walked where you wished; but when you are old, you will stretch out your hands, and another will gird you and carry you where you do not wish" (John 21:18). Jesus had revealed ahead of time that the disciple's hands would be stretched out on the cross.

As a Jew and foreigner, Peter was condemned to be scourged and crucified. In looking ahead to this fearful death, the apostle remembered his sin in denying Jesus in the hour of His trial. Once he had been unready to acknowledge the cross, but now he counted it a joy to yield up his life for the gospel. Yet he felt that to die in the same way his Master had died was too great an honor. He had been forgiven by Christ, but he could never forgive himself. Nothing could lessen the bitterness of his sorrow and repentance. As a last favor he asked his executioners to nail him to the cross with his head downward. They granted this request, and so the great apostle Peter died in this way.

John, the Beloved Disciple

John is known as "the disciple whom Jesus loved" (John 21:20). He was one of the three chosen to witness Christ's glory on the mount of transfiguration and His agony in Gethsemane, and it was to his care that our Lord entrusted His mother in those last hours of anguish on the cross.

John clung to Christ like a vine clings to a stately pillar. He braved the dangers of the judgment hall and lingered near the cross, and when the news came that Christ had risen, he ran to the tomb, getting there even before Peter.

John did not naturally possess a beautiful character. He was proud, self-assertive, ambitious for honor, reckless, and resentful when he thought others did not treat him well. He and his brother were called "Sons of Thunder" (Mark 3:17). Evil temper and desire for revenge were in the beloved disciple, but beneath this the divine Teacher saw the sincere, loving heart. Jesus rebuked John's self-seeking, disappointed his ambitions, and tested his faith, but He revealed to him the beauty of holiness, the transforming power of love.

John's defects came out strongly on several occasions. At one time Christ sent messengers to a Samaritan village to ask for refreshments for Him and His disciples. But when the Savior approached the town, instead of inviting Him to be their guest, the Samaritans refused to give the courtesies they would have offered a common traveler.

Such coldness and disrespect to their Master filled the disciples with anger. In their zeal James and John said, "Lord, do You want us to command fire to come down from heaven and consume them, just as Elijah did?" Their words brought Jesus pain. "You do not know what manner of spirit you are of. For the Son of Man did not come to destroy men's lives but to save them" (Luke 9:54–56).

Christ Wants Only Willing Surrender

Christ does not force people to receive Him. Satan and those under his spirit try to compel the conscience. Under a pretended zeal for righteousness, some people who are working with evil angels bring suffering on other human beings in order to "convert" them to their ideas of religion. But Christ always seeks to win by revealing His love. He wants only the willing surrender of the heart under the influence of love.

On another occasion James and

John used their mother to ask for the highest positions in Christ's kingdom. These young disciples held onto the hope that He would take His throne and kingly power as the people wanted Him to do.

But the Savior answered, "You do not know what you ask. Are you able to drink the cup that I drink, and be baptized with the baptism that I am baptized with?" They answered confidently, "We are able."

"You will indeed drink the cup that I drink, and with the baptism I am baptized with you will be baptized," Christ declared. Ahead of Him was a cross instead of a throne! James and John would in fact share their Master's suffering—one destined to swift-coming death by beheading, the other, longest of all to follow his Master in labor, in being spoken against, and in persecution. "But to sit on My right hand or on My left," He continued, "is not Mine to give, but it is for those for whom it is prepared." (Mark 10:38–40.)

Jesus rebuked the pride and ambition of the two disciples. "Whoever desires to become great among you, let him be your servant. And whoever desires to be first among you, let him be your slave" (Matthew 20:26, 27). In the kingdom of God, position results from character. The crown and the throne are evidences of having conquered self through the grace of Christ.

Many years later, the Lord Jesus revealed to John how to come near to His kingdom: "To him who overcomes I will grant to sit with Me on My throne, as I also overcame and sat down with My Father on His throne" (Revelation 3:21).

The one who stands nearest to Christ will be the one who has drunk most deeply of His spirit of self-sacrificing love—love that moves the disciple to work and sacrifice even to death to help save humanity.

John Learned His Lessons Well

At another time, James and John met someone who was not an acknowledged follower of Christ but was casting out devils in His name. The disciples forbade the man to work and thought they were right. But Christ rebuked them: "Do not forbid him, for no one who works a miracle in My name can soon afterward speak evil of Me" (Mark 9:39). James and John thought they were defending Christ's honor, but they began to see they were jealous for their own. They admitted their error and accepted the rebuke.

John treasured every lesson and tried to bring his life into harmony with God's pattern. He had begun to recognize the glory of Christ—"the glory as of the only begotten of the Father, full of grace and truth" (John 1:14).

John's affection for his Master did not cause Christ's love for him—it was the effect of that love. Under the transforming love of Christ he became subdued and humble. Self was hid in Jesus. More than all his companions, John yielded himself to the power of that awe-inspiring life. His Master's lessons were engraved on his heart. When he testified about the Savior's grace, his simple language was eloquent with the love that saturated his whole being.

The Savior loved all the Twelve,

but John had the most receptive spirit. Younger than the others, with more of the child's simple trust, he opened his heart to Jesus. In this way he came more into sympathy with Christ, and it was he who communicated the Savior's deepest spiritual teaching to the people. John could talk of the Father's love as none of the other disciples could. The beauty of holiness that had transformed him gleamed with Christ-like radiance from his face, and fellowship with Christ became his one desire.

"Beloved, now we are children of God; and it has not yet been revealed what we shall be, but we know that when He is revealed, we shall be like Him, for we shall see Him as He is" (1 John 3:2).

John, Faithful Witness for Christ*

John experienced the Spirit's outpouring on the Day of Pentecost with the other disciples, and with fresh power he continued to speak the words of life to the people. He was a powerful preacher, on fire for the Lord, and deeply in earnest. In beautiful language and with a musical voice he told about Christ in a way that impressed hearts. The soaring power of the truths he spoke and the zeal that characterized his teachings gave him access to all classes, and his life was in harmony with his teachings.

Christ had asked the disciples to love one another as He had loved them. "A new commandment I give to you," He had said, "that you love one another; as I have loved you, that you also love one another" (John 13:34). After they had witnessed Christ's sufferings, and after the Holy Spirit had rested on them at Pentecost, they had a clearer concept of what kind of love they must have for one another. Then John could say: "By this we know love, because He laid down His life for us. And we also ought to lay down our lives for the brethren."

After Pentecost, when the disciples went out to proclaim a living Savior, they rejoiced in the sweetness of fellowship with other believers. They were tender, thoughtful, self-denying, revealing the love that Christ had urged on them. By unselfish words and deeds they worked to kindle this love in other hearts.

The believers were always to cherish love like this. Their lives were to magnify a Savior who could justify them by His righteousness.

But gradually a change came. Dwelling on mistakes, speaking and listening to unkind criticism, the believers lost sight of the Savior and His love. They became more particular about the theory of the faith than its practice. They lost brotherly love, and, saddest of all, did not know that they had lost it. They did not realize that happiness and joy were going out of their lives and that they would soon walk in darkness.

A Tragic Change Comes Into the Early Church

John realized that Christian love was dying out of the church. "Beloved, let us love one another," he wrote, "for love is of God; and everyone who loves is born of God and knows God. He who does not love does not know

---

* This chapter is based on the letters of John.

God, for God is love. In this the love of God was manifested toward us, that God has sent His only begotten Son into the world, that we might live through Him. In this is love, not that we loved God, but that He loved us and sent His Son to be the propitiation for our sins. Beloved, if God so loved us, we also ought to love one another."

"Whoever hates his brother is a murderer, and you know that no murderer has eternal life abiding in him.

"By this we know love, because He laid down His life for us. And we also ought to lay down our lives for the brethren."

The opposition of the world is not the greatest danger to the church. It is the evil cherished in the hearts of believers that brings their worst disaster and most certainly sets back God's cause. There is no surer way to weaken spirituality than by cherishing envy, fault-finding, and evil thoughts about others' motives. The strongest evidence that God has sent His Son into the world is the existence of harmony and union among people of different natures who form His church. But in order to bear this witness, their characters must conform to Christ's character and their wills to His will.

In the church today, many who claim to love the Savior do not love one another. Unbelievers are watching to see if the faith of professed Christians is having a sanctifying influence on their lives. Christians must not make it possible for the enemy to say, These people hate one another. The tie that binds together all the children of the same heavenly Father should be very close and tender.

Divine love calls us to show the same compassion that Christ showed. True Christians will not willingly permit someone in danger and need to go unwarned, uncared for. They will not be unfriendly or distant, leaving the mistaken one to plunge farther into unhappiness and discouragement.

Those who have never experienced the tender love of Christ cannot lead others to the fountain of life. Christ's love in the heart leads people to reveal Him in conversation, in a spirit of pity, in uplifting lives. Heaven measures the fitness of Christian workers by their ability to love as Christ loved.

"Let us not love in word or in tongue," the apostle wrote, "but in deed and in truth." We have completeness of character when the impulse to help others springs constantly from within. It is this love that makes the believers "the aroma of life leading to life" and enables God to bless their work. (2 Corinthians 2:16.)

True Love, the Best Gift God Can Give Us

Supreme love for God and unselfish love for one another—this is the best gift our heavenly Father can bestow. This love is not an impulse but a divine principle. It is found only in the heart where Jesus reigns. "We love Him because He first loved us." Love modifies the character, governs the impulses and passions, and ennobles the affections. This love sweetens the life and spreads a refining influence on all around.

John worked to lead the believers to understand that this love, filling the heart, would control every other motive and raise those who possessed it above the corrupting influences of the world. As this love became the central power in the life, their trust and confidence in God would be complete. They could know that they would receive from Him everything they needed for their present and eternal good. "Love has been perfected among us in this," John writes, "that we may have boldness on the day of judgment; because as he is, so are we in this world. There is no fear in love, but perfect love casts out fear." "If we ask anything according to his will, he hears us. And if we know that he hears us . . . , we know that we have obtained the requests made of him" (NRSV).

"If we confess our sins, He is faithful and just to forgive us our sins and to cleanse us from all unrighteousness." The Lord does not require us to do some hard thing in order to gain forgiveness. We do not need to make long, tiring pilgrimages or perform painful acts of penance to find forgiveness for our sins. "Whoever confesses and forsakes" his sin "will have mercy" (Proverbs 28:13).

In heaven above, Christ is pleading for His church—those for whom He paid the redemption price of His blood. Neither life nor death can separate us from the love of God, not because we hold Him so firmly, but because He holds us so securely. If our salvation depended on our own efforts, we could not be saved, but it depends on the One who is behind all the promises. Our grasp on Him may seem weak, but as long as we stay united to Him, no one can pluck us out of His hand.

As the years went by and the number of believers grew, John worked even more faithfully and earnestly. Satan's delusions existed everywhere. By misrepresentation and falsehood, Satan's agents tried to stir up opposition against the doctrines of Christ, and as a result arguments and heresies were threatening the church. Some who professed Christ claimed that His love released them from obedience to the law of God. On the other hand, many taught that merely keeping the law, without faith in the blood of Christ, was enough to save them. Some held that Christ was a good man but denied His divinity. Some, living in their sins, were bringing heresies into the church. Many people were being led into skepticism and false teaching.

John Saw the Dangers Threatening the Church

John was sad to see these poisonous errors creeping into the church, and he met the emergency promptly and decisively. His letters breathe the spirit of love, as if he wrote with a pen dipped in love, but when he came in contact with those who were breaking God's law while claiming to live without sin, he did not hesitate to warn them of their dangerous deception.

Writing to an influential woman, he said: "Many deceivers have gone out into the world who do not confess Jesus Christ as coming in the flesh. This is a deceiver and an antichrist. . . . He who abides in the doctrine of Christ has both the Father and the Son. If anyone comes to you and does not bring this doctrine, do not receive him into your house nor greet him; for he who greets him shares in his evil deeds."

In these last days there are evils similar to those that threatened the early church. "You must have love," is the cry heard everywhere, especially from those who claim to be sanctified. But true love is too pure to cover unconfessed sin. While we are to love people, we are to make no compromise with evil. We are not to unite with the rebellious and call this love. God requires His people to stand for the right as firmly as John did in opposing soul-destroying errors.

The apostle teaches that we are to deal with sin and sinners clearly and directly. This is not inconsistent with true love. "Whoever commits sin," he wrote, "also commits lawlessness, and sin is lawlessness. And you know that He was manifested to take away our sins, and in Him there is no sin. Whoever abides in Him does not sin. Whoever sins has neither seen Him nor known Him."

As a witness for Christ, John did not enter into long, drawn-out arguments. He declared what he knew. He had been closely associated with Christ and had witnessed His miracles. For him the darkness had passed away; the true Light was shining. He spoke from the abundance of a heart overflowing with love for the Savior, and no power could stop his words.

"That which was from the beginning," he declared, "which we have heard, which we have seen with our eyes, which we have looked upon, and our hands have handled, concerning the Word of life . . . we declare to you."

Like John, all true believers may bear witness to what they have seen and heard and felt of the power of Christ.

John's Secret of True Sanctification

John's life gives us an example of true sanctification. During the years he associated closely with Christ, the Savior often warned him, and he accepted these reproofs. He saw his weaknesses, and the revelation humbled him. Day by day his heart was drawn out to Christ, until love for his Master made him lose sight of self. The strength and patience that he saw in the Son of God filled him with admiration. He yielded his resentful, ambitious temper to Christ, and divine love transformed his character.

The experience of Judas provides a striking contrast to this. He professed to be a disciple of Christ but had only the appearance of godliness. As he listened to the Savior's words, he often came under conviction, but he would not humble his heart or confess his sins. By resisting the divine influence, he dishonored the Master.

John battled earnestly against his faults, but Judas violated his conscience, fastening his habits of evil more securely on himself. The truth Christ taught did not match with Judas's desires, and he could not yield his ideas. He cherished covetousness, revengeful passions, and dark and moody thoughts, until Satan gained full control of him.

John and Judas had the same opportunities. Both associated closely with Jesus. Each had serious defects of character, and each had access to divine grace. But while one was learning from Jesus, the other just listened and did not change. One, overcoming sin each day, was sanctified through the truth; the other, resisting the transforming power of grace and indulging his selfish desires, became a slave to Satan.

Transformation like we see in John results from fellowship with Christ. There may be defects in our characters, yet when we become true disciples of Christ, we are changed until we become like Him whom we adore.

In his letters, John wrote, "Everyone who has this hope in Him purifies himself, just as He is pure." "He who says he abides in Him ought himself also to walk just as He walked." (1 John 3:3; 2:6.) As God is holy in His sphere, so we fallen human beings, through faith in Christ, are to be holy in our sphere.

Sanctification is God's purpose in all His dealings with His people. He has chosen them from eternity, so that they can be holy. He gave His Son to die for them to rid them of all the littleness of self. They can honor God only as they are transformed into His image and controlled by His Spirit. Then they can tell others what divine grace has done for them.

True sanctification comes as God develops in us the principle of love. "God is love, and he who abides in love abides in God, and God in him" (1 John 4:16). When Christ lives in the heart, He brings nobility into the life. Pure doctrine will blend with works of righteousness.

Those who want to have the blessings of sanctification must first learn the meaning of self-sacrifice. The cross of Christ is the central pillar on which hangs the "eternal weight of glory." "If anyone desires to come after Me," Christ says, "let him deny himself, and take up his cross, and follow Me." (2 Corinthians 4:17; Matthew 16:24.) God supports and strengthens anyone who is willing to follow in Christ's way.

True Sanctification Is a Lifework

Sanctification is not the work of a moment, an hour, a day, but of a lifetime. It does not come from a happy turn of feeling, but results from constantly dying to sin and constantly living for Christ. We will overcome not by occasional efforts, but by persevering discipline and hard conflict. As long as Satan reigns, we will have self to subdue and persistent sins to overcome. As long as life lasts, there will be no point that we can reach and then say, "I have fully arrived." Sanctification results from lifelong obedience.

None of the apostles or prophets ever claimed to be without sin. Men who have lived nearest to God, who would sacrifice life itself rather than knowingly commit a wrong act, have confessed the sinfulness of their nature. They have claimed no righteousness of their own but have trusted completely in Christ's righteousness.

The more clearly we recognize the purity of Christ's character, the more clearly we will see how very sinful sin is. We will be continually confessing our sins and humbling our hearts before Him. At every step forward our repentance will deepen. We will confess, "I know that in me (that is, in my flesh) nothing good dwells." "God forbid that I should boast except in the cross of our Lord Jesus Christ." (Romans 7:18; Galatians 6:14.) May no human lips dishonor God by saying, "I am sinless; I am holy." Sanctified lips will never give voice to such boastful, untrue words.

Those who feel inclined to claim great holiness should look into the mirror of God's law. As they understand its work as a revealer of the thoughts and motives of the heart, they will not boast of sinlessness. "If we say that we have no sin," John wrote, "we deceive ourselves, and the truth is not in us." "If we say that we have not sinned, we make Him a liar." "If we confess our sins, He is faithful and just to forgive us our sins and to cleanse us from all unrighteousness." (1 John 1:8, 10, 9.)

Some people profess to be holy and claim a right to the promises of God while they refuse to obey His commandments. But this is presumption. We will show that we have true love for God when we obey all His commandments. "He who says, 'I know Him,' and does not keep His commandments, is a liar, and the truth is not in him." "He who keeps His commandments abides in Him, and He in him." (1 John 2:4; 3:24.)

John did not teach that we earn salvation by obedience, but obedience is the fruit of faith and love. "You know that He was manifested to take away our sins; and in Him there is no sin. Whoever abides in Him does not sin. Whoever sins has neither seen Him nor known Him" (1 John 3:5, 6). If we abide in Christ, our feelings, our thoughts, our actions, will be in harmony with the will of God. The sanctified heart is in harmony with the teachings of God's law.

Faith Is the Key to Overcoming

Many who try to obey God's commandments have little peace or joy. These people do not correctly represent sanctification. The Lord wants all His sons and daughters to be happy, peaceful, and obedient. Through faith the believer possesses these blessings. Through faith, every lack in our characters can be filled, every defilement cleansed, every fault corrected, every excellence developed.

Prayer is heaven's appointed way to success in developing character. For forgiveness of sin, for the Holy Spirit, for a Christlike temper, for wisdom and strength to do His work, for any gift He has promised, we may ask, and the promise is, "You will receive."

It is in personal, private fellowship with Him that we are to think deeply about God's glorious ideal for human- ity. In all ages, as people have prayed and turned their thoughts to heaven, God has worked out His purpose for His children by unfolding the doctrines of grace gradually to their minds.

True sanctification means perfect love, perfect obedience, perfect conformity to God's will. We are to be sanctified through obeying the truth. It is our privilege to cut away from the entanglements of self and sin and move forward to perfection.

Many interpret the will of God to be what they want to do. These people have no conflicts with self. Others may sincerely struggle for a time against their selfish desire for pleasure and ease, but then they get tired of dying to self every day and of endless trouble. Death to self seems repulsive, and instead of resisting temptation, they fall under its power.

The Word of God leaves no room for compromise with evil. At whatever sacrifice of convenience or selfish indulgence, of effort or suffering, Christ's followers must continue to wage a constant battle with self.

The greatest praise we can bring to God is to become consecrated channels through whom He can work. Let us not refuse to give God that which, though we cannot gain merit by giving it, will bring us ruin if we deny it to Him. He asks for a whole heart—give it. It is His, both by creation and redemption. He asks for your intellect—give it. It is His. He asks for your money—give it. It is His. "Do you not know that . . . you are not your own? For you were bought at a price" (1 Corinthians 6:19, 20). God holds up before us the highest ideal—perfection. He asks us to be absolutely and completely for Him in this world, as He is for us in the presence of God.

"This is the will of God" concerning you, "your sanctification" (1 Thessalonians 4:3). Is it your will also? If you humble your heart and confess your sins, trusting in the merits of Jesus, He will forgive and cleanse you. God demands entire obedience to His law. Let your heart be filled with an intense longing for His righteousness.

As you contemplate the unimaginable riches of God's grace, you will come into possession of them, and your life will reveal the merits of the Savior's sacrifice, the protection of His righteousness, and His power to present you before the Father "without spot and blameless" (2 Peter 3:14).

John Is Exiled to Lonely Patmos

After more than half a century the enemies of the gospel succeeded in persuading the Roman emperor to use his power against the Christians. In the terrible persecution that followed, the apostle John did much to help other Christians courageously meet the trials that came to them. The old, tested servant of Jesus repeated the story of the crucified and risen Savior powerfully and eloquently. From his lips came the same glad message: "That which was from the beginning, which we have heard, which we have seen with our eyes, which we have looked upon, and our hands have handled, concerning the Word of life— . . . that which we have seen and heard we declare to you" (1 John 1:1–3).

John lived to be very old. He witnessed the destruction of Jerusalem and the temple. As the last surviving disciple who had been closely connected with the Savior, his message had great influence. His teachings led many to turn from unbelief.

The Jews were filled with bitter hatred against him. They said that their efforts would be useless as long as John's testimony kept ringing in the ears of the people. In order to help people forget the miracles and teachings of Jesus, they must silence the

voice of this bold witness. So John was summoned to Rome. His enemies hoped to bring about his death by accusing him of teaching traitorous heresies.

John answered for himself in a clear, convincing manner. But the more convincing his testimony, the more deeply his opposers hated him. The emperor Domitian was filled with rage. He could not dispute the reasoning of Christ's faithful representative, yet he determined to silence his voice.

John was thrown into a pot of boiling oil, but the Lord preserved His faithful servant as He preserved the three Hebrews in the fiery furnace. As the words were spoken, Thus perish all who believe in that deceiver, Jesus Christ, John declared, My Master gave His life to save the world. I am honored to suffer for His sake. I am a weak, sinful man. Christ was holy, harmless, undefiled.

Saved From the Boiling Oil

These words had their influence, and John was removed from the oil by the very men who had thrown him in.

Again by the emperor's decree, John was banished to the Isle of Patmos "for the word of God and for the testimony of Jesus Christ" (Revelation

1:9). Here, his enemies thought, he will surely die of hardship and distress. Patmos, a barren island in the Aegean Sea, was a place to banish criminals, but to John this gloomy spot became the gate of heaven. Shut away from the active work of his younger years, he had the companionship of God and heavenly angels. They outlined before him the events that would take place in the closing scenes of earth's history, and on that island he wrote out the visions he received from God. The messages given him on that barren coast were to reveal the established plans of the Lord concerning every nation on earth.

Among the cliffs and rocks of Patmos, John had fellowship with his Maker. Peace filled his heart. He could say in faith, "We know that we have passed from death to life" (1 John 3:14).

In his isolated home John was able to study the book of nature more closely. He was surrounded by scenes that many would think were gloomy and uninteresting. But to John it was not so. While his surroundings might be desolate, the blue heavens above were as beautiful as the skies over his beloved Jerusalem. In the wild, rugged rocks, in the mysteries of the sea, in the glories of the sky, he read important lessons of God's power and glory.

John Was Happy in His Exile

Around him the apostle saw evidences of the Flood that had covered the earth—rocks thrown up from the great deep and from the earth by the gushing waters. The mighty waves in turmoil, restrained by an invisible

hand, spoke of the control of an infinite Power. And in contrast he realized the weakness and folly of mortals who glory in their supposed wisdom and strength and set their hearts against the Ruler of the universe. The deepest longing of the heart after God, the most fervent prayers, went up from the exiled apostle.

The history of John illustrates the way God can use older workers. Many thought that John was long past service, an old and broken reed, ready to fall at any time. But the Lord saw fit to use him still. In Patmos he made friends and converts. His was a message of joy, proclaiming a risen Savior interceding for His people until He would return to take them to Himself. After John had grown old in the service of his Lord, he received more communications from heaven than during all the earlier years of his life.

Older workers who have given their lives to the work of God may have physical weaknesses, but they still possess talents that qualify them to stand in their place in God's cause. From their failures they have learned to avoid errors and dangers, and so they are well able to give wise counsel. Though they have lost some of their vigor, the Lord does not lay them aside. He gives them special grace and wisdom.

Those who endured poverty and remained faithful when there were few to stand for truth are to be honored and respected. The Lord desires younger workers to gain wisdom and maturity by associating with these faithful men. Let the younger workers give them an honored place in their councils. God wants the old and tested workers to do their part to save men and women from being swept away by the mighty current of evil. He wants them to keep the armor on until He asks them to lay it down.

Trials Are Worth the Pain They Cost

In the experience of the apostle John there is a lesson of wonderful strength and comfort. God causes the plottings of wicked men to work for good to those who maintain their faith and loyalty amid the storms of persecution, bitter opposition, and unfair accusations. God brings His children near to Him so that He can teach them to lean on Him. In this way He prepares them to fill positions of trust and to accomplish the great purpose for which He gave them their powers.

In all ages God's witnesses have run the risk of being falsely accused and persecuted. Joseph was slandered and persecuted because he would not compromise his virtue and integrity. David was hunted like a wild animal by his enemies. Daniel was thrown into a den of lions. Job's body was so afflicted that his relatives and friends abhorred him. Jeremiah's testimony enraged the king and princes so greatly that he was thrown into a terrible pit. Stephen was stoned. Paul was imprisoned, beaten, stoned, and finally executed. And John was banished to Patmos.

These examples of human faithfulness tell us of God's abiding presence and sustaining grace. They testify to the power of faith to resist the powers of the world. In the darkest hour our Father is in control of our lives.

Jesus calls on His people to follow Him in the path of self-denial and shame. He was opposed by evil men and evil angels in an unpitying alliance. The fact that He was so unlike the world provoked the most bitter hostility. This is how it will be with all who are filled with the Spirit of Christ. The type of persecution changes with the times, but the spirit behind it is the same that has killed the Lord's chosen ones ever since the days of Abel.

Satan has tortured the people of God and put them to death, but in dying they bore witness to the power of One who is stronger than Satan. Wicked people cannot touch the life that is hid with Christ in God. Prison walls cannot bind the spirit.

Believers in Christ, persecuted by the world, are educated and disciplined in the school of Christ. On earth they follow Christ through severe conflicts; they endure self-denial and bitter disappointments; but in this way they learn how terrible sin is, and they look on it with horror. As participants in Christ's sufferings, they look beyond the gloom to the glory, saying, "I consider that the sufferings of this present time are not worthy to be compared with the glory which shall be revealed in us" (Romans 8:18).

John Sees the Visions of the Revelation

In the days of the apostles, the Christians worked so untiringly that in spite of the fierce opposition, in a short time they took the gospel to all the inhabited earth. The Bible has recorded their zeal to encourage the believers in every age. The Lord Jesus used the church at Ephesus as a symbol of the church in that age of the apostles:

"I know your works, your labor, your patience, and that you cannot bear those who are evil. And you have tested those who say they are apostles and are not, and have found them liars; and you have persevered and have patience, and have labored for My name's sake and have not become weary" (Revelation 2:2, 3).

At first the believers tried to obey every word of God. With love overflowing for their Redeemer, their highest aim was to win others to Christ. They did not think of hoarding the precious treasure of Christ's grace. Feeling the weight of the message, "On earth peace, goodwill toward men!" they burned with eagerness to carry the good news to earth's farthest territories. Sinful human beings—repentant, pardoned, cleansed, and sanctified—were brought into partnership with God. In every city the work went forward. People were converted, and then they, too, felt they could not rest until the light was shining on others. They made inspired personal appeals to the sinners and outcasts.

But after a time the believers' zeal and love for God and for one another grew less. One by one the old Christians died at their post. Some of the younger workers who might have shared the burdens of these pioneers, and in this way have been prepared to offer wise leadership, became tired of the same old truths. In their desire for something new and startling, they tried to introduce doctrines that were not in harmony with the basic principles of the gospel. In their spiritual blindness they failed to see that these appealing but false ideas would lead many to question the experiences of the past, and this would lead to confusion and unbelief.

The Revelation Comes When Needed

As some urged these false doctrines, differences sprang up. The discussion of unimportant points occupied time that the believers should have spent in proclaiming the gospel. Instead, they left the masses of people unwarned. True devotion was rapidly dying out, and Satan seemed about to gain control. At this critical time John was sentenced to banishment. Nearly all his former associates had died as martyrs. To all outward appearances the day was not far off when the enemies of the church would win.

But the Lord's unseen hand was moving in the darkness. John was placed where Christ could give him a wonderful revelation of Himself and divine truth for the churches. The exiled disciple received a message whose influence would strengthen the church till the end of time. Those who banished John became instruments in God's hand to carry out Heaven's purpose. The very effort to extinguish the light made the truth stand out boldly.

It was on the Sabbath that the Lord of glory appeared to the exiled apostle. John kept the Sabbath as sacredly on Patmos as he had in Judea. He claimed the precious promises given about that day. "I was in the Spirit on the Lord's Day, and I heard behind me a loud voice, as of a trumpet. . . .

"Then I turned to see the voice that spoke with me. And having turned I saw seven golden lampstands, and in the midst of the seven lampstands One like the Son of Man" (Revelation 1:10–13).

This beloved disciple had seen his Master in Gethsemane, His face marked with the blood drops of agony, His "visage . . . marred more than any man, and His form more than the sons of men" (Isaiah 52:14). He had seen Him hanging on the cross, the object of mockery and abuse. Now John gazes on his Lord once more. But He is no longer a Man of Sorrows, humiliated by men. He is wearing a garment of heavenly brightness, "His eyes like a flame of fire" (Revelation 1:14). Out of His mouth flashes a sharp two-edged sword, a symbol of the power of His word.

Then before John's amazed vision, the glories of heaven opened. He was permitted to see the throne of God, and looking beyond the conflicts of earth, he saw the white-robed assembly of the redeemed. He heard the music of angels and the victory songs of those who had overcome by the blood of the Lamb. Scene after scene of thrilling interest unfolded before him, down to the close of time. In figures and symbols, he saw subjects of vast importance presented, so that the people of God in his age and in future ages could have guidance and comfort and an intelligent understanding of the dangers and conflicts ahead of them.

Sincere Students Can Understand Revelation

Religious teachers have declared that Revelation is a sealed book and that its secrets cannot be explained. But God does not want His people to consider the book sealed. It is "the Revelation of Jesus Christ, which God gave Him, to show His servants—things which must shortly take place." "Blessed is he who reads and those who hear the words of this prophecy, and keep those things which are written in it; for the time is near" (verses 1, 3). "He who testifies to these things says, 'Surely I am coming quickly'" (Revelation 22:20).

The very name given to its inspired pages, "the Revelation," contradicts the statement that this is a sealed book. A revelation is something revealed. Its truths are addressed to those living in the last days, as well as to those living in the days of John. Some of the scenes it shows are in the past, and some are now taking place. Some bring to view the close of the great conflict, and some reveal the joys of the redeemed in the earth made new.

We should not think it is useless for us to search this book to know the meaning of the truth it contains. Those whose hearts are open to truth will be enabled to understand its teachings.

In the Revelation all the books of the Bible meet and end. Here is the book that corresponds to the book of Daniel. One is a prophecy, the other a revelation. The book that was sealed is not the Revelation; the angel commanded, "But you, Daniel, shut up the words, and seal the book until the time of the end" (Daniel 12:4).

"What you see, write in a book," Christ commanded John, "and send it to the seven churches." "Write . . . the things which are, and the things which will take place after this. . . . The seven stars are the angels of the seven churches, and the seven lampstands which you saw are the seven churches." (Revelation 1:11, 19, 20.)

The names of the seven churches are symbolic of the church's condition in different periods of history. The number seven indicates completeness—the messages extend to the end of time.

Christ walks in the middle of the golden lampstands. This symbolizes His constant communication with His people. He knows their true condition, their ways, their devotion. Although He is High Priest in the sanctuary above, He is represented as walking in the midst of His churches on earth. He watches with constant vigilance. If the lampstands were left to human care alone, the flickering flame would shrink and die, but He is the true caretaker. His continued care and sustaining grace are the source of life and light.

"These things says He who holds the seven stars in His right hand" (Revelation 2:1). These words are spoken to the teachers in the church—those entrusted with weighty responsibilities. The stars of heaven are under God's control. He fills them with light and guides their movements. If He did not do this, they would become fallen stars. It is the same with His ministers. Through them His light is to shine out. If they will look to the Savior as He looked to the Father, He will give them His brightness to reflect to the world.

Christ Preserves His Church Today

Early in the history of the church the mystery of iniquity that Paul had foretold began its dreadful work, and false doctrines ensnared many believers. At the time John received this revelation, many had lost their first love of gospel truth. "Remember," God pleaded, "from where you have fallen; repent and do the first works" (verse 5).

The church needed stern rebuking and even punishment. But the rebuke that God sends is always spoken in tender love and with the promise of peace to every repentant believer. "If anyone hears My voice and opens the door, I will come in to him and dine with him, and he with Me" (Revelation 3:20). He warned the believers, "Be watchful, and strengthen the things which remain, that are ready to die." "I am coming quickly! Hold fast what you have, that no one may take your crown." (Verses 2, 11.)

Looking down through long centuries of darkness, the elderly exile saw many Christians dying as martyrs. But he also saw that Jesus, who sustained His early witnesses, would not abandon His faithful followers during the centuries that must pass before the close of time. "Do not fear any of those things which you are about to suffer," the Lord said. "Indeed, the devil is about to throw some of you into prison, that you may be tested, and you will have tribulation. . . . Be faithful until death, and I will give you the crown of life" (Revelation 2:10).

John heard the promises: "To him who overcomes I will give to eat from the tree of life." "I will not blot out his name from the Book of Life; but I will confess his name before My Father and before His angels." I will "grant [him] to sit with Me on My throne." (Revelation 2:7; 3:5, 21.) John saw sinners finding a Father in the God whom they had feared because of their sins.

In vision John saw the Savior presented in the symbols of "the Lion of the tribe of Judah," and of "a Lamb as though it had been slain" (Revelation 5:5, 6). These symbols represent the combination of omnipotent power and self-sacrificing love. The Lion of Judah, terrifying to those who reject God's grace, will be the Lamb of God to the faithful. The pillar of fire that means terror and wrath to those who disobey God's law is a sign of mercy and deliverance to those who have kept His commandments. God's angels "will gather together His elect . . . from one end of heaven to the other" (Matthew 24:31).

When God's People Will Be the Majority

In comparison with the billions of people in the world, God's people will be a little flock, but God will be their refuge. When the sound of the last trumpet penetrates the prison house of the dead, and the righteous come out, standing then with the loyal and true of all ages, the children of God will be far in the majority.

Christ's true disciples follow Him through self-denial and bitter disappointment, but this teaches them to hate the guilt and woe of sin. Taking part in Christ's sufferings, they are destined to take part in His glory. In holy vision the prophet saw the ultimate triumph of God's remnant church.

"I saw something like a sea of glass mingled with fire, and those who have the victory . . . standing on the sea of glass, having harps of God" (Revelation 15:2).

"Then I looked, and behold, a Lamb standing on Mount Zion, and with Him one hundred and forty-four thousand, having His Father's name written on their foreheads" (Revelation 14:1). In this world they served God with their minds and with their hearts, and now He can place His name "on their foreheads." Christ welcomes them as His children, saying, "Enter into the joy of your Lord" (Matthew 25:21).

"These are the ones who follow the Lamb wherever He goes" (Revelation 14:4). But all who follow the Lamb in heaven must first follow Him on earth, not complainingly or unpredictably, but in loving, willing obedience, as the flock follows the shepherd. "In their mouth was found no deceit, for they are without fault before the throne of God" (verse 5).

"Then I, John, saw the holy city, New Jerusalem, coming down out of heaven from God, prepared as a bride adorned for her husband" (Revelation 21:2).

"Blessed are those who do His commandments, that they may have the right to the tree of life, and may enter through the gates into the city" (Revelation 22:14).

A Glorious Future Is Before Us

Many centuries have passed since the apostles rested from their labors, but the history of their sacrifices for Christ is still among the most precious treasures of the church. As these messengers of the cross went out to preach the gospel, there was a revelation of God's glory like no one had ever seen before. They carried the gospel to every nation in a single generation.

At the beginning, some of the apostles were uneducated men, but under the instruction of their Master they gained a preparation for the great work committed to them. Grace and truth ruled in their hearts, and they lost sight of self.

How closely they stood by the side of God and connected their personal honor to His throne! Any attack on the gospel seemed to cut deeply into their hearts, and with every power they had they battled for the cause of Christ. They expected much, and they attempted much. Their understanding of truth and their power to withstand opposition increased the more they followed God's will. Whenever they spoke, Jesus was the theme. As they proclaimed Christ their words moved hearts, and multitudes who had cursed the Savior's name now identified themselves as disciples of the Crucified One.

The apostles encountered hardship, grief, slander, and persecution, but they rejoiced that they were called to suffer for Christ. They were willing to commit everything to their Lord, and the victories they won for Christ revealed the grace of heaven.

The apostles built the church on the foundation that Christ had established. Peter says, "Coming to Him as to a living stone, rejected indeed by men, but chosen by God and precious, you also, as living stones, are being built up a spiritual house, a holy priesthood, to offer up spiritual sacrifices acceptable to God through Jesus Christ" (1 Peter 2:4, 5).

In the quarry of the Jewish and the Gentile world the apostles worked, bringing out "stones" to lay on the foundation. Paul said, "You are . . . built on the foundation of the apostles and prophets, Jesus Christ Himself being the chief cornerstone, in whom the whole building, being fitted together, grows into a holy temple in the Lord" (Ephesians 2:19–21).

"I have laid the foundation, and another builds on it. But let each one take heed how he builds on it. For no other foundation can anyone lay than that which is laid, which is Jesus Christ" (1 Corinthians 3:10, 11).

The apostles built upon the Rock of Ages. To this foundation they brought the stones that they quarried from the world. The enemies of Christ made their work very difficult. They had to struggle against bigotry, prejudice, and hatred. Kings and governors, priests and rulers, tried to destroy the temple of God. But faithful Christians carried the work forward, and the structure grew, beautiful and symmetrical. Sometimes the workers were almost blinded by the mists of superstition around them or were almost overpowered by the violence of their opponents. But with faith and courage they kept moving forward.

One after another the builders fell. Stephen was stoned, James was killed by the sword, Paul was beheaded, Peter was crucified, John was exiled. Yet the church grew. New workers took the place of those who fell, and they added stone after stone to the building.

Centuries of fierce persecution followed, but always there were Christians who considered the building of God's temple more important than life itself. The enemy stopped at nothing to halt the work committed to the Lord's builders. But God raised up workers who defended the faith clearly and powerfully. Like the apostles, many died in the line of duty, but the building of the temple went steadily forward.

The Waldenses, John Wycliffe, Huss and Jerome, Martin Luther and Zwingli, Cranmer, Latimer, Knox, the Huguenots, John and Charles Wesley, and many others brought to the foundation material that will endure for eternity. And those who so nobly promoted the distribution of God's Word and in heathen lands have prepared the way for the last great message—these also have helped to build the structure.

We may look back through the centuries and see the living stones of God's temple gleaming like beams of light through the darkness. Throughout eternity these precious jewels will shine with increasing brilliance, revealing the contrast between the gold of truth and the dross of error.

How We Help the Building

Paul, the other apostles, and all the righteous since them have acted their part in building the temple. But the structure is not yet complete. We who are living in this age are to bring to the foundation material that will stand the test of fire—gold, silver, and precious stones. To those who build this way for God, Paul speaks words of encouragement: "If anyone's work which he has built on it endures, he will receive a reward. If anyone's work is burned, he will suffer loss; but he himself will be saved, yet so as through fire" (1 Corinthians 3:14, 15). The Christian who presents the word of life faithfully is bringing to the foundation material that will last, and in the kingdom he will be honored as a wise builder.

As Christ sent His disciples out, so today He sends the members of His church. If they will rely on God, they will not work in vain. God said to Jeremiah, "Do not say, 'I am a youth,' for you shall go to all to whom I send you." Then the Lord touched His servant's mouth, saying, "Behold, I have put My words in your mouth." (Jeremiah 1:7, 9.) And He tells us to go out to speak the words He gives us, feeling His holy touch on our lips. There is nothing that the Savior wants more than people who will represent His Spirit and His character to the world.

The church is God's agency to proclaim His truth, and if she is loyal to Him, obedient to all His commandments, no power can stand against her.

Zeal for God and His cause moved the disciples to give the gospel message with mighty power. Should not a similar zeal ignite our hearts with a determination to tell the story of Christ and Him crucified? It is the privilege of every Christian not only to look for but to hasten the coming of the Savior.

Nothing Can Stop the Triumph of Truth

If the church will put on the robe of Christ's righteousness and withdraw from all allegiance with the world, she will be ready to enter the dawn of a glorious day. Truth, passing by those who reject it, will win. When the message of God meets opposition, He gives it additional force. Filled with divine energy, it will cut its way through the strongest barriers and triumph over every obstacle.

What sustained Jesus during His life of toil and sacrifice? Looking into eternity, He saw the happiness of those who had received pardon and everlasting life through His humiliation.

We may have a vision of the future, the blessedness of heaven. By faith we may stand on the threshold of the eternal city and hear the gracious welcome given to those who cooperated with Christ in this life. As the words are spoken, "Come, you blessed of My Father" (Matthew 25:34), they throw their crowns at the feet of the Redeemer, exclaiming,

"Worthy is the Lamb who was slain
To receive power and riches and
    wisdom,
And strength and honor and glory
    and blessing!"
                                    Revelation 5:12

Then the redeemed greet the ones who led them to the Savior, and all of them unite in praising Jesus who died so that human beings could have the life that is measured by the life of God. The conflict is over! Songs of victory fill all heaven.

"These are the ones who come out of the great tribulation, and washed their robes and made them white in the blood of the Lamb. Therefore they are before the throne of God, and serve Him day and night in His temple. And He who sits on the throne will dwell among them. . . . The Lamb who is in the midst of the throne will shepherd them and lead them to living fountains of waters. And God will wipe away every tear from their eyes" (Revelation 7:14–17).